I0329491

C-1609 CAREER EXAMINATION SERIES

This is your PASSBOOK for...

Data Conversion Operator (USPS)

Test Preparation Study Guide
Questions & Answers

NLC®

NATIONAL LEARNING CORPORATION®

212 Michael Drive, Syosset, NY 11791
(516) 921-8888 • www.passbooks.com
E-mail: info@passbooks.com

PUBLISHED IN THE UNITED STATES OF AMERICA

COPYRIGHT NOTICE

PASSBOOK® SERIES

THE *PASSBOOK® SERIES* has been created to prepare applicants and candidates for the ultimate academic battlefield – the examination room.

At some time in our lives, each and every one of us may be required to take an examination – for validation, matriculation, admission, qualification, registration, certification, or licensure.

Based on the assumption that every applicant or candidate has met the basic formal educational standards, has taken the required number of courses, and read the necessary texts, the *PASSBOOK® SERIES* furnishes the one special preparation which may assure passing with confidence, instead of failing with insecurity. Examination questions – together with answers – are furnished as the basic vehicle for study so that the mysteries of the examination and its compounding difficulties may be eliminated or diminished by a sure method.

This book is meant to help you pass your examination provided that you qualify and are serious in your objective.

The entire field is reviewed through the huge store of content information which is succinctly presented through a provocative and challenging approach – the question-and-answer method.

A climate of success is established by furnishing the correct answers at the end of each test.

You soon learn to recognize types of questions, forms of questions, and patterns of questioning. You may even begin to anticipate expected outcomes.

You perceive that many questions are repeated or adapted so that you can gain acute insights, which may enable you to score many sure points.

You learn how to confront new questions, or types of questions, and to attack them confidently and work out the correct answers.

You note objectives and emphases, and recognize pitfalls and dangers, so that you may make positive educational adjustments.

Moreover, you are kept fully informed in relation to new concepts, methods, practices, and directions in the field.

You discover that you are actually taking the examination all the time: you are preparing for the examination by "taking" an examination, not by reading extraneous and/or supererogatory textbooks.

In short, this PASSBOOK®, used directedly, should be an important factor in helping you to pass your test.

DATA CONVERSION OPERATOR (USPS)
CLERICAL ABILITIES 710

DUTIES

Operates electronic data entry equipment from source documents to an input suitable for computer processing. Reports to data conversion supervisor, supervisor of computer operations or other designated supervisor.

EXAMPLES OF TYPICAL TASKS

Performs a mechanical verification of information; selects correct program format and operating mode for each data entry system job application; records machine utilization information and submits to the supervisor; performs other job-related tasks in support of primary duties.

HOW TO TAKE A TEST

I. YOU MUST PASS AN EXAMINATION

A. WHAT EVERY CANDIDATE SHOULD KNOW

Examination applicants often ask us for help in preparing for the written test. What can I study in advance? What kinds of questions will be asked? How will the test be given? How will the papers be graded?

As an applicant for a civil service examination, you may be wondering about some of these things. Our purpose here is to suggest effective methods of advance study and to describe civil service examinations.

Your chances for success on this examination can be increased if you know how to prepare. Those "pre-examination jitters" can be reduced if you know what to expect. You can even experience an adventure in good citizenship if you know why civil service exams are given.

B. WHY ARE CIVIL SERVICE EXAMINATIONS GIVEN?

Civil service examinations are important to you in two ways. As a citizen, you want public jobs filled by employees who know how to do their work. As a job seeker, you want a fair chance to compete for that job on an equal footing with other candidates. The best-known means of accomplishing this two-fold goal is the competitive examination.

Exams are widely publicized throughout the nation. They may be administered for jobs in federal, state, city, municipal, town or village governments or agencies.

Any citizen may apply, with some limitations, such as the age or residence of applicants. Your experience and education may be reviewed to see whether you meet the requirements for the particular examination. When these requirements exist, they are reasonable and applied consistently to all applicants. Thus, a competitive examination may cause you some uneasiness now, but it is your privilege and safeguard.

C. HOW ARE CIVIL SERVICE EXAMS DEVELOPED?

Examinations are carefully written by trained technicians who are specialists in the field known as "psychological measurement," in consultation with recognized authorities in the field of work that the test will cover. These experts recommend the subject matter areas or skills to be tested; only those knowledges or skills important to your success on the job are included. The most reliable books and source materials available are used as references. Together, the experts and technicians judge the difficulty level of the questions.

Test technicians know how to phrase questions so that the problem is clearly stated. Their ethics do not permit "trick" or "catch" questions. Questions may have been tried out on sample groups, or subjected to statistical analysis, to determine their usefulness.

Written tests are often used in combination with performance tests, ratings of training and experience, and oral interviews. All of these measures combine to form the best-known means of finding the right person for the right job.

II. HOW TO PASS THE WRITTEN TEST

A. NATURE OF THE EXAMINATION

To prepare intelligently for civil service examinations, you should know how they differ from school examinations you have taken. In school you were assigned certain definite pages to read or subjects to cover. The examination questions were quite detailed and usually emphasized memory. Civil service exams, on the other hand, try to discover your present ability to perform the duties of a position, plus your potentiality to learn these duties. In other words, a civil service exam attempts to predict how successful you will be. Questions cover such a broad area that they cannot be as minute and detailed as school exam questions.

In the public service similar kinds of work, or positions, are grouped together in one "class." This process is known as *position-classification*. All the positions in a class are paid according to the salary range for that class. One class title covers all of these positions, and they are all tested by the same examination.

B. FOUR BASIC STEPS

1) Study the announcement

How, then, can you know what subjects to study? Our best answer is: "Learn as much as possible about the class of positions for which you've applied." The exam will test the knowledge, skills and abilities needed to do the work.

Your most valuable source of information about the position you want is the official exam announcement. This announcement lists the training and experience qualifications. Check these standards and apply only if you come reasonably close to meeting them.

The brief description of the position in the examination announcement offers some clues to the subjects which will be tested. Think about the job itself. Review the duties in your mind. Can you perform them, or are there some in which you are rusty? Fill in the blank spots in your preparation.

Many jurisdictions preview the written test in the exam announcement by including a section called "Knowledge and Abilities Required," "Scope of the Examination," or some similar heading. Here you will find out specifically what fields will be tested.

2) Review your own background

Once you learn in general what the position is all about, and what you need to know to do the work, ask yourself which subjects you already know fairly well and which need improvement. You may wonder whether to concentrate on improving your strong areas or on building some background in your fields of weakness. When the announcement has specified "some knowledge" or "considerable knowledge," or has used adjectives like "beginning principles of..." or "advanced ... methods," you can get a clue as to the number and difficulty of questions to be asked in any given field. More questions, and hence broader coverage, would be included for those subjects which are more important in the work. Now weigh your strengths and weaknesses against the job requirements and prepare accordingly.

3) Determine the level of the position

Another way to tell how intensively you should prepare is to understand the level of the job for which you are applying. Is it the entering level? In other words, is this the position in which beginners in a field of work are hired? Or is it an intermediate or advanced level? Sometimes this is indicated by such words as "Junior" or "Senior" in the class title. Other jurisdictions use Roman numerals to designate the level – Clerk I, Clerk II, for example. The word "Supervisor" sometimes appears in the title. If the level is not indicated by the title, check the description of duties. Will you be working under very close supervision, or will you have responsibility for independent decisions in this work?

4) Choose appropriate study materials

Now that you know the subjects to be examined and the relative amount of each subject to be covered, you can choose suitable study materials. For beginning level jobs, or even advanced ones, if you have a pronounced weakness in some aspect of your training, read a modern, standard textbook in that field. Be sure it is up to date and has general coverage. Such books are normally available at your library, and the librarian will be glad to help you locate one. For entry-level positions, questions of appropriate difficulty are chosen – neither highly advanced questions, nor those too simple. Such questions require careful thought but not advanced training.

If the position for which you are applying is technical or advanced, you will read more advanced, specialized material. If you are already familiar with the basic principles of your field, elementary textbooks would waste your time. Concentrate on advanced textbooks and technical periodicals. Think through the concepts and review difficult problems in your field.

These are all general sources. You can get more ideas on your own initiative, following these leads. For example, training manuals and publications of the government agency which employs workers in your field can be useful, particularly for technical and professional positions. A letter or visit to the government department involved may result in more specific study suggestions, and certainly will provide you with a more definite idea of the exact nature of the position you are seeking.

III. KINDS OF TESTS

Tests are used for purposes other than measuring knowledge and ability to perform specified duties. For some positions, it is equally important to test ability to make adjustments to new situations or to profit from training. In others, basic mental abilities not dependent on information are essential. Questions which test these things may not appear as pertinent to the duties of the position as those which test for knowledge and information. Yet they are often highly important parts of a fair examination. For very general questions, it is almost impossible to help you direct your study efforts. What we can do is to point out some of the more common of these general abilities needed in public service positions and describe some typical questions.

1) General information

Broad, general information has been found useful for predicting job success in some kinds of work. This is tested in a variety of ways, from vocabulary lists to questions about current events. Basic background in some field of work, such as sociology or economics, may be sampled in a group of questions. Often these are principles which have become familiar to most persons through exposure rather than through formal training. It is difficult to advise you how to study for these questions; being alert to the world around you is our best suggestion.

2) Verbal ability

An example of an ability needed in many positions is verbal or language ability. Verbal ability is, in brief, the ability to use and understand words. Vocabulary and grammar tests are typical measures of this ability. Reading comprehension or paragraph interpretation questions are common in many kinds of civil service tests. You are given a paragraph of written material and asked to find its central meaning.

3) Numerical ability

Number skills can be tested by the familiar arithmetic problem, by checking paired lists of numbers to see which are alike and which are different, or by interpreting charts and graphs. In the latter test, a graph may be printed in the test booklet which you are asked to use as the basis for answering questions.

4) Observation

A popular test for law-enforcement positions is the observation test. A picture is shown to you for several minutes, then taken away. Questions about the picture test your ability to observe both details and larger elements.

5) Following directions

In many positions in the public service, the employee must be able to carry out written instructions dependably and accurately. You may be given a chart with several columns, each column listing a variety of information. The questions require you to carry out directions involving the information given in the chart.

6) Skills and aptitudes

Performance tests effectively measure some manual skills and aptitudes. When the skill is one in which you are trained, such as typing or shorthand, you can practice. These tests are often very much like those given in business school or high school courses. For many of the other skills and aptitudes, however, no short-time preparation can be made. Skills and abilities natural to you or that you have developed throughout your lifetime are being tested.

Many of the general questions just described provide all the data needed to answer the questions and ask you to use your reasoning ability to find the answers. Your best preparation for these tests, as well as for tests of facts and ideas, is to be at your physical and mental best. You, no doubt, have your own methods of getting into an exam-taking mood and keeping "in shape." The next section lists some ideas on this subject.

IV. KINDS OF QUESTIONS

Only rarely is the "essay" question, which you answer in narrative form, used in civil service tests. Civil service tests are usually of the short-answer type. Full instructions for answering these questions will be given to you at the examination. But in case this is your first experience with short-answer questions and separate answer sheets, here is what you need to know:

1) Multiple-choice Questions

Most popular of the short-answer questions is the "multiple choice" or "best answer" question. It can be used, for example, to test for factual knowledge, ability to solve problems or judgment in meeting situations found at work.

A multiple-choice question is normally one of three types—

- It can begin with an incomplete statement followed by several possible endings. You are to find the one ending which *best* completes the statement, although some of the others may not be entirely wrong.
- It can also be a complete statement in the form of a question which is answered by choosing one of the statements listed.

- It can be in the form of a problem – again you select the best answer.

Here is an example of a multiple-choice question with a discussion which should give you some clues as to the method for choosing the right answer:

When an employee has a complaint about his assignment, the action which will *best* help him overcome his difficulty is to
A. discuss his difficulty with his coworkers
B. take the problem to the head of the organization
C. take the problem to the person who gave him the assignment
D. say nothing to anyone about his complaint

In answering this question, you should study each of the choices to find which is best. Consider choice "A" – Certainly an employee may discuss his complaint with fellow employees, but no change or improvement can result, and the complaint remains unresolved. Choice "B" is a poor choice since the head of the organization probably does not know what assignment you have been given, and taking your problem to him is known as "going over the head" of the supervisor. The supervisor, or person who made the assignment, is the person who can clarify it or correct any injustice. Choice "C" is, therefore, correct. To say nothing, as in choice "D," is unwise. Supervisors have and interest in knowing the problems employees are facing, and the employee is seeking a solution to his problem.

2) True/False Questions

The "true/false" or "right/wrong" form of question is sometimes used. Here a complete statement is given. Your job is to decide whether the statement is right or wrong.

SAMPLE: A roaming cell-phone call to a nearby city costs less than a non-roaming call to a distant city.

This statement is wrong, or false, since roaming calls are more expensive.

This is not a complete list of all possible question forms, although most of the others are variations of these common types. You will always get complete directions for answering questions. Be sure you understand *how* to mark your answers – ask questions until you do.

V. RECORDING YOUR ANSWERS

Computer terminals are used more and more today for many different kinds of exams.

For an examination with very few applicants, you may be told to record your answers in the test booklet itself. Separate answer sheets are much more common. If this separate answer sheet is to be scored by machine – and this is often the case – it is highly important that you mark your answers correctly in order to get credit.

An electronic scoring machine is often used in civil service offices because of the speed with which papers can be scored. Machine-scored answer sheets must be marked with a pencil, which will be given to you. This pencil has a high graphite content which responds to the electronic scoring machine. As a matter of fact, stray dots may register as answers, so do not let your pencil rest on the answer sheet while you are pondering the correct answer. Also, if your pencil lead breaks or is otherwise defective, ask for another.

Since the answer sheet will be dropped in a slot in the scoring machine, be careful not to bend the corners or get the paper crumpled.

The answer sheet normally has five vertical columns of numbers, with 30 numbers to a column. These numbers correspond to the question numbers in your test booklet. After each number, going across the page are four or five pairs of dotted lines. These short dotted lines have small letters or numbers above them. The first two pairs may also have a "T" or "F" above the letters. This indicates that the first two pairs only are to be used if the questions are of the true-false type. If the questions are multiple choice, disregard the "T" and "F" and pay attention only to the small letters or numbers.

Answer your questions in the manner of the sample that follows:

32. The largest city in the United States is
    - A. Washington, D.C.
    - B. New York City
    - C. Chicago
    - D. Detroit
    - E. San Francisco

1) Choose the answer you think is best. (New York City is the largest, so "B" is correct.)
2) Find the row of dotted lines numbered the same as the question you are answering. (Find row number 32)
3) Find the pair of dotted lines corresponding to the answer. (Find the pair of lines under the mark "B.")
4) Make a solid black mark between the dotted lines.

VI. BEFORE THE TEST

Common sense will help you find procedures to follow to get ready for an examination. Too many of us, however, overlook these sensible measures. Indeed, nervousness and fatigue have been found to be the most serious reasons why applicants fail to do their best on civil service tests. Here is a list of reminders:

- Begin your preparation early – Don't wait until the last minute to go scurrying around for books and materials or to find out what the position is all about.
- Prepare continuously – An hour a night for a week is better than an all-night cram session. This has been definitely established. What is more, a night a week for a month will return better dividends than crowding your study into a shorter period of time.
- Locate the place of the exam – You have been sent a notice telling you when and where to report for the examination. If the location is in a different town or otherwise unfamiliar to you, it would be well to inquire the best route and learn something about the building.
- Relax the night before the test – Allow your mind to rest. Do not study at all that night. Plan some mild recreation or diversion; then go to bed early and get a good night's sleep.
- Get up early enough to make a leisurely trip to the place for the test – This way unforeseen events, traffic snarls, unfamiliar buildings, etc. will not upset you.
- Dress comfortably – A written test is not a fashion show. You will be known by number and not by name, so wear something comfortable.

- Leave excess paraphernalia at home – Shopping bags and odd bundles will get in your way. You need bring only the items mentioned in the official notice you received; usually everything you need is provided. Do not bring reference books to the exam. They will only confuse those last minutes and be taken away from you when in the test room.
- Arrive somewhat ahead of time – If because of transportation schedules you must get there very early, bring a newspaper or magazine to take your mind off yourself while waiting.
- Locate the examination room – When you have found the proper room, you will be directed to the seat or part of the room where you will sit. Sometimes you are given a sheet of instructions to read while you are waiting. Do not fill out any forms until you are told to do so; just read them and be prepared.
- Relax and prepare to listen to the instructions
- If you have any physical problem that may keep you from doing your best, be sure to tell the test administrator. If you are sick or in poor health, you really cannot do your best on the exam. You can come back and take the test some other time.

VII. AT THE TEST

The day of the test is here and you have the test booklet in your hand. The temptation to get going is very strong. Caution! There is more to success than knowing the right answers. You must know how to identify your papers and understand variations in the type of short-answer question used in this particular examination. Follow these suggestions for maximum results from your efforts:

1) Cooperate with the monitor

The test administrator has a duty to create a situation in which you can be as much at ease as possible. He will give instructions, tell you when to begin, check to see that you are marking your answer sheet correctly, and so on. He is not there to guard you, although he will see that your competitors do not take unfair advantage. He wants to help you do your best.

2) Listen to all instructions

Don't jump the gun! Wait until you understand all directions. In most civil service tests you get more time than you need to answer the questions. So don't be in a hurry. Read each word of instructions until you clearly understand the meaning. Study the examples, listen to all announcements and follow directions. Ask questions if you do not understand what to do.

3) Identify your papers

Civil service exams are usually identified by number only. You will be assigned a number; you must not put your name on your test papers. Be sure to copy your number correctly. Since more than one exam may be given, copy your exact examination title.

4) Plan your time

Unless you are told that a test is a "speed" or "rate of work" test, speed itself is usually not important. Time enough to answer all the questions will be provided, but this does not mean that you have all day. An overall time limit has been set. Divide the total time (in minutes) by the number of questions to determine the approximate time you have for each question.

5) Do not linger over difficult questions

If you come across a difficult question, mark it with a paper clip (useful to have along) and come back to it when you have been through the booklet. One caution if you do this – be sure to skip a number on your answer sheet as well. Check often to be sure that you have not lost your place and that you are marking in the row numbered the same as the question you are answering.

6) Read the questions

Be sure you know what the question asks! Many capable people are unsuccessful because they failed to *read* the questions correctly.

7) Answer all questions

Unless you have been instructed that a penalty will be deducted for incorrect answers, it is better to guess than to omit a question.

8) Speed tests

It is often better NOT to guess on speed tests. It has been found that on timed tests people are tempted to spend the last few seconds before time is called in marking answers at random – without even reading them – in the hope of picking up a few extra points. To discourage this practice, the instructions may warn you that your score will be "corrected" for guessing. That is, a penalty will be applied. The incorrect answers will be deducted from the correct ones, or some other penalty formula will be used.

9) Review your answers

If you finish before time is called, go back to the questions you guessed or omitted to give them further thought. Review other answers if you have time.

10) Return your test materials

If you are ready to leave before others have finished or time is called, take ALL your materials to the monitor and leave quietly. Never take any test material with you. The monitor can discover whose papers are not complete, and taking a test booklet may be grounds for disqualification.

VIII. EXAMINATION TECHNIQUES

1) Read the general instructions carefully. These are usually printed on the first page of the exam booklet. As a rule, these instructions refer to the timing of the examination; the fact that you should not start work until the signal and must stop work at a signal, etc. If there are any *special* instructions, such as a choice of questions to be answered, make sure that you note this instruction carefully.

2) When you are ready to start work on the examination, that is as soon as the signal has been given, read the instructions to each question booklet, underline any key words or phrases, such as *least*, *best*, *outline*, *describe* and the like. In this way you will tend to answer as requested rather than discover on reviewing your paper that you *listed without describing*, that you selected the *worst* choice rather than the *best* choice, etc.

3) If the examination is of the objective or multiple-choice type – that is, each question will also give a series of possible answers: A, B, C or D, and you are called upon to select the best answer and write the letter next to that answer on your answer paper – it is advisable to start answering each question in turn. There may be anywhere from 50 to 100 such questions in the three or four hours allotted and you can see how much time would be taken if you read through all the questions before beginning to answer any. Furthermore, if you come across a question or group of questions which you know would be difficult to answer, it would undoubtedly affect your handling of all the other questions.

4) If the examination is of the essay type and contains but a few questions, it is a moot point as to whether you should read all the questions before starting to answer any one. Of course, if you are given a choice – say five out of seven and the like – then it is essential to read all the questions so you can eliminate the two that are most difficult. If, however, you are asked to answer all the questions, there may be danger in trying to answer the easiest one first because you may find that you will spend too much time on it. The best technique is to answer the first question, then proceed to the second, etc.

5) Time your answers. Before the exam begins, write down the time it started, then add the time allowed for the examination and write down the time it must be completed, then divide the time available somewhat as follows:
    - If 3-1/2 hours are allowed, that would be 210 minutes. If you have 80 objective-type questions, that would be an average of 2-1/2 minutes per question. Allow yourself no more than 2 minutes per question, or a total of 160 minutes, which will permit about 50 minutes to review.
    - If for the time allotment of 210 minutes there are 7 essay questions to answer, that would average about 30 minutes a question. Give yourself only 25 minutes per question so that you have about 35 minutes to review.

6) The most important instruction is to *read each question* and make sure you know what is wanted. The second most important instruction is to *time yourself properly* so that you answer every question. The third most important instruction is to *answer every question.* Guess if you have to but include something for each question. Remember that you will receive no credit for a blank and will probably receive some credit if you write something in answer to an essay question. If you guess a letter – say "B" for a multiple-choice question – you may have guessed right. If you leave a blank as an answer to a multiple-choice question, the examiners may respect your feelings but it will not add a point to your score. Some exams may penalize you for wrong answers, so in such cases *only,* you may not want to guess unless you have some basis for your answer.

7) Suggestions
    a. Objective-type questions
        1. Examine the question booklet for proper sequence of pages and questions
        2. Read all instructions carefully
        3. Skip any question which seems too difficult; return to it after all other questions have been answered
        4. Apportion your time properly; do not spend too much time on any single question or group of questions

5. Note and underline key words – *all, most, fewest, least, best, worst, same, opposite,* etc.
6. Pay particular attention to negatives
7. Note unusual option, e.g., unduly long, short, complex, different or similar in content to the body of the question
8. Observe the use of "hedging" words – *probably, may, most likely,* etc.
9. Make sure that your answer is put next to the same number as the question
10. Do not second-guess unless you have good reason to believe the second answer is definitely more correct
11. Cross out original answer if you decide another answer is more accurate; do not erase until you are ready to hand your paper in
12. Answer all questions; guess unless instructed otherwise
13. Leave time for review

b. Essay questions
1. Read each question carefully
2. Determine exactly what is wanted. Underline key words or phrases.
3. Decide on outline or paragraph answer
4. Include many different points and elements unless asked to develop any one or two points or elements
5. Show impartiality by giving pros and cons unless directed to select one side only
6. Make and write down any assumptions you find necessary to answer the questions
7. Watch your English, grammar, punctuation and choice of words
8. Time your answers; don't crowd material

8) Answering the essay question

Most essay questions can be answered by framing the specific response around several key words or ideas. Here are a few such key words or ideas:

M's: manpower, materials, methods, money, management
P's: purpose, program, policy, plan, procedure, practice, problems, pitfalls, personnel, public relations

a. Six basic steps in handling problems:
1. Preliminary plan and background development
2. Collect information, data and facts
3. Analyze and interpret information, data and facts
4. Analyze and develop solutions as well as make recommendations
5. Prepare report and sell recommendations
6. Install recommendations and follow up effectiveness

b. Pitfalls to avoid
1. *Taking things for granted* – A statement of the situation does not necessarily imply that each of the elements is necessarily true; for example, a complaint may be invalid and biased so that all that can be taken for granted is that a complaint has been registered

2. *Considering only one side of a situation* – Wherever possible, indicate several alternatives and then point out the reasons you selected the best one
3. *Failing to indicate follow up* – Whenever your answer indicates action on your part, make certain that you will take proper follow-up action to see how successful your recommendations, procedures or actions turn out to be
4. *Taking too long in answering any single question* – Remember to time your answers properly

IX. AFTER THE TEST

Scoring procedures differ in detail among civil service jurisdictions although the general principles are the same. Whether the papers are hand-scored or graded by machine we have described, they are nearly always graded by number. That is, the person who marks the paper knows only the number – never the name – of the applicant. Not until all the papers have been graded will they be matched with names. If other tests, such as training and experience or oral interview ratings have been given, scores will be combined. Different parts of the examination usually have different weights. For example, the written test might count 60 percent of the final grade, and a rating of training and experience 40 percent. In many jurisdictions, veterans will have a certain number of points added to their grades.

After the final grade has been determined, the names are placed in grade order and an eligible list is established. There are various methods for resolving ties between those who get the same final grade – probably the most common is to place first the name of the person whose application was received first. Job offers are made from the eligible list in the order the names appear on it. You will be notified of your grade and your rank as soon as all these computations have been made. This will be done as rapidly as possible.

People who are found to meet the requirements in the announcement are called "eligibles." Their names are put on a list of eligible candidates. An eligible's chances of getting a job depend on how high he stands on this list and how fast agencies are filling jobs from the list.

When a job is to be filled from a list of eligibles, the agency asks for the names of people on the list of eligibles for that job. When the civil service commission receives this request, it sends to the agency the names of the three people highest on this list. Or, if the job to be filled has specialized requirements, the office sends the agency the names of the top three persons who meet these requirements from the general list.

The appointing officer makes a choice from among the three people whose names were sent to him. If the selected person accepts the appointment, the names of the others are put back on the list to be considered for future openings.

That is the rule in hiring from all kinds of eligible lists, whether they are for typist, carpenter, chemist, or something else. For every vacancy, the appointing officer has his choice of any one of the top three eligibles on the list. This explains why the person whose name is on top of the list sometimes does not get an appointment when some of the persons lower on the list do. If the appointing officer chooses the second or third eligible, the No. 1 eligible does not get a job at once, but stays on the list until he is appointed or the list is terminated.

X. HOW TO PASS THE INTERVIEW TEST

The examination for which you applied requires an oral interview test. You have already taken the written test and you are now being called for the interview test – the final part of the formal examination.

You may think that it is not possible to prepare for an interview test and that there are no procedures to follow during an interview. Our purpose is to point out some things you can do in advance that will help you and some good rules to follow and pitfalls to avoid while you are being interviewed.

What is an interview supposed to test?

The written examination is designed to test the technical knowledge and competence of the candidate; the oral is designed to evaluate intangible qualities, not readily measured otherwise, and to establish a list showing the relative fitness of each candidate – as measured against his competitors – for the position sought. Scoring is not on the basis of "right" and "wrong," but on a sliding scale of values ranging from "not passable" to "outstanding." As a matter of fact, it is possible to achieve a relatively low score without a single "incorrect" answer because of evident weakness in the qualities being measured.

Occasionally, an examination may consist entirely of an oral test – either an individual or a group oral. In such cases, information is sought concerning the technical knowledges and abilities of the candidate, since there has been no written examination for this purpose. More commonly, however, an oral test is used to supplement a written examination.

Who conducts interviews?

The composition of oral boards varies among different jurisdictions. In nearly all, a representative of the personnel department serves as chairman. One of the members of the board may be a representative of the department in which the candidate would work. In some cases, "outside experts" are used, and, frequently, a businessman or some other representative of the general public is asked to serve. Labor and management or other special groups may be represented. The aim is to secure the services of experts in the appropriate field.

However the board is composed, it is a good idea (and not at all improper or unethical) to ascertain in advance of the interview who the members are and what groups they represent. When you are introduced to them, you will have some idea of their backgrounds and interests, and at least you will not stutter and stammer over their names.

What should be done before the interview?

While knowledge about the board members is useful and takes some of the surprise element out of the interview, there is other preparation which is more substantive. It *is* possible to prepare for an oral interview – in several ways:

1) Keep a copy of your application and review it carefully before the interview

This may be the only document before the oral board, and the starting point of the interview. Know what education and experience you have listed there, and the sequence and dates of all of it. Sometimes the board will ask you to review the highlights of your experience for them; you should not have to hem and haw doing it.

2) Study the class specification and the examination announcement

Usually, the oral board has one or both of these to guide them. The qualities, characteristics or knowledges required by the position sought are stated in these documents. They offer valuable clues as to the nature of the oral interview. For example, if the job involves supervisory responsibilities, the announcement will usually indicate that knowledge of modern supervisory methods and the qualifications of the candidate as a supervisor will be tested. If so, you can expect such questions, frequently in the form of a hypothetical situation which you are expected to solve. NEVER go into an oral without knowledge of the duties and responsibilities of the job you seek.

3) Think through each qualification required

Try to visualize the kind of questions you would ask if you were a board member. How well could you answer them? Try especially to appraise your own knowledge and background in each area, *measured against the job sought*, and identify any areas in which you are weak. Be critical and realistic – do not flatter yourself.

4) Do some general reading in areas in which you feel you may be weak

For example, if the job involves supervision and your past experience has NOT, some general reading in supervisory methods and practices, particularly in the field of human relations, might be useful. Do NOT study agency procedures or detailed manuals. The oral board will be testing your understanding and capacity, not your memory.

5) Get a good night's sleep and watch your general health and mental attitude

You will want a clear head at the interview. Take care of a cold or any other minor ailment, and of course, no hangovers.

What should be done on the day of the interview?

Now comes the day of the interview itself. Give yourself plenty of time to get there. Plan to arrive somewhat ahead of the scheduled time, particularly if your appointment is in the fore part of the day. If a previous candidate fails to appear, the board might be ready for you a bit early. By early afternoon an oral board is almost invariably behind schedule if there are many candidates, and you may have to wait. Take along a book or magazine to read, or your application to review, but leave any extraneous material in the waiting room when you go in for your interview. In any event, relax and compose yourself.

The matter of dress is important. The board is forming impressions about you – from your experience, your manners, your attitude, and your appearance. Give your personal appearance careful attention. Dress your best, but not your flashiest. Choose conservative, appropriate clothing, and be sure it is immaculate. This is a business interview, and your appearance should indicate that you regard it as such. Besides, being well groomed and properly dressed will help boost your confidence.

Sooner or later, someone will call your name and escort you into the interview room. *This is it.* From here on you are on your own. It is too late for any more preparation. But remember, you asked for this opportunity to prove your fitness, and you are here because your request was granted.

What happens when you go in?

The usual sequence of events will be as follows: The clerk (who is often the board stenographer) will introduce you to the chairman of the oral board, who will introduce you to the other members of the board. Acknowledge the introductions before you sit down. Do not be surprised if you find a microphone facing you or a stenotypist sitting by. Oral interviews are usually recorded in the event of an appeal or other review.

Usually the chairman of the board will open the interview by reviewing the highlights of your education and work experience from your application – primarily for the benefit of the other members of the board, as well as to get the material into the record. Do not interrupt or comment unless there is an error or significant misinterpretation; if that is the case, do not hesitate. But do not quibble about insignificant matters. Also, he will usually ask you some question about your education, experience or your present job – partly to get you to start talking and to establish the interviewing "rapport." He may start the actual questioning, or turn it over to one of the other members. Frequently, each member undertakes the questioning on a particular area, one in which he is perhaps most competent, so you can expect each member to participate in the examination. Because time is limited, you may also expect some rather abrupt switches in the direction the questioning takes, so do not be upset by it. Normally, a board member will not pursue a single line of questioning unless he discovers a particular strength or weakness.

After each member has participated, the chairman will usually ask whether any member has any further questions, then will ask you if you have anything you wish to add. Unless you are expecting this question, it may floor you. Worse, it may start you off on an extended, extemporaneous speech. The board is not usually seeking more information. The question is principally to offer you a last opportunity to present further qualifications or to indicate that you have nothing to add. So, if you feel that a significant qualification or characteristic has been overlooked, it is proper to point it out in a sentence or so. Do not compliment the board on the thoroughness of their examination – they have been sketchy, and you know it. If you wish, merely say, "No thank you, I have nothing further to add." This is a point where you can "talk yourself out" of a good impression or fail to present an important bit of information. Remember, *you close the interview yourself.*

The chairman will then say, "That is all, Mr. ______, thank you." Do not be startled; the interview is over, and quicker than you think. Thank him, gather your belongings and take your leave. Save your sigh of relief for the other side of the door.

How to put your best foot forward

Throughout this entire process, you may feel that the board individually and collectively is trying to pierce your defenses, seek out your hidden weaknesses and embarrass and confuse you. Actually, this is not true. They are obliged to make an appraisal of your qualifications for the job you are seeking, and they want to see you in your best light. Remember, they must interview all candidates and a non-cooperative candidate may become a failure in spite of their best efforts to bring out his qualifications. Here are 15 suggestions that will help you:

1) Be natural – Keep your attitude confident, not cocky

If you are not confident that you can do the job, do not expect the board to be. Do not apologize for your weaknesses, try to bring out your strong points. The board is interested in a positive, not negative, presentation. Cockiness will antagonize any board member and make him wonder if you are covering up a weakness by a false show of strength.

2) Get comfortable, but don't lounge or sprawl

Sit erectly but not stiffly. A careless posture may lead the board to conclude that you are careless in other things, or at least that you are not impressed by the importance of the occasion. Either conclusion is natural, even if incorrect. Do not fuss with your clothing, a pencil or an ashtray. Your hands may occasionally be useful to emphasize a point; do not let them become a point of distraction.

3) Do not wisecrack or make small talk

This is a serious situation, and your attitude should show that you consider it as such. Further, the time of the board is limited – they do not want to waste it, and neither should you.

4) Do not exaggerate your experience or abilities

In the first place, from information in the application or other interviews and sources, the board may know more about you than you think. Secondly, you probably will not get away with it. An experienced board is rather adept at spotting such a situation, so do not take the chance.

5) If you know a board member, do not make a point of it, yet do not hide it

Certainly you are not fooling him, and probably not the other members of the board. Do not try to take advantage of your acquaintanceship – it will probably do you little good.

6) Do not dominate the interview

Let the board do that. They will give you the clues – do not assume that you have to do all the talking. Realize that the board has a number of questions to ask you, and do not try to take up all the interview time by showing off your extensive knowledge of the answer to the first one.

7) Be attentive

You only have 20 minutes or so, and you should keep your attention at its sharpest throughout. When a member is addressing a problem or question to you, give him your undivided attention. Address your reply principally to him, but do not exclude the other board members.

8) Do not interrupt

A board member may be stating a problem for you to analyze. He will ask you a question when the time comes. Let him state the problem, and wait for the question.

9) Make sure you understand the question

Do not try to answer until you are sure what the question is. If it is not clear, restate it in your own words or ask the board member to clarify it for you. However, do not haggle about minor elements.

10) Reply promptly but not hastily

A common entry on oral board rating sheets is "candidate responded readily," or "candidate hesitated in replies." Respond as promptly and quickly as you can, but do not jump to a hasty, ill-considered answer.

11) Do not be peremptory in your answers

A brief answer is proper – but do not fire your answer back. That is a losing game from your point of view. The board member can probably ask questions much faster than you can answer them.

12) Do not try to create the answer you think the board member wants

He is interested in what kind of mind you have and how it works – not in playing games. Furthermore, he can usually spot this practice and will actually grade you down on it.

13) Do not switch sides in your reply merely to agree with a board member

Frequently, a member will take a contrary position merely to draw you out and to see if you are willing and able to defend your point of view. Do not start a debate, yet do not surrender a good position. If a position is worth taking, it is worth defending.

14) Do not be afraid to admit an error in judgment if you are shown to be wrong

The board knows that you are forced to reply without any opportunity for careful consideration. Your answer may be demonstrably wrong. If so, admit it and get on with the interview.

15) Do not dwell at length on your present job

The opening question may relate to your present assignment. Answer the question but do not go into an extended discussion. You are being examined for a *new* job, not your present one. As a matter of fact, try to phrase ALL your answers in terms of the job for which you are being examined.

Basis of Rating

Probably you will forget most of these "do's" and "don'ts" when you walk into the oral interview room. Even remembering them all will not ensure you a passing grade. Perhaps you did not have the qualifications in the first place. But remembering them will help you to put your best foot forward, without treading on the toes of the board members.

Rumor and popular opinion to the contrary notwithstanding, an oral board wants you to make the best appearance possible. They know you are under pressure – but they also want to see how you respond to it as a guide to what your reaction would be under the pressures of the job you seek. They will be influenced by the degree of poise you display, the personal traits you show and the manner in which you respond.

ABOUT THIS BOOK

This book contains tests divided into Examination Sections. Go through each test, answering every question in the margin. We have also attached a sample answer sheet at the back of the book that can be removed and used. At the end of each test look at the answer key and check your answers. On the ones you got wrong, look at the right answer choice and learn. Do not fill in the answers first. Do not memorize the questions and answers, but understand the answer and principles involved. On your test, the questions will likely be different from the samples. Questions are changed and new ones added. If you understand these past questions you should have success with any changes that arise. Tests may consist of several types of questions. We have additional books on each subject should more study be advisable or necessary for you. Finally, the more you study, the better prepared you will be. This book is intended to be the last thing you study before you walk into the examination room. Prior study of relevant texts is also recommended. NLC publishes some of these in our Fundamental Series. Knowledge and good sense are important factors in passing your exam. Good luck also helps. So now study this Passbook, absorb the material contained within and take that knowledge into the examination. Then do your best to pass that exam.

EXAMINATION SECTION

EXAMINATION SECTION
TEST 1

DIRECTIONS: Each question or incomplete statement is followed by several suggested answers or completions. Select the one that BEST answers the question or completes the statement. *PRINT THE LETTER OF THE CORRECT ANSWER IN THE SPACE AT THE RIGHT.*

Questions 1 -3
For questions 1 through 3, there is a name or code provided along with four other names or codes listed in alphabetical/numerical order. Find the correct space for the given name or code so that it will be in proper order with the rest of the list.

1. Roggen, Sam 1.____

A. _
Rogers, Arthur L
B. _
Roghani, Fada
C. _
Rogovin, H.T.
D. _
Rogowski, Marie R.
E. _

2. 05076012 2.____

A. _
05076004
B. _
05076007
C. _
05076010
D. _
05076021
E. _

3. CBA-1875 3.____

A. _
CAA-1720
B. _
CAB-1819
C. _
CAC-1804
D. _
CAD-1402
E. _

Questions 4-8
Questions 4 through 8 require you to compare names, addresses or codes. In each line below there are three items that are very much alike. Compare the three and answer as follows:

Answer "A" if all three are exactly alike;
Answer "B" if only the FIRST and SECOND items are exactly alike;
Answer "C" if only the FIRST and THIRD items are exactly alike;
Answer "D" if only the SECOND AND THIRD items are exactly alike;
Answer "E" if all three names are different.

4.	Helene Bedell	Helene Beddell	Helene Beddell	4.___
5.	FT. Wedemeyer	FT. Wedemeyer	FT. Wedmeyer	5.___
6.	3214 W. Beaumont St.	3214 W. Beaumount St.	3214 Beaumont St.	6.___
7.	BC3105T-5	BC3015T-5	BC3105T-5	7.___
8.	4460327	4460327	4460327	8.___

For questions 9 through 11, find the correct spelling of the word and write the correct letter in the space at the right.

9. A. accomodate B. acommodate C. accommadate D. none of the above 9.___

10. A. manageble B. manageable C. manegeable D. none of the above 10.___

11. A. reccommend B. recommend C. recammend D. none of the above 11.___

12. 32 + 26 = 12.___

A. 69
B. 59
C. 58
D. 54
E. none of the above

13. 57-15 = 13.___

A. 72
B. 62
C. 54
D. 44
E. none of the above

14. 23x7 = 14.___

A. 164
B. 161
C. 154
D. 141
E. none of the above

15. 160/5 = 15.___

A. 32

B. 30
C. 25
D. 21
E. none of the above

16. 17.8 + 13.3 = 16.____

A. 30.1
B. 31.0
C. 31.1
D. 33.3

Questions 17-19

Questions 17 through 19 test the ability to follow instructions. Following the directions in each item will lead you to identify or create a specific letter-number combination. Next, use the "Look-Up Table" to find the letter that corresponds with your letter-number combination. Mark this letter in the space at the right.

For example, if the combination is "P1," the answer would be "A" because this is the letter indicated in the box where "P" and "1" meet in the table.

LOOK-UP TABLE

	P	Q	R	S	T
1	A	B	c,	D	E
2	B	C	D	E	A
3	C	D	E	A	B
4	D	E	A	B	C
5	E	A	B	C	D
6-	A	B	C	D	E
7	B	C	D	E	A
8	C	D	E	A	B
9	D	E	A	B	C
10	E	A	B	C	D

17. Look at the letter-number combinations below. Draw a circle around the third combination from the left. Write that letter-number combination in this space: ______ 17.____

T1 S5 P2 Q5 P5 R2

18. Draw a line under each letter that appears only once in the line. Write the letter "Q" and the number of lines you drew here: ______ 18.____

S T Q T Q P T Q

19. Look again at the line of letters in question 16. Draw a circle around each "Q." Write the letter that appears at the beginning of the line and the number of circles you drew here: 19.____

______

20. Select the sentence which is MOST APPROPRIATE with respect to grammar, usage and punctuation suitable for a formal letter or report: 20.____

A. Major repairs has caused the cafeteria to be closed until late October.
B. The cafeteria will be closed until late October on account of major repairs.

C. The cafeteria will be closed for major repairs until late October.
D. The closing of the cafeteria until late October due to the completion of major repairs.

In questions 21 through 23, identify the most similar meaning to the highlighted word:

21. The staff was **amazed** by the news. 21.___

A. pleased
B. surprised
C. saddened
D. relieved

22. Please **delete** the second paragraph. 22.___

A. retype
B. reread
C. revise
D. remove

23. Did you **duplicate** the information as written? 23.___

A. type
B. copy
C. remember
D. understand

24. "It is a simple matter to find and correct the errors made by a typist, but often a file clerk's errors are not discovered until something which is needed cannot be found. For this reason, the work of every file clerk should be checked at regular intervals." 24.___
The paragraph BEST supports the statement that filing

A. may contain errors that are not immediately noticeable
B. should be organized by typists rather than file clerks
C. is a more difficult process than typing
D. should be checked for errors more frequently than typing

25. "The most efficient method for performing a task is not always easily determined. That which is economical in terms of time must be carefully distinguished from that which is economical in terms of expended energy. In short, the quickest method may require a degree of physical effort that may be neither essential nor desirable." The paragraph BEST supports the statement that 25.___

A. it is more efficient to perform a task slowly than rapidly
B. skill in performing a task should not be acquired at the expense of time
C. the most efficient execution of a task is not always the one done in the shortest time
D. energy and time cannot both be considered in the performance of a single task

KEY (CORRECT ANSWERS)

1. B
2. D
3. E
4. D
5. B

6. E
7. C
8. A
9. D
10. B

11. B
12. C
13. E
14. B
15. A

16. C
17. B
18. C
19. A
20. C

21. B
22. D
23. B
24. A
25. C

CLERICAL ABILITIES TEST

Clerical aptitude involves the ability to perceive pertinent detail in verbal or tabular material, to observe differences in copy, to proofread words and numbers, and to avoid perceptual errors in arithmetic computation.

NATURE OF THE TEST

Four types of clerical aptitude questions are presented in the Clerical Abilities Test. There are 120 questions with a short time limit. The test contains 30 questions on name and number checking, 30 on the arrangement of names in correct alphabetical order, 30 on simple arithmetic, and 30 on inspecting groups of letters and numbers. The questions have been arranged in groups or cycles of five questions of each type. The Clerical Abilities Test is primarily a test of speed in carrying out relatively simple clerical tasks. While accuracy on these tasks is important and will be taken into account in the scoring, experience has shown that many persons are so concerned about accuracy that they do the test more slowly than they should. Competitors should be cautioned that speed as well as accuracy is important to achieve a good score.

HOW THE TEST IS ADMINISTERED

Each competitor should be given a copy of the test booklet with sample questions on the cover page, an answer sheet, and a medium No. 2 pencil. Ten minutes are allowed to study the directions and sample questions and to answer the questions in the proper boxes on the two pages.

The separate answer sheet should be used for the test proper. Fifteen minutes are allowed for the test.

HOW THE TEST IS SCORED

The correct answers should be counted and recorded. The number of incorrect answers must also be counted because one-fourth of the number of incorrect answers is subtracted from the number of right answers. An omission is considered as neither a right nor a wrong answer. The score on this test is the number of right answers minus one-fourth of the number of wrong answers (fractions of one-half or less are dropped). For example, if an applicant had answered 89 questions correctly and 10 questions incorrectly, and had omitted 1 question, his score would be 87.

EXAMINATION SECTION

DIRECTIONS: This test contains four kinds of questions. There are some of each kind on each page in the booklet. The time limit for the test will be announced by the examiner.
Use the special pencil furnished by the examiner in marking your answers on the separate answer sheet. For each question, there are five suggested answers. Decide which answer is correct, find the number of the question on the answer sheet, and make a solid black mark between the dotted lines just below the letter of your answer. If you wish to change your answer, erase the first mark completely, do not merely cross it out.

SAMPLE QUESTIONS

In each line across the page there are three names or numbers that are much alike. Compare the three names or numbers and decide which ones are exactly alike. On the Sample Answer Sheet at the right, mark the answer

A. if ALL THREE names or numbers are exactly ALIKE
B. if only the FIRST and SECOND names or numbers are exactly ALIKE
C. if only the FIRST and THIRD names or numbers are exactly ALIKE
D. if only the SECOND and THIRD names or numbers are exactly ALIKE
E. if ALL THREE names or numbers are DIFFERENT

I.	Davis Hazen	David Hozen	David Hazen
II.	Lois Appel	Lois Appel	Lois Apfel
III.	June Allan	Jane Allan	Jane Allan
IV.	10235	10235	10235
V.	32614	32164	32614

SAMPLE ANSWER SHEET

	A	B	C	D	E
I					
II					
III					
IV					
V					
VI					
VII					

It will be to your advantage to learn what A, B, C, D, and E stand for. If you finish the sample questions before you are told to turn to the test, study them.

2

In the next group of sample questions, there is a name in a box at the left, and four other names in alphabetical order at the right. Find the correct space for the boxed name so that it will be in alphabetical order with the others, and mark the letter of that space as your answer.

VI. | Jones, Jane |

A. →
Goodyear, G.L.
B. →
Haddon, Harry
C. →
Jackson, Mary
D. →
Jenkins, William
E. →

VII. | Kessler, Neilson |

A. →
Kessel, Carl
B. →
Kessinger, D.J.
C. →
Kessler, Karl
D. →
Kessner, Lewis
E. →

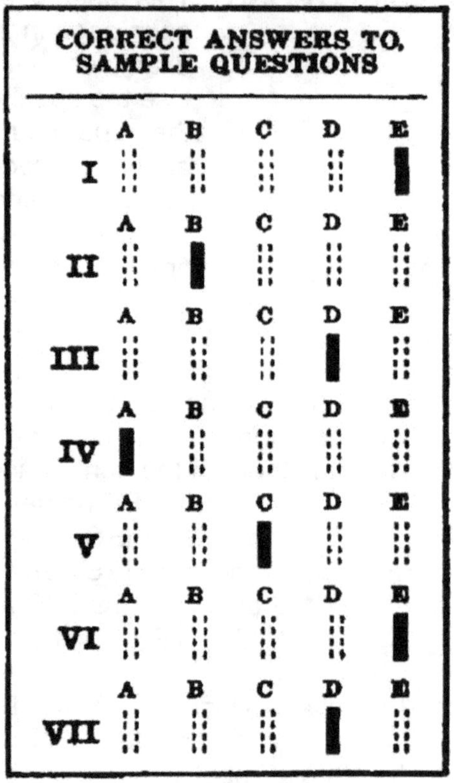

DIRECTIONS: In the following questions, complete the equation and find your answer among the list of suggested answers. Mark the Sample Answer Sheet A, B, C, or D for the answer you obtained; or if your answer is not among these, mark E for that question.

VIII. Add: 22
+33

A. 44 B. 45 C. 54 D. 55 E. None of these

IX. Subtract: 24
- 3

A. 20 B. 21 C. 27 D. 29 E. None of these

X. Multiply: 25
x 5

A. 100 B. 115 C. 125 D. 135 E. None of these

XI. Divide: $6\overline{)126}$

A. 20   B. 22   C. 24   D. 26   E. None of these

DIRECTIONS: There is one set of suggested answers for the next group of sample questions. Do not try to memorize these answers, because there will be a different set on each age in the test.

To find the answer to a question, find which suggested answer contains numbers and letters, all of which appear in the question. If no suggested answer fits, mark E for that question.

XII. 8 N K 9 G T 4 6

XIII. T 9 7 Z 6 L 3 K

XIV. Z 7 G K 3 9 8 N

XV. 3 K 9 4 6 G Z L

XVI. Z N 7 3 8 K T 9

Suggested Answers
A = 7, 9, G, K
B = 8, 9, T, Z
C = 6, 7, K, Z
D = 6, 8, G, T
E = None of the above

	SAMPLE ANSWER SHEET					CORRECT ANSWERS TO SAMPLE QUESTIONS				
	A	B	C	D	E	A	B	C	D	E
VIII									▮	
IX							▮			
X								▮		
XI										▮
XII									▮	
XIII								▮		
XIV						▮				
XV										▮
XVI							▮			

After you have marked your answers to all the questions on the Sample Answer Sheets on this page and on the front page of the booklet, check them with the answers in the boxes marked Correct Answers To Sample Questions.

Questions 1-5.

In Questions 1 through 5, compare the three names or numbers, and mark
A. if ALL THREE names or numbers are exactly ALIKE
B. if only the FIRST and SECOND names or numbers are exactly ALIKE
C. if only the FIRST and THIRD names or numbers are exactly ALIKE
D. if only the SECOND and THIRD names or numbers are exactly ALIKE
E. if ALL THREE names or numbers are DIFFERENT

1.	5261383	5261383	5261338
2.	8125690	8126690	8125609
3.	W.E. Johnston	W.E. Johnson	W.E. Johnson
4.	Vergil L. Muller	Vergil L. Muller	Vergil L. Muller

5. Atherton R. Warde Asheton R. Warde Atherton P. Warde

Questions 6-10.

In Questions 6 through 10, find the correct place for the name in the box

6. | Hackett, Gerald |

A. →
Habert, James
B. →
Hachett, J.J.
C. →
Hachetts, K. Larson
D. →
Hachettson, Leroy
E. →

7. | Margenroth, Alvin |

A. →
Margeroth, Albert
B. →
Margestein, Dan
C. →
Margestein, David
D. →
Margue, Edgar
E. →

8. | Bobbitt, Olivier E. |

A. →
Bobbitt, D. Olivier
B. →
Bobbitt, Olivia B
C. →
Bobbitt, Olivia H.
D. →
Bobbitt, R. Olivia
E. →

9. | Mosley, Werner |

A. →
Mosely, Albert J.
B. →
Mosley, Alvin
C. →
Mosley, S.M.
D. →
Mozley, Vinson N.
E. →

10. | Youmuns, Frank L. |

A. →
Youmons, Frank G.
B. →
Youmons, Frank H.
C. →
Youmons, Frank K.
D. →
Youmons, Frank M.
E. →

Questions 11-15.

11. Add: 43
+32

A. 55 B. 65 C. 66 D. 75 E. None of these

12. Subtract: 83
- 4

A. 73 B. 79 C. 80 D. 89 E. None of these

13. Multiply: 41
x 7

A. 281 B. 287 C. 291 D. 297 E. None of these

14. Divide: $6\overline{)306}$

A. 44 B. 51 C. 52 D. 60 E. None of these

15. Add: 37
+15

A. 42 B. 52 C. 53 D. 62 E. None of these

Questions 16-20.

In Questions 16 through 20, find which one of the suggested answers appears in that question.

16. 6 2 5 K 4 P T G

17. L 4 7 2 T 6 V K

18. 3 5 4 L 9 V T G

19. G 4 K 7 L 3 5 Z

SUGGESTED ANSWERS
A = 4, 5, K, T
B = 4, 7, G, K
C = 2, 5, G, L
D = 2, 7, L, T
E = None of the above

20. 4 K 2 9 N 5 T G

Questions 21-25.

In Questions 21 through 25, compare the three names or numbers, and mark

A. if ALL THREE names or numbers are exactly ALIKE
B. if only the FIRST and SECOND names or numbers are exactly ALIKE
C. if only the FIRST and THIRD names or numbers are exactly ALIKE
D. if only the SECOND and THIRD names or numbers are exactly ALIKE
E. if ALL THREE names or numbers are DIFFERENT

21.	2395890	2395890	2395890
22.	1926341	1926347	1926314
23.	E. Owens McVey	E. Owen McVey	E. Owen McVay
24.	Emily Neal Rouse	Emily Neal Rowse	Emily Neal Rowse
25.	H. Merritt Audubon	H. Merriott Audubon	H. Merritt Audubon

Questions 26-30.

In Questions 26 through 30, find the correct place for the name in the box.

26. Watters, N.O.

A. →
Waters, Charles L.
B. →
Waterson, Nina P.
C. →
Watson, Nora J.
D. →
Wattwood, Paul A.
E. →

27. Johnston, Edward

A. →
Johnston, Edgar R.
B. →
Johnston, Edmond
C. →
Johnston, Edmund
D. →
Johnstone, Edmund A.
E. →

28. Rensch, Adeline

A. →
Ramsay, Amos
B. →
Remschel, Augusta
C. →
Renshaw, Austin
D. →
Rentzel, Becky
E. →

29. Schnyder, Maurice

A. →
Schneider, Martin
B. →
Schneider, Mertens
C. →
Schnyder, Newman
D. →
Schreibner, Norman
E. →

30. Freedenburg, C. Erma

A. →
Freedenberg, Emerson
B. →
Freedenberg, Erma
C. →
Freedenberg, Erma E.
D. →
Freedinberg, Erma F.
E. →

Questions 31-35.

31. Subtract: $\begin{array}{r} 68 \\ \underline{-\ 47} \end{array}$

A. 10 B. 11 C. 20 D. 22 E. None of these

32. Multiply: $\begin{array}{r} 50 \\ \underline{\times\ 8} \end{array}$

A. 400 B. 408 C. 450 D. 458 E. None of these

33. Divide: $9\overline{)180}$

A. 20 B. 29 C. 30 D. 39 E. None of these

34. Add: $\begin{array}{r} 78 \\ \underline{+\ 63} \end{array}$

A. 131 B. 140 C. 141 D. 151 E. None of these

35. Add: 89
 - 70

A. 9 B. 18 C. 19 D. 29 E. None of these

Questions 36-40.

In Questions 36 through 40, find which one of the suggested answers appears in that question.

36. 9 G Z 3 L 4 6 N

37. L 5 N K 4 3 9 V

38. 8 2 V P 9 L Z 5

39. V P 9 Z 5 L 8 7

40. 5 T 8 N 2 9 V L

SUGGESTED ANSWERS
A = 4, 9, L, V
B = 4, 5, N, Z
C = 5, 8, L, Z
D = 8, 9, N, V
E = None of the above

Questions 41-45.

In Questions 41 through 45, compare the three names or numbers, and mark
- A. if ALL THREE names or numbers are exactly ALIKE
- B. if only the FIRST and SECOND names or numbers are exactly ALIKE
- C. if only the FIRST and THIRD names or numbers are exactly ALIKE
- D. if only the SECOND and THIRD names or numbers are exactly ALIKE
- E. if ALL THREE names or numbers are DIFFERENT

41.	6219354	621354	6219354
42.	2312793	2312793	2312793
43.	1065407	1065407	1065047
44.	Francis Ransdell	Frances Ramsdell	Francis Ramsdell
45.	Cornelius Detwiler	Cornelius Detwiler	Cornelius Detwiler

Questions 46-50.

In Questions 46 through 50, find the correct place for the name in the box.

46. | DeMattia, Jessica |

A. →
DeLong, Jesse
B. →
DeMatteo, Jessie
C. →
Derby, Jessie S.
D. →
DeShazo, L.M.
E. →

47. | Theriault, Louis |

A. →
Therien, Annette
B. →
Therien, Elaine
C. →
Thibeault, Gerald
D. →
Thiebeault, Pierre
E. →

48. | Gaston, M. Hubert |

A. →
Gaston, Dorothy M.
B. →
Gaston, Henry N.
C. →
Gaston, Isabel
D. →
Gaston, M. Melvin
E. →

49. | SanMiguel, Carlos |

A. →
SanLuis, Juana
B. →
Santilli, Laura
C. →
Stinnett, Nellie
D. →
Stoddard, Victor
E. →

50. DeLaTour, Hall F.

A. →
DeLargy, Harold
B. →
DeLathouder, Hilda
C. →
Lathrop, Hillary
D. →
LaTour, Hulbert E.
E. →

Questions 51-55.

51. Multiply: $\begin{array}{r} 62 \\ \underline{\times\ 5} \end{array}$

A. 300 B. 310 C. 315 D. 360 E. None of these

52. Divide: $3\overline{)153}$

A. 41 B. 43 C. 51 D. 53 E. None of these

53. Add: $\begin{array}{r} 47 \\ \underline{+21} \end{array}$

A. 58 B. 59 C. 67 D. 68 E. None of these

54. Subtract: $\begin{array}{r} 87 \\ \underline{-42} \end{array}$

A. 34 B. 35 C. 44 D. 45 E. None of these

55. Multiply: $\begin{array}{r} 37 \\ \underline{\times\ 3} \end{array}$

A. 91 B. 101 C. 104 D. 114 E. None of these

Questions 56-60.

For Questions 56 through 60, find which one of the suggested answers appears in that question.

56. N 5 4 7 T K 3 Z
57. 8 5 3 V L 2 Z N
58. 7 2 5 N 9 K L V
59. 9 8 L 2 5 Z K V
60. Z 6 5 V 9 3 P N

SUGGESTED ANSWERS
A = 3, 8, K, N
B = 5, 8, N, V
C = 3, 9, V, Z
D = 5, 9, K, Z
E = None of the above

Questions 61-65.

In Questions 61 through 65, compare the three names or numbers, and mark
A. if ALL THREE names or numbers are exactly ALIKE
B. if only the FIRST and SECOND names or numbers are exactly ALIKE
C. if only the FIRST and THIRD names or numbers are exactly ALIKE
D. if only the SECOND and THIRD names or numbers are exactly ALIKE
E. if ALL THREE names or numbers are DIFFERENT

61.	6452054	6452654	6452054
62.	8501268	8501268	8501286
63	Ella Burk Newham	Ella Burk Newnham	Elena Burk Newnham
64.	Jno. K. Ravencroft	Jno. H. Ravencroft	Jno. H. Ravencoft
65.	Martin Wills Pullen	Martin Wills Pulen	Martin Wills Pullen

Questions 66-70.

In Questions 66 through 70, find the correct place for the name in the box.

66. O'Bannon, M.J.

A. →
O'Beirne, B.B.
B. →
Oberlin, E.L.
C. →
Oberneir, L.P.
D. →
O'Brian, S.F.
E. →

67. Entsminger, Jacob

A. →
Ensminger, J.
B. →
Entsminger, J.A.
C. →
Entsminger, Jack
D. →
Entsminger, James
E. →

68. Iacone, Pete R.

A. →
Iacone, Pedro
B. →
Iacone, Pedro M.
C. →
Iacone, Peter F.
D. →
Iascone, Peter W.
E. →

69. Sheppard, Gladys

A. →
Shepard, Dwight
B. →
Shepard, F.H.
C. →
Shephard, Louise
D. →
Shepperd, Stella
E. →

70. Thackton, Melvin T.

A. →
Thackston, Milton G.
B. →
Thackston, Milton W.
C. →
Thackston, Theodore
D. →
Thackston, Thomas G.
E. →

Questions 71-75.

71. Divide: $7\overline{)357}$

A. 51 B. 52 C. 53 D. 54 E. None of these

72. Add: 58
+27

A. 75 B. 84 C. 85 D. 95 E. None of these

73. Subtract: 86
- 57

A. 18 B. 29 C. 38 D. 39 E. None of these

74. Multiply: $\begin{array}{r} 68 \\ \underline{\times\ 4} \end{array}$

A. 242 B. 264 C. 272 D. 274 E. None of these

75. Divide: $9\overline{)639}$

A. 71 B. 73 C. 81 D. 83 E. None of these

Questions 76-80.

For Questions 76 through 80, find which one of the suggested answers appears in that question.

76. 6 Z T N 8 7 4 V

77. V 7 8 6 N 5 P L

78. N 7 P V 8 4 2 L

79. 7 8 G 4 3 V L T

80. 4 8 G 2 T N 6 L

SUGGESTED ANSWERS
A = 2, 7, L, N
B = 2, 8, T, V
C = 6, 8, L, T
D = 6, 7, N, V
E = None of the above

Questions 81-85.

In Questions 81 through 85, compare the three names or numbers, and mark
A. if ALL THREE names or numbers are exactly ALIKE
B. if only the FIRST and SECOND names or numbers are exactly ALIKE
C. if only the FIRST and THIRD names or numbers are exactly ALIKE
D. if only the SECOND and THIRD names or numbers are exactly ALIKE
E. if ALL THREE names or numbers are DIFFERENT

81.	3457988	3457986	3457986
82.	4695682	4695862	4695682
83.	Stricklund Kanedy	Stricklund Kanedy	Stricklund Kanedy
84.	Joy Harbor Witner	Joy Harloe Witner	Joy Harloe Witner
85.	R.M.O. Uberroth	R.M.O. Uberroth	R.N.O. Uberroth

Questions 86-90.

In Questions 86 through 90, find the correct place for the name in the box.

86. | Dunlavey, M. Hilary |

A. →
Dunleavy, Hilary G.
B. →
Dunleavy, Hilary K.
C. →
Dunleavy, Hilary S.
D. →
Dunleavy, Hilery W.
E. →

87. | Yarbrough, Maria |

A. →
Yabroudy, Margy
B. →
Yarboro, Marie
C. →
Yarborough, Marina
D. →
Yarborough, Mary
E. →

88. | Prouty, Martha |

A. →
Proutey, Margaret
B. →
Proutey, Maude
C. →
Prouty, Myra
D. →
Prouty, Naomi
E. →

89. | Pawlowicz, Ruth M. |

A. →
Pawalek, Edward
B. →
Pawelek, Flora G.
C. →
Pawlowski, Joan M.
D. →
Pawtowski, Wanda
E. →

90. Vanstory, George

A. →
Vanover, Eva
B. →
VanSwinderen, Floyd
C. →
VanSyckle, Harry
D. →
Vanture, Laurence
E. →

Questions 91-95

91. Add: 28
+35

A. 53 B. 62 C. 64 D. 73 E. None of these

92. Subtract: 78
-69

A. 7 B. 8 C. 18 D. 19 E. None of these

93. Multiply: 86
x 6

A. 492 B. 506 C. 516 D. 526 E. None of these

94. Divide: $8\overline{)648}$

A. 71 B. 76 C. 81 D. 89 E. None of these

95. Add: 97
+34

A. 131 B. 132 C. 140 D. 141 E. None of these

Questions 96-100.

For Questions 96 through 100, find which one of the suggested answers appears in that question.

96. V 5 7 Z N 9 4 T

97. 4 6 P T 2 N K 9

98. 6 4 N 2 P 8 Z K

99. 7 P 5 2 4 N K T

100. K T 8 5 4 N 2 P

SUGGESTED ANSWERS
A = 2, 5, N, Z
B = 4, 5, N, P
C = 2, 9, P, T
D = 4, 9, T, Z
E = None of the above

Questions 101-105.

In Questions 101 through 105, compare the three names or numbers, and mark
A. if ALL THREE names or numbers are exactly ALIKE
B. if only the FIRST and SECOND names or numbers are exactly ALIKE
C. if only the FIRST and THIRD names or numbers are exactly ALIKE
D. if only the SECOND and THIRD names or numbers are exactly ALIKE
E. if ALL THREE names or numbers are DIFFERENT

101. 1592514	1592574	1592574
102. 2010202	2010202	2010220
103. 6177396	6177936	6177396
104. Drusilla S. Ridgeley	Drusilla S. Ridgeley	Drusilla S. Ridgeley
105. Andrei I. Toumantzev	Andrei I. Tourmantzev	Andrei I. Toumantzov

Questions 106-110.

In Questions 106 through 110, find the correct place for the name in the box.

106. Fitzsimmons, Hugh

A. →
Fitts, Harold
B. →
Fitzgerald, June
C. →
FitzGibbon, Junius
D. →
FitzSimons, Martin
E. →

107. D'Amato, Vincent

A. →
Daly, Steven
B. →
D'Amboise, S. Vincent
C. →
Daniel, Vail
D. →
DeAlba, Valentina
E. →

108. Schaeffer, Roger D.

A. →
Schaffert, Evelyn M.
B. →
Schaffner, Margaret M.
C. →
Schafhirt, Milton G.
D. →
Shafer, Richard E.
E. →

109. White-Lewis, Cecil

A. →
Whitelaw, Cordelia
B. →
White-Leigh, Nancy
C. →
Whitely, Rodney
D. →
Whitlock, Warren
E. →

110. VanDerHeggen, Don

A. →
VanDemark, Doris
B. →
Vandenberg, H.E.
C. →
VanDercook, Marie
D. →
vanderLinden, Robert
E. →

Questions 111-115.

111. Add: 75
+49

A. 124 B. 125 C. 134 D. 225 E. None of these

112. Subtract: 69
- 45

A. 14 B. 23 C. 24 D. 26 E. None of these

113. Multiply: 36
x 8

A. 246 B. 262 C. 288 D. 368 E. None of these

114. Divide: $8\overline{)328}$

A. 31 B. 41 C. 42 D. 48 E. None of these

115. Multiply: 58
x 9

A. 472 B. 513 C. 521 D. 522 E. None of these

Questions 116-120.

For Questions 116 through 120, find which one of the suggested answers appears in that question.

116. Z 3 N P G 5 4 2

117. 6 N 2 8 G 4 P T

118. 6 N 4 T V G 8 2

119. T 3 P 4 N 8 G 2

120. 6 7 K G N 2 L 5

SUGGESTED ANSWERS:
A = 2, 3, G, N
B = 2, 6, N, T
C = 3, 4, G, K
D = 4, 6, K, T
E = None of the above

KEY (CORRECT ANSWERS)

1.	B	21	A	41.	A	61	C	81	D	101.	D
2.	E	22.	E	42.	A	62.	B	82.	C	102.	B
3.	D	23.	E	43.	B	63.	E	83.	A	103.	C
4.	A	24.	D	44.	E	64.	E	84.	D	104.	A
5.	E	25.	C	45.	A	65.	C	85.	B	105.	E
6.	E	26.	D	46.	C	66.	A	86.	A	106.	D
7.	A	27.	D	47.	A	667.	D	87.	E	107.	B
8.	D	28.	C	48.	D	68.	C	88.	C	108.	A
9.	B	29.	C	49.	B	69.	D	89.	C	109.	C
10.	E	30.	D	50.	C	70.	E	90.	B	110.	D
11.	D	31.	E	51.	B	71.	A	91.	E	111.	A
12.	B	32.	A	52.	C	72.	C	92.	E	112.	C
13.	B	33.	A	53.	D	73.	B	93.	C	113.	C
14.	B	34.	C	54.	D	74.	C	94.	C	114.	B
15.	B	35.	C	55.	E	75.	A	95.	A	115.	D
16.	A	36.	E	56.	E	76.	D	96.	D	116.	A
17.	D	37.	A	57.	B	77.	D	97.	C	117.	B
18.	E	38.	C	58.	E	78.	A	98.	E	118.	B
19.	B	39.	C	59.	D	79.	E	99.	B	119.	A
20.	A	40.	D	60.	C	80.	C	100.	B	120.	E

CLERICAL ABILITIES TEST

EXAMINATION SECTION

TEST 1

DIRECTIONS: Each question or incomplete statement is followed by several suggested answers or completions. Select the one that BEST answers the question or completes the statement. *PRINT THE LETTER OF THE CORRECT ANSWER IN THE SPACE AT THE RIGHT.*

Questions 1-10.

DIRECTIONS: Questions 1 through 10 consist of lines of names, dates, and numbers. For each question, you are to choose the option (A, B, C, or D) in Column II which EXACTLY matches the information in Column I. *PRINT THE LETTER OF THE CORRECT ANSWER IN THE SPACE AT THE RIGHT.*

SAMPLE QUESTION

Column I	Column II
Schneider 11/16/75 581932	A. Schneider 11/16/75 518932
	B. Schneider 11/16/75 581932
	C. Schnieder 11/16/75 581932
	D. Shnieder 11/16/75 518932

The correct answer is B. Only Option B shows the name, date, and number exactly as they are in Column I. Option A has a mistake in the number. Option C has a mistake in the name. Option D has a mistake in the name and in the number. Now answer Questions 1 through 10 in the same manner.

	Column I	Column II	
1.	Johnston 12/26/74 659251	A. Johnson 12/23/74 659251	1.____
		B. Johston 12/26/74 659251	
		C. Johnston 12/26/74 695251	
		D. Johnston 12/26/74 659251	
2.	Allison 1/26/75 9939256	A. Allison 1/26/75 9939256	2.____
		B. Alisson 1/26/75 9939256	
		C. Allison 1/26/76 9399256	
		D. Allison 1/26/75 9993356	
3.	Farrell 2/12/75 361251	A. Farell 2/21/75 361251	3.____
		B. Farrell 2/12/75 361251	
		C. Farrell 2/21/75 361251	
		D. Farrell 2/12/75 361151	

4. Guerrero 4/28/72 105689

A. Guererro 4/28/72 105689
B. Guererro 4/28/72 105986
C. Guerrero 4/28/72 105869
D. Guerrero 4/28/72 105689

4.____

5. McDonnell 6/05/73 478215

A. McDonnell 6/15/73 478215
B. McDonnell 6/05/73 478215
C. McDonnell 6/05/73 472815
D. MacDonell 6/05/73 478215

5.____

6. Shepard 3/31/71 075421

A. Sheperd 3/31/71 075421
B. Shepard 3/13/71 075421
C. Shepard 3/31/71 075421
D. Shepard 3/13/71 075241

6.____

7. Russell 4/01/69 031429

A. Russell 4/01/69 031429
B. Russell 4/10/69 034129
C. Russell 4/10/69 031429
D. Russell 4/01/69 034129

7.____

8. Phillips 10/16/68 961042

A. Philipps 10/16/68 961042
B. Phillips 10/16/68 960142
C. Phillips 10/16/68 961042
D. Philipps 10/16/68 916042

8.____

9. Campbell 11/21/72 624856

A. Campbell 11/21/72 624856
B. Campbell 11/21/72 624586
C. Campbell 11/21/72 624686
D. Campbel 11/21/72 624856

9.____

10. Patterson 9/18/71 76199176

A. Patterson 9/18/72 76191976
B. Patterson 9/18/71 76199176
C. Patterson 9/18/72 76199176
D. Patterson 9/18/71 76919176

10.____

Questions 11-15.

DIRECTIONS: Questions 11 through 15 consist of groups of numbers and letters which you are to compare. For each question, you are to choose the option (A, B,C, or D) in Column I which EXACTLY matches the group of numbers and letters given in Column I.

SAMPLE QUESTION

Column I
B92466

Column II
A. B92644
B. B94266
C. A92466
D. B92466

The correct answer is D. Only Option D in Column II shows the group of numbers and letters EXACTLY as it appears in Column I. Now answer Questions 11 through 15 in the same manner.

	Column I	Column II	
11.	925AC5	A. 952CA5 B. 925AC5 C. 952AC5 D. 925CA6	11.____
12.	Y006925	A. Y060925 B. Y006295 C. Y006529 D. Y006925	12.____
13.	J236956	A. J236956 B. J326965 C. J239656 D. J932656	13.____
14.	AB6952	A. AB6952 B. AB9625 C. AB9652 D. AB6925	14.____
15.	X259361	A. X529361 B. X259631 C. X523961 D. X259361	15.____

Questions 16-25.

DIRECTIONS: Each of questions 16 through 25 consists of three lines of code letters and three lines of numbers. The numbers on each line should correspond with the code letters on the same line in accordance with the table below.

Code Letter	S	V	W	A	Q	M	X	E	G	K
Corresponding Number	0	1	2	3	4	5	5	7	8	9

On some of the lines, an error exists in the coding. Compare the letters and numbers in each question carefully. If you find an error or errors on:

only one of the lines in the question, mark your answer A;
any two lines in the question, mark your answer B;
all three lines in the question, mark your answer C;
none of the lines in the question, mark your answer D.

SAMPLE QUESTION

WQGKSXG	2489068
XEKVQMA	6591453
KMAESXV	9527061

In the above sample, the first line is correct since each code letter listed has the correct corresponding number. On the second line, an error exists because code letter E should have the number 7 instead of the number 5. On the third line, an error exists because the code letter A should have the number 3 instead of the number 2. Since there are errors in two of the three lines, the correct answer is B. Now answer Questions 16 through 25 in the same manner.

16.	SWQEKGA	0247983	16.____
	KEAVSXM	9731065	
	SSAXGKQ	0036894	
17.	QAMKMVS	4259510	17.____
	MGGEASX	5897306	
	KSWMKWS	9125920	
18.	WKXQWVE	2964217	18.____
	QKXXQVA	4966413	
	AWMXGVS	3253810	
19.	GMMKASE	8559307	19.____
	AWVSKSW	3210902	
	QAVSVGK	4310189	
20.	XGKQSMK	6894049	20.____
	QSVKEAS	4019730	
	GSMXKMV	8057951	
21.	AEKMWSG	3195208	21.____
	MKQSVQK	5940149	
	XGQAEVW	6843712	
22.	XGMKAVS	6858310	22.____
	SKMAWEQ	0953174	
	GVMEQSA	8167403	
23.	VQSKAVE	1489317	23.____
	WQGKAEM	2489375	
	MEGKAWQ	5689324	
24.	XMQVSKG	6541098	24.____
	QMEKEWS	4579720	
	KMEVGKG	9571983	

25. GKVAMEW 88912572 25.____
AXMVKAE 3651937
KWAGMAV 9238531

Questions 26-35.

DIRECTIONS: Each of Questions 26 through 35 consists of a column of figures. For each question, add the column of figures and choose the correct answer from the four choices given.

26. 5,665.43 26.____
2,356.69
6,447.24
7,239.65

A. 20,698.01
B. 21,709.01
C. 21,718.01
D. 22,609.01

27. 817,209.55 27.____
264,354.29
82,368.76
849,964.89

A. 1,893.977.49
B. 1,989,988.39
C. 2,009,077.39
D. 2,013,897.49

28. 156,366.89 28.____
249,973.23
823,229.49
56,869.45

A. 1,286,439.06
B. 1,287,521.06
C. 1,297,539.06
D. 1,296,421.06

29. 23,422.15 29.____
149,696.24
238,377.53
86,289.79
505,533.63

A. 989,229.34
B. 999,879.34
C. 1,003,330.34
D. 1,023,329.34

30. 2,468,926.70
656,842.28
49,723.15
832,369.59 30.____

A. 3,218,062.72
B. 3,808,092.72
C. 4,007,861.72
D. 4,818,192.72

31. 524,201.52
7,775,678.51
8,345,299.63
40,628,898.08
31,374,670.07 31.____

A. 88,646,647.81
B. 88,646,747.91
C. 88,648,647.91
D. 88,648,747.81

32. 6,824,829.40
682,482.94
5,542,015.27
775,678.51
7,732,507.25 32.____

A. 21,557,513.37
B. 21,567,513.37
C. 22,567,503.37
D. 22,567,513.37

33. 22,109,405.58
6,097,093.43
5,050,073.99
8,118,050.05
4,313,980.82 33.____

A. 45,688,593.87
B. 45,688,603.87
C. 45,689,593.87
D. 45,689,603.87

34. 79,324,114.19
99,848,129.74
43,331,653.31
41,610,207.14 34.____

A. 264,114,104.38
B. 264,114,114.38
C. 265,114,114.38
D. 265,214,104.38

35. 33,729,653.94 35.____
5,959,342.58
26,052,715.47
4,452,669.52
7,079,953.59

A. 76,374,334.10
B. 76,375,334.10
C. 77,274,335.10
D. 77,275,335.10

Questions 36-40.

DIRECTIONS: Each of Questions 36 through 40 consists of a single number in Column I and four options in Column II. For each question, you are to choose the option (A, B, C, or D) in Column II which EXACTLY matches the number in Column I.

SAMPLE QUESTION

Column I	Column II
5965121	A. 5956121
	B. 5965121
	C. 5966121
	D. 5965211

The correct answer is B. Only Option B shows the number EXACTLY as it appears in Column I. Now answer Questions 36 through 40 in the same manner.

	Column I	Column II	
36.	9643242	A. 9643242	36.____
		B. 9462342	
		C. 9642442	
		D. 9463242	
37.	3572477	A. 3752477	37.____
		B. 3725477	
		C. 3572477	
		D. 3574277	
38.	5276101	A. 5267101	38.____
		B. 5726011	
		C. 5271601	
		D. 5276101	
39.	4469329	A. 4496329	39.____
		B. 4469329	
		C. 4496239	
		D. 4469239	

40. 2326308

A. 2236308
B. 2233608
C. 2326308
D. 2323608

40.____

KEY (CORRECT ANSWERS)

1.	D	11.	B	21.	A	31.	D
2.	A	12.	D	22.	C	32.	A
3.	B	13.	A	23.	B	33.	B
4.	D	14.	A	24.	D	34.	A
5.	B	15.	D	25.	A	35.	C
6.	C	16.	D	26.	B	36.	A
7.	A	17.	C	27.	D	37.	C
8.	C	18.	A	28.	A	38.	D
9.	A	19.	D	29.	C	39.	B
10.	B	20.	B	30.	C	40.	C

TEST 2

DIRECTIONS: Each question or incomplete statement is followed by several suggested answers or completions. Select the one that BEST answers the question or completes the statement. *PRINT THE LETTER OF THE CORRECT ANSWER IN THE SPACE AT THE RIGHT.*

Questions 1-5.

DIRECTIONS: Each of Questions 1 through 5 consists of a name and a dollar amount. In each question, the name and dollar amount in Column II should be an EXACT copy of the name and dollar amount in Column I. If there is:
a mistake only in the name, mark your answer A;
a mistake only in the dollar amount, mark your answer B;
a mistake in both the name and the dollar amount, mark your answer C;
no mistake in either the name or the dollar amount, mark your answer D.

SAMPLE QUESTION

Column I	Column II
George Peterson $125.50	George Petersson $125.50

Compare the name and dollar amount in Column II with the name and dollar amount in Column I. The name *Petersson* in Column II is spelled *Peterson* in Column I. The amount is the same in both columns. Since there is a mistake only in the name, the answer to the sample question is A. Now answer Questions 1 through 5 in the same manner.

	Column I	Column II	
1.	Susanne Shultz $3440	Susanne Schultz $3440	1.____
2.	Anibal P. Contrucci $2121.61	Anibel P. Contrucci $2112.61	2.____
3.	Eugenio Mendoza $12.45	Eugenio Mendozza $12.45	3.____
4.	Maurice Gluckstadt $4297	Maurice Gluckstadt $4297	4.____
5.	John Pampellonne $4656.94	John Pammpellonne $4566.94	5.____

Questions 6-11.

DIRECTIONS: Each of Questions 6 through 11 consist of a set of names and addresses, which you are to compare. In each question, the name and addresses in Column II should be an EXACT copy of the name and address in Column I. If there is:
a mistake only in the name, mark your answer A;
a mistake only in the address, mark your answer B;
a mistake in both the name and address, mark your answer C;
no mistake in either the name or address, mark your answer D.

SAMPLE QUESTION

Column I	Column II
Michael Filbert 456 Reade Street New York, N.Y. 10013	Michael Filbert 645 Reade Street New York, N.Y. 10013

Since there is a mistake only in the address (the street number should be 456 instead of 645), the answer to the sample question is B. Now answer Questions 6 through 11 in the same manner.

	Column I	Column II	
6.	Hilda Goettelmann 55 Lenox Rd. Brooklyn, N.Y. 11226	Hilda Goettelman 55 Lenox Ave. Brooklyn, N.Y. 11226	6.____
7.	Arthur Sherman 2522 Batchelder St. Brooklyn, N.Y. 11235	Arthur Sharman 2522 Batcheder St. Brooklyn, N.Y. 11253	7.____
8.	Ralph Barnett 300 West 28 Street New York, New York 10001	Ralph Barnett 300 West 28 Street New York, New York 10001	8.____
9.	George Goodwin 135 Palmer Avenue Staten Island, New York 10302	George Godwin 135 Palmer Avenue Staten Island, New York 10302	9.____
10.	Alonso Ramirez 232 West 79 Street New York, N.Y. 10024	Alonso Ramirez 223 West 79 Street New York, N.Y. 10024	10.____
11.	Cynthia Graham 149-34 83 Street Howard Beach, N.Y. 11414	Cynthia Graham 149-35 83 Street Howard Beach, N.Y. 11414	11.____

Questions 12-20.

DIRECTIONS: Questions 12 through 20 are problems in subtraction. For each question do the subtraction and select your answer from the four choices given.

12. 232,921.85
-179,587.68 12.____

A. 52,433.17
B. 52,434.17
C. 53,334.17
D. 53,343,17

13. 5,531,876.29
-3,897,158.36 13.____

A. 1,634,717.93
B. 1,644,718.93
C. 1,734,717.93
D. 1,7234,718.93

14. 1,482,658.22
-937,925.76 14.____

A. 544,633.46
B. 544,732.46
C. 545,632.46
D. 545,732.46

15. 937,828.17
-259,673.88 15.____

A. 678,154.29
B. 679,154.29
C. 688,155.39
D. 699,155.39

16. 760,412.38
-263,465.95 16.____

A. 496,046.43
B. 496,946.43
C. 496,956.43
D. 497,046.43

17. 3,203,902.26
-2,933,087.96 17.____

A. 260,814.30
B. 269,824.30
C. 270,814.30
D. 270,824.30

18. 1,023,468.71
-934,678.88 18.____

A. 88,780.83
B. 88,789.83
C. 88,880.83
D. 88,889.83

19. 831,549.47 19.____
-772,814.78

A. 58,734.69
B. 58,834.69
C. 59,735.69
D. 59,834.69

20. 6,306,181.74 20.____
-3,617,376.99

A. 2,687,904.99
B. 2,688,904.99
C. 2,689,804.99
D. 2,799,905.99

Questions 21-30.

DIRECTIONS: Each of Questions 21 through 30 consists of three lines of code letters and three lines of numbers. The numbers on each line should correspond with the code letters on the same line in accordance with the table below.

Code Letter	J	U	B	T	Y	D	K	R	L	P
Corresponding Number	0	1	2	3	4	5	5	7	8	9

On some of the lines, an error exists in the coding. Compare the letters and numbers in each question carefully. If you find an error or errors on:
only *one* of the lines in the question, mark your answer A;
any *two* lines in the question, mark your answer B;
all *three* lines in the question, mark your answer C;
none of the lines in the question, mark your answer D.

SAMPLE QUESTION

BJRPYUR 2079417
DTBPYKJ 5328460
YKLDBLT 4685283

In the above sample, the first line is correct since each code letter listed has the correct corresponding number. On the second line, an error exists because code letter P should have the number 9 instead of the number 8. The third line is correct since each code letter listed has the correct corresponding number. Since there is an error in *one* of the three lines, the correct answer is A. Now answer Questions 21 through 30 in the same manner.

21. BYPDTJL 2495308 21.____
PLRDTJU 9815301
DTJRYLK 5207486

22. RPBYRJK 7934706 22.____
PKTYLBU 9624821
KDLPJYR 6489047

23.	TPYBUJR BYRKPTU DUKPYDL	3942107 2476931 5169458	23.____
24.	KBYDLPL BLRKBRU JTULDYB	6345898 2876261 0318542	24.____
25.	LDPYDKR BDKDRJL BDRPLUJ	8594567 2565708 2679810	25.____
26.	PLRLBPU LPYKRDJ TDKPDTR	9858291 88936750 3569527	26.____
27.	RKURPBY RYUKPTJ RTKPTJD	7617924 7426930 7369305	27.____
28.	DYKPBJT KLPJBTL TKPLBJP	5469203 6890238 3698209	28.____
29.	BTPRJYL LDKUTYR YDBLRPJ	2397148 8561347 4528190	29.____
30.	ULPBKYT KPDTRBJ YLKJPTB	1892643 6953720 4860932	30.____

KEY (CORRECT ANSWERS)

1.	A	11.	D	21.	B
2.	C	12.	C	22.	C
3.	A	13.	A	23.	D
4.	D	14.	B	24.	B
5.	C	15.	A	25.	A
6.	C	16.	B	26.	C
7.	C	17.	C	27.	A
8.	D	18.	B	28.	D
9.	A	19.	A	29.	B
10.	B	20.	B	30.	D

CLERICAL ABILITIES

EXAMINATION SECTION

TEST 1

DIRECTIONS: Each question or incomplete statement is followed by several suggested answers or completions. Select the one that BEST answers the question or completes the statement. *PRINT THE LETTER OF THE CORRECT ANSWER IN THE SPACE AT THE RIGHT.*

Questions 1-4.

DIRECTIONS: Questions 1 through 4 are to be answered on the basis of the information given below.

The most commonly used filing system and the one that is easiest to learn is alphabetical filing. This involves putting records in an A to Z order, according to the letters of the alphabet. The name of a person is filed by using the following order: first, the surname or last name; second, the first name; third, the middle name or middle initial. For example, *Henry C. Young* is filed under *Y* and thereafter under *Young, Henry C.* The name of a company is filed in the same way. For example, *Long Cabinet Co.* is filed under *L* while *John T. Long Cabinet Co.* is filed under *L* and thereafter under *Long, John T. Cabinet Co.*

1. The one of the following which lists the names of persons in the CORRECT alphabetical order is: 1.____
   A. Mary Carrie, Helen Carrol, James Carson, John Carter
   B. James Carson, Mary Carrie, John Carter, Helen Carrol
   C. Helen Carrol, James Carson, John Carter, Mary Carrie
   D. John Carter, Helen Carrol, Mary Carrie, James Carson

2. The one of the following which lists the names of persons in the CORRECT alphabetical order is: 2.____
   A. Jones, John C.; Jones, John A.; Jones, John P.; Jones, John K.
   B. Jones, John P.; Jones, John K.; Jones, John C.; Jones, John A.
   C. Jones, John A.; Jones, John C.; Jones, John K.; Jones, John P.
   D. Jones, John K.; Jones, John C.; Jones, John A.; Jones, John P.

3. The one of the following which lists the names of the companies in the CORRECT alphabetical order is: 3.____
   A. Blane Co., Blake Co., Block Co., Blear Co.
   B. Blake Co., Blane Co., Blear Co., Block Co.
   C. Block Co., Blear Co., Blane Co., Blake Co.
   D. Blear Co., Blake Co., Blane Co., Block Co.

4. You are to return to the file an index card on *Barry C. Wayne Materials and Supplies Co.* 4.____
Of the following, the CORRECT alphabetical group that you should return the index card to is
   A. A to G B. H to M C. N to S D. T to Z

Questions 5-10.

DIRECTIONS: In each of Questions 5 through 10, the names of four people are given. For each question, choose as your answer the one of the four names given which should be filed FIRST according to the usual system of alphabetical filing of names, as described in the following paragraph.

In filing names, you must start with the last name. Names are filed in order of the first letter of the last name, then the second letter, etc. Therefore, BAILY would be filed before BROWN, which would be filed before COLT. A name with fewer letters of the same type comes first, i.e., Smith before Smithe. If the last names are the same, the names are filed alphabetically by the first name. If the first name is an initial, a name with an initial would come before a first name that starts with the same letter as the initial. Therefore, I. BROWN would come before IRA BROWN. Finally, if both last name and first name are the same, the name would be filed alphabetically by the middle name, once again an initial coming before a middle name which starts with the same letter as the initial. If there is no middle name at all, the name would come before those with middle initials or names.

SAMPLE QUESTION: A. Lester Daniels
B. William Dancer
C. Nathan Danzig
D. Dan Lester

The last names beginning with D are filed before the last name beginning with L. Since DANIELS, DANCER, and DANZIG all begin with the same three letters, you must look at the fourth letter of the last name to determine which name should be filed first. C comes before I or Z in the alphabet, so DANCER is filed before DANIELS or DANZIG. Therefore, the answer to the above sample question is B.

5. A. Scott Biala 5.____
B. Mary Byala
C. Martin Baylor
D. Francis Bauer

6. A. Howard J. Black 6.____
B. Howard Black
C. J. Howard Black
D. John H. Black

7. A. Theodora Garth Kingston 7.____
B. Theadore Barth Kingston
C. Thomas Kingston
D. Thomas T. Kingston

8. A. Paulette Mary Huerta 8.____
B. Paul M. Huerta
C. Paulette L. Huerta
D. Peter A. Huerta

9. A. Martha Hunt Morgan 9.____
B. Martin Hunt Morgan
C. Mary H. Morgan
D. Martine H. Morgan

10. A. James T. Meerschaum 10.____
B. James M. Mershum
C. James F. Mearshaum
D. James N. Meshum

Questions 11-14.

DIRECTIONS: Questions 11 through 14 are to be answered SOLELY on the basis of the following information.

You are required to file various documents in file drawers which are labeled according to the following pattern:

DOCUMENTS

MEMOS		LETTERS	
File	Subject	File	Subject
84PM1	(A-L)	84PC1	(A-L)
84PM2	(M-Z)	84PC2	(M-Z)

REPORTS		INQUIRIES	
File	Subject	File	Subject
84PR1	(A-L)	84PQ1	(A-L)
84PR2	(M-Z)	84PQ2	(M-Z)

11. A letter dealing with a burglary should be filed in the drawer labeled 11.____
A. 84PM1 B. 84PC1 C. 84PR1 D. 84PQ2

12. A report on Statistics should be found in the drawer labeled 12.____
A. 84PM1 B. 84PC2 C. 84PR2 D. 84PQS

13. An inquiry is received about parade permit procedures. It should be filed in the drawer labeled 13.____
A. 84PM2 B. 84PC1 C. 84PR1 D. 84PQ2

14. A police officer has a question about a robbery report you filed. You should pull this file from the drawer labeled 14.____
A. 84PM1 B. 84PM2 C. 84PR1 D. 84PR2

Questions 15-22.

DIRECTIONS: Each of Questions 15 through 22 consists of four or six numbered names. For each question, choose the option (A, B, C, or D) which indicates the order in which the names should be filed in accordance with the following filing instructions:

- File alphabetically according to last name, then first name, then middle initial.
- File according to each successive letter within a name.
- When comparing two names in which the letters in the longer name are identical to the corresponding letters in the shorter name, the shorter name is filed first.
- When the last names are the same, initials are always filed before names beginning with the same letter.

15. I. Ralph Robinson
    II. Alfred Ross
    III. Luis Robles
    IV. James Roberts

    The CORRECT filing sequence for the above names should be
    A. IV, II, I, III B. I, IV, III, II C. III, IV, I, II D. IV, I, III, II

15.____

16. I. Irwin Goodwin
    II. Inez Gonzalez
    III. Irene Goodman
    IV. Ira S. Goodwin
    V. Ruth I. Goldstein
    VI. M.B. Goodman

    The CORRECT filing sequence for the above names should be
    A. V, II, I, IV, III, VI B. V, II, VI, III, IV, I
    C. V, II, III, VI, IV, I D. V, II, III, VI, I, IV

16.____

17. I. George Allan
    II. Gregory Allen
    III. Gary Allen
    IV. George Allen

    The CORRECT filing sequence for the above names should be
    A. IV, III, I, II B. I, IV, II, III C. III, IV, I, II D. I, III, IV, II

17.____

18. I. Simon Kauffman 18.____
II. Leo Kaufman
III. Robert Kaufmann
IV. Paul Kauffmann

The CORRECT filing sequence for the above names should be
A. I, IV, II, III B. II, IV, III, I C. III, II, IV, I D. I, II, III, IV

19. I. Roberta Williams 19.____
II. Robin Wilson
III. Roberta Wilson
IV. Robin Williams

The CORRECT filing sequence for the above names should be
A. III, II, IV, I B. I, IV, III, II C. I, II, III, IV D. III, I, II, IV

20. I. Lawrence Shultz 20.____
II. Albert Schultz
III. Theodore Schwartz
IV. Thomas Schwarz
V. Alvin Schultz
VI. Leonard Shultz

The CORRECT filing sequence for the above names should be
A. II, V, III, IV, I, VI
B. IV, III, V, I, II, VI
C. II, V, I, VI, III, IV
D. I, VI, II, V, III, IV

21. I. McArdle 21.____
II. Mayer
III. Maletz
IV. McNiff
V. Meyer
VI. MacMahon

The CORRECT filing sequence for the above names should be
A. I, IV, VI, III, II, V
B. II, I, IV, VI, III, V
C. VI, III, II, I, IV, V
D. VI, III, II, V, I, IV

22. I. Jack E. Johnson 22.____
II. R.H. Jackson
III. Bertha Jackson
IV. J.T. Johnson
V. Ann Johns
VI. John Jacobs

The CORRECT filing sequence for the above names should be
A. II, III, VI, V, IV, I
B. III, II, VI, V, IV, I
C. VI, II, III, I, V, IV
D. III, II, VI, IV, V, I

Questions 23-30.

DIRECTIONS: The code table below shows 10 letters with matching numbers. For each question, there are three sets of letters. Each set of letters is followed by a set of numbers which may or may not match their correct letter according to the code table. For each question, check all three sets of letters and numbers and mark your answer:

A. if no pairs are correctly matched
B. if only one pair is correctly matched
C. if only two pairs are correctly matched
D. if all three pairs are correctly matched

CODE TABLE

T	M	V	D	S	P	R	G	B	H
1	2	3	4	5	6	7	8	9	0

SAMPLE QUESTION: TMVDSP – 123456
RGBHTM – 789011
DSPRGB – 256789

In the sample question above, the first set of numbers correctly match its set of letters. But the second and third pairs contain mistakes. In the second pair, M is correctly matched with number 1. According to the code table, letter M should be correctly matched with number 2. In the third pair, the letter D is incorrectly matched with number 2. According to the code table, letter D should be correctly matched with number 4. Since only one of the pairs is correctly matched, the answer to this sample question is B.

23. RSBMRM – 759262
GDSRVH – 845730
VDBRTM - 349713

23.____

24. TGVSDR – 183247
SMHRDP – 520647
TRMHSR - 172057

24.____

25. DSPRGM – 456782
MVDBHT – 234902
HPMDBT - 062491

25.____

26. BVPTRD – 936184
GDPHMB – 807029
GMRHMV - 827032

26.____

27. MGVRSH – 283750
TRDMBS – 174295
SPRMGV - 567283

27.____

28. SGBSDM – 489542 28.____
MGHPTM – 290612
MPBMHT - 269301

29. TDPBHM – 146902 29.____
VPBMRS – 369275
GDMBHM - 842902

30. MVPTBV – 236194 30.____
PDRTMB – 47128
BGTMSM - 981232

KEY (CORRECT ANSWERS)

1.	A	11.	B	21.	C
2.	C	12.	C	22.	B
3.	B	13.	D	23.	B
4.	D	14.	D	24.	B
5.	D	15.	D	25.	C
6.	B	16.	C	26.	A
7.	B	17.	D	27.	D
8.	B	18.	A	28.	A
9.	A	19.	B	29.	D
10.	C	20.	A	30.	A

TEST 2

DIRECTIONS: Each question or incomplete statement is followed by several suggested answers or completions. Select the one that BEST answers the question or completes the statement. *PRINT THE LETTER OF THE CORRECT ANSWER IN THE SPACE AT THE RIGHT.*

Questions 1-10.

DIRECTIONS: Questions 1 through 10 each consists of two columns, each containing four lines of names, numbers and/or addresses. For each question, compare the lines in Column I with the lines in Column II to see if they match exactly, and mark your answer A, B, C, or D, according to the following instructions:

A. all four lines match exactly
B. only three lines match exactly
C. only two lines match exactly
D. only one line matches exactly

		COLUMN I	COLUMN II	
1.	I.	Earl Hodgson	Earl Hodgson	1.____
	II.	1409870	1408970	
	III.	Shore Ave.	Schore Ave.	
	IV.	Macon Rd.	Macon Rd.	
2.	I.	9671485	9671485	2.____
	II.	470 Astor Court	470 Astor Court	
	III.	Halprin, Phillip	Halperin, Phillip	
	IV.	Frank D. Poliseo	Frank D. Poliseo	
3.	I.	Tandem Associates	Tandom Associates	3.____
	II.	144-17 Northern Blvd.	144-17 Northern Blvd.	
	III.	Alberta Forchi	Albert Forchi	
	IV.	Kings Park, NY 10751	Kings Point, NY 10751	
4.	I.	Bertha C. McCormack	Bertha C. McCormack	4.____
	II.	Clayton, MO	Clayton, MO	
	III.	976-4242	976-4242	
	IV.	New City, NY 10951	New City, NY 10951	
5.	I.	George C. Morill	George C. Morrill	5.____
	II.	Columbia, SC 29201	Columbia, SD 29201	
	III.	Louis Ingham	Louis Ingham	
	IV.	3406 Forest Ave.	3406 Forest Ave.	
6.	I.	506 S. Elliott Pl.	506 S. Elliott Pl.	6.____
	II.	Herbert Hall	Hurbert Hall	
	III.	4712 Rockaway Pkway	4712 Rockaway Pkway	
	IV.	169 E. 7 St.	169 E. 7 St.	

7.	I.	345 Park Ave.	345 Park Pl.	7.____
	II.	Colman Oven Corp.	Coleman Oven Corp.	
	III.	Robert Conte	Robert Conti	
	IV.	6179846	6179846	
8.	I.	Grigori Schierber	Grigori Schierber	8.____
	II.	Des Moines, Iowa	Des Moines, Iowa	
	III.	Gouverneur Hospital	Gouverneur Hospital	
	IV.	91-35 Cresskill Pl.	91-35 Cresskill Pl.	
9.	I.	Jeffery Janssen	Jeffrey Janssen	9.____
	II.	8041071	8041071	
	III.	40 Rockefeller Plaza	40 Rockafeller Plaza	
	IV.	407 6 St.	406 7 St.	
10.	I.	5971996	5871996	10.____
	II.	3113 Knickerbocker Ave.	31123 Knickerbocker Ave.	
	III.	8434 Boston Post Rd.	8424 Boston Post Rd.	
	IV.	Penn Station	Penn Station	

Questions 11-14.

DIRECTIONS: Questions 11 through 14 are to be answered by looking at the four groups of names and addresses listed below (I, II, III, and IV), and then finding out the number of groups that have their corresponding numbered lies exactly the same.

	GROUP I	GROUP II
Line 1.	Richmond General Hospital	Richman General Hospital
Line 2.	Geriatric Clinic	Geriatric Clinic
Line 3.	3975 Paerdegat St.	3975 Peardegat St.
Line 4.	Loudonville, New York 11538	Londonville, New York 11538

	GROUP III	GROUP IV
Line 1.	Richmond General Hospital	Richmend General Hospital
Line 2.	Geriatric Clinic	Geriatric Clinic
Line 3.	3795 Paerdegat St.	3975 Paerdegat St.
Line 4.	Loudonville, New York 11358	Loudonville, New York 11538

1. In how many groups is line one exactly the same? 11.____
   A. Two B. Three C. Four D. None

12. In how many groups is line two exactly the same? 12.____
   A. Two B. Three C. Four D. None

13. In how many groups is line three exactly the same? 13.____
   A. Two B. Three C. Four D. None

14. In how many groups is line four exactly the same? 14.____
    A. Two B. Three C. Four D. None

Questions 15-18.

DIRECTIONS: Each of Questions 15 through 18 has two lists of names and addresses. Each list contains three sets of names and addresses. Check each of the three sets in the list on the right to see if they are the same as the corresponding set in the list on the left. Mark your answers:
A. if none of the sets in the right list are the same as those in the left list
B. if only one of the sets in the right list is the same as those in the left list
C. if only two of the sets in the right list are the same as those in the left list
D. if all three sets in the right list are the same as those in the left list

15.	Mary T. Berlinger 2351 Hampton St. Monsey, N.Y. 20117	Mary T. Berlinger 2351 Hampton St. Monsey, N.Y. 20117	15.____
	Eduardo Benes 483 Kingston Avenue Central Islip, N.Y. 11734	Eduardo Benes 473 Kingston Avenue Central Islip, N.Y. 11734	
	Alan Carrington Fuchs 17 Gnarled Hollow Road Los Angeles, CA 91635	Alan Carrington Fuchs 17 Gnarled Hollow Road Los Angeles, CA 91685	
16.	David John Jacobson 178 34 St. Apt. 4C New York, N.Y. 00927	David John Jacobson 178 53 St. Apt. 4C New York, N.Y. 00927	16.____
	Ann-Marie Calonella 7243 South Ridge Blvd. Bakersfield, CA 96714	Ann-Marie Calonella 7243 South Ridge Blvd. Bakersfield, CA 96714	
	Pauline M. Thompson 872 Linden Ave. Houston, Texas 70321	Pauline M. Thomson 872 Linden Ave. Houston, Texas 70321	
17.	Chester LeRoy Masterton 152 Lacy Rd. Kankakee, Ill. 54532	Chester LeRoy Masterson 152 Lacy Rd. Kankakee, Ill. 54532	17.____
	William Maloney S. LaCrosse Pla. Wausau, Wisconsin 52136	William Maloney S. LaCross Pla. Wausau, Wisconsin 52146	
	Cynthia V. Barnes 16 Pines Rd. Greenpoint, Miss. 20376	Cynthia V. Barnes 16 Pines Rd. Greenpoint,, Miss. 20376	

18.	Marcel Jean Frontenac 8 Burton On The Water Calender, Me. 01471	Marcel Jean Frontenac 6 Burton On The Water Calender, Me. 01471	18.____
	J. Scott Marsden 174 S. Tipton St. Cleveland, Ohio	J. Scott Marsden 174 Tipton St. Cleveland, Ohio	
	Lawrence T. Haney 171 McDonough St. Decatur, Ga. 31304	Lawrence T. Haney 171 McDonough St. Decatur, Ga. 31304	

Questions 19-26.

DIRECTIONS: Each of Questions 19 through 26 has two lists of numbers. Each list contains three sets of numbers. Check each of the three sets in the list on the right to see if they are the same as the corresponding set in the list on the left. Mark your answers:

A. if none of the sets in the right list are the same as those in the left list
B. if only one of the sets in the right list is the same as those in the left list
C. if only two of the sets in the right list are the same as those in the left list
D. if all three sets in the right list are the same as those in the left lists

19.	7354183476 4474747744 5791430231	7354983476 4474747774 57914302311	19.____
20.	7143592185 8344517699 9178531263	7143892185 8344518699 9178531263	20.____
21.	2572114731 8806835476 8255831246	257214731 8806835476 8255831246	21.____
22.	331476853821 6976658532996 3766042113715	331476858621 6976655832996 3766042113745	22.____
23.	8806663315 74477138449 211756663666	88066633115 74477138449 211756663666	23.____

24. 990006966996 53022219743 4171171117717	99000696996 53022219843 4171171177717	24.____
25. 24400222433004 5300030055000355 20000075532002022	24400222433004 5300030055500355 20000075532002022	25.____
26. 611166640660001116 7111300117001100733 26666446664476518	61116664066001116 7111300117001100733 26666446664476518	26.____

Questions 27-30.

DIRECTIONS: Questions 27 through 30 are to be answered by picking the answer which is in the correct numerical order, from the lowest number to the highest number, in each question.

27. A. 44533, 44518, 44516, 44547
B. 44516, 44518, 44533, 44547
C. 44547, 44533, 44518, 44516
D. 44518, 44516, 44547, 44533

27.____

28. A. 95587, 95593, 95601, 95620
B. 95601, 95620, 95587, 95593
C. 95593, 95587, 95601. 95620
D. 95620, 95601, 95593, 95587

28.____

29. A. 232212, 232208, 232232, 232223
B. 232208, 232223, 232212, 232232
C. 232208, 232212, 232223, 232232
D. 232223, 232232, 232208, 232208

29.____

30. A. 113419, 113521, 113462, 113462
B. 113588, 113462, 113521, 113419
C. 113521, 113588, 113419, 113462
D. 113419, 113462, 113521, 113588

30.____

KEY (CORRECT ANSWERS)

1.	C	11.	A	21.	C
2.	B	12.	C	22.	A
3.	D	13.	A	23.	D
4.	A	14.	A	24.	A
5.	C	15.	C	25.	C
6.	B	16.	B	26.	C
7.	D	17.	B	27.	B
8.	A	18.	B	28.	A
9.	D	19.	B	29.	C
10.	C	20.	B	30.	D

NAME AND NUMBER COMPARISONS

COMMENTARY

This test seeks to measure your ability and disposition to do a job carefully and accurately, your attention to exactness and preciseness of detail, your alertness and versatility in discerning similarities and differences between things, and your power in systematically handling written language symbols.

It is actually a test of your ability to do academic and/or clerical work, using the basic elements of verbal (qualitative) and mathematical (quantitative) learning—words and numbers.

EXAMINATION SECTION

TEST 1

DIRECTIONS: In each line across the page there are three names or numbers that are much alike. Compare the three names or numbers and decide which ones are exactly alike. *PRINT IN THE SPACE AT THE RIGHT THE LETTER:*

A. if all THREE names or numbers are exactly alike
B. if only the FIRST and SECOND names or numbers are ALIKE
C. if only the FIRST and THIRD names or numbers are alike
D. if only the SECOND or THIRD names or numbers are alike
E. if ALL THREE names or numbers are DIFFERENT

1.	Davis Hazen	David Hozen	David Hazen	1.____
2.	Lois Appel	Lois Appel	Lois Apfel	2.____
3.	June Allan	Jane Allan	Jane Allan	3.____
4.	10235	10235	10235	4.____
5.	32614	32164	32614	5.____

TEST 2

1.	2395890	2395890	2395890	1.____
2.	1926341	1926347	1926314	2.____
3.	E. Owens McVey	E. Owen McVey	E. Owen McVay	3.____
4.	Emily Neal Rouse	Emily Neal Rowse	Emily Neal Rowse	4.____
5.	H. Merritt Audubon	H. Merriott Audubon	H. Merritt Audubon	5.____

TEST 3

1.	6219354	6219354	6219354	1.____
2.	231793	2312793	2312793	2.____
3.	1065407	1065407	1065047	3.____
4.	Francis Ransdell	Frances Ramsdell	Francis Ramsdell	4.____
5.	Cornelius Detwiler	Cornelius Detwiler	Cornelius Detwiler	5.____

TEST 4

1.	6452054	6452564	6542054	1.____
2.	8501268	8501268	8501286	2.____
3.	Ella Burk Newham	Ella Burk Newnham	Elena Burk Newnham	3.____
4.	Jno. K. Ravencroft	Jno. H. Ravencroft	Jno. H. Ravencoft	4.____
5.	Martin Wills Pullen	Martin Wills Pulen	Martin Wills Pullen	5.____

TEST 5

1.	3457988	3457986	3457986	1.____
2.	4695682	4695862	4695682	2.____
3.	Stricklund Kaneydy	Sticklund Kanedy	Stricklund Kanedy	3.____
4.	Joy Harlor Witner	Joy Harloe Witner	Joy Harloe Witner	4.____
5.	R.M.O. Uberroth	R.M.O. Uberroth	R.N.O. Uberroth	5.____

TEST 6

1.	1592514	1592574	1592574	1.____
2.	2010202	2010202	2010220	2.____
3.	6177396	6177936	6177396	3.____
4.	Drusilla S. Ridgeley	Drusilla S. Ridgeley	Drusilla S. Ridgeley	4.____
5.	Andrei I. Tooumantzev	Andrei I. Tourmantzev	Andrei I. Toumantzov	5.____

TEST 7

1.	5261383	5261383	5261338	1.____
2.	8125690	8126690	8125609	2.____
3.	W.E. Johnston	W.E. Johnson	W.E. Johnson	3.____
4.	Vergil L. Muller	Vergil L. Muller	Vergil L. Muller	4.____
5.	Atherton R. Warde	Asheton R. Warde	Atherton P. Warde	5.____

TEST 8

1.	013469.5	023469.5	02346.95	1.____
2.	33376	333766	333766	2.____
3.	Ling-Temco-Vought	Ling-Tenco-Vought	Ling-Temco Vought	3.____
4.	Lorilard Corp.	Lorillard Corp.	Lorrilard Corp.	4.____
5.	American Agronomics Corporation	American Agronomics Corporation	American Agronomic Corporation	5.____

TEST 9

1.	436592864	436592864	436592864	1.____
2.	197765123	197755123	197755123	2.____
3.	Dewaay Cortvriendt International S.A.	Deway Cortvriendt International S.A.	Deway Corturiendt International S.A.	3.____
4.	Crédit Lyonnais	Crèdit Lyonnais	Crèdit Lyonais	4.____
5.	Algemene Bank Nederland N.V.	Algamene Bank Nederland N.V.	Algemene Bank Naderland N.V.	5.____

TEST 10

1.	00032572	0.0032572	00032522	1.____
2.	399745	399745	398745	2.____
3.	Banca Privata Finanziaria S.p.A.	Banca Privata Finanzaria S.P.A.	Banca Privata Finanziaria S.P.A.	3.____
4.	Eastman Dillon, Union Securities & Co.	Eastman Dillon, Union Securities Co.	Eastman Dillon, Union Securities & Co.	4.____
5.	Arnhold and S. Bleichroeder, Inc.	Arnhold & S. Bleichroeder, Inc.	Arnold and S. Bleichroeder, Inc.	5.____

TEST 11

DIRECTIONS: Answer the questions below on the basis of the following instructions: For each such numbered set of names, addresses, and numbers listed in Columns I and II, select your answer from the following options:

A. The names in Columns I and II are different
B. The addresses in Columns I and II are different
C. The numbers in Columns I and II are different
D. The names, addresses and numbers are identical

1.	Francis Jones 62 Stately Avenue 96-12446	Francis Jones 62 Stately Avenue 96-21446	1.____
2.	Julio Montez 19 Ponderosa Road 56-73161	Julio Montez 19 Ponderosa Road 56-71361	2.____
3.	Mary Mitchell 2314 Melbourne Drive 68-92172	Mary Mitchell 2314 Melbourne Drive 68-92172	3.____
4.	Harry Patterson 25 Dunne Street 14-33430	Harry Patterson 25 Dunne Street 14-34330	4.____
5.	Patrick Murphy 171 West Hosmer Street 93-81214	Patrick Murphy 171 West Hosmer Street 93-18214	5.____

6

TEST 12

1.	August Schultz 816 St. Clair Avenue 53-40149	August Schultz 816 St. Claire Avenue 53-40149	1.____
2.	George Taft 72 Runnymede Street 47-04033	George Taft 72 Runnymede Street 47-04023	2.____
3.	Angus Henderson 1418 Madison Street 81-76375	Angus Henderson 1418 Madison Street 81-76375	3.____
4.	Carolyn Mazur 12 Rivenlew Road 38-99615	Carolyn Mazur 12 Rivervane Road 38-99615	4.____
5.	Adele Russell 1725 Lansing Lane 72-91962	Adela Russell 1725 Lansing Lane 72-91962	5.____

TEST 13

DIRECTIONS: The following questions are based on the instructions given below. In each of the following questions, the 3-line name and address in Column I is the master-list entry, and the 3-line entry in Column II is the information to be checked against the master list.
If there is one line that is NOT exactly alike, mark your answer A.
If there are two lines NOT exactly alike, mark your answer B.
If there are three lines NOT exactly alike, mark your answer C.
If the lines ALL are exactly alike, mark your answer D.

	Column I	Column II	
1.	Jerome A. Jackson 1243 14th Avenue New York, N.Y. 10023	Jerome A. Johnson 1234 14th Avenue New York, N.Y. 10023	1.____
2.	Sophie Strachtheim 33-28 Connecticut Ave. Far Rockaway, N.Y. 11697	Sophie Strachtheim 33-28 Connecticut Ave. Far Rockaway, N.Y. 11697	2.____
3.	Elisabeth NT. Gorrell 256 Exchange St New York, N.Y. 10013	Elizabeth NT. Correll 256 Exchange St. New York, N.Y. 10013	3.____
4.	Maria J. Gonzalez 7516 E. Sheepshead Rd. Brooklyn, N.Y. 11240	Maria J. Gonzalez 7516 N. Shepshead Rd. Brooklyn, N.Y. 11240	4.____
5.	Leslie B. Brautenweiler 21-57A Seller Terr. Flushing, N.Y. 11367	Leslie B. Brautenwieler 21-75ASeiler Terr. Flushing, N.J. 11367	5.____

KEY (CORRECT ANSWERS)

TEST 1	TEST 2	TEST 3	TEST 4	TEST 5	TEST 6	TEST 7
1. E	1. A	1. A	1. E	1. D	1. D	1. B
2. B	2. E	2. A	2. B	2. C	2. B	2. E
3. D	3. E	3. B	3. E	3. E	3. C	3. D
4. A	4. D	4. E	4. E	4. D	4. A	4. A
5. C	5. C	5. A	5. C	5. B	5. E	5. E

TEST 8	TEST 9	TEST 10	TEST 11	TEST 12	TEST 13
1. E	1. A	1. E	1. C	1. B	1. B
2. D	2. D	2. B	2. C	2. C	2. D
3. E	3. E	3. E	3. D	3. D	3. A
4. E	4. E	4. C	4. C	4. B	4. A
5. B	5. E	5. E	5. C	5. A	5. C

NAME AND NUMBER CHECKING

EXAMINATION SECTION

TEST 1

DIRECTIONS: Questions 1 through 17 consist of sets of names and addresses. In each question, the name and address in Column II should be an exact copy of the name and address in Column I.
If there is:
a mistake only in the name, mark your answer A;
a mistake only in the address, mark your answer B;
a mistake in both name and address, mark your answer C;
No mistake in either name or address, mark your answer D.

Sample Question

Column I	Column II
Christina Magnusson 288 Greene Street New York, N.Y. 10003	Christina Magnusson 288 Greene Street New York, N.Y. 10013

Since there is a mistake only in the address (the zip code should be 10003 instead of 10013), the answer to the sample question is B.

	COLUMN I	COLUMN II	
1.	Ms. Joan Kelly 313 Franklin Avenue Brooklyn, N.Y. 11202	Ms. Joan Kielly 318 Franklin Ave. Brooklyn, N.Y. 11202	1.____
2.	Mrs. Eileen Engel 47-24 86 Road Queens, N.Y. 11122	Mrs. Ellen Engel 47-24 86 Road Queens, New York 11122	2.____
3.	Marcia Michaels 213 E. 81 St. New York, N.Y. 10012	Marcia Michaels 213 E. 81 St. New York, N.Y. 10012	3.____
4.	Rev. Edward J. Smyth 1401 Brandeis Street San Francisco, Calif. 96201	Rev. Edward J. Smyth 1401 Brandies Street San Francisco, Calif. 96201	4.____
5.	Alicia Rodriguez 24-68 82 St. Elmhurst, N.Y. 11122	Alicia Rodriguez 2468 81 St. Elmhurst, N.Y. 11122	5.____

	COLUMN I	COLUMN II	
6.	Ernest Eisemann 21 Columbia St. New York, N.Y. 10007	Ernest Eisermann 21 Columbia St. New York, N.Y. 10007	6.____
7.	Mr. & Mrs. George Petersson 87-11 91st Avenue Woodhaven, N.Y. 11421	Mr. & Mrs. George Peterson 87-11 91st Avenue Woodhaven, N.Y. 11421	7.____
8.	Mr. Ivan Klebnikov 1848 Newkirk Avenue Brooklyn, N.Y. 11226	Mr. Ivan Klebikov 1848 Newkirk Avenue Brooklyn, N.Y. 11622	8.____
9.	Mr. Samuel Rothfleisch 71 Pine Street New York, N.Y. 10005	Samuel Rothfleisch 71 Pine Street New York, N.Y. 100005	9.____
10.	Mrs. Isabel Tonnessen 198 East 185th Street Bronx, N.Y. 10458	Mrs. Isabel Tonnessen 189 East 185th Street Bronx, N.Y. 10348	10.____
11.	Esteban Perez 173 Eighth Street Staten Island, N.Y. 10306	Estaban Perez 173 Eighth Street Staten Island, N.Y. 10306	11.____
12.	Esta Wong 141 West 68 St. New York, N.Y. 10023	Esta Wang 141 West 68 St. New York, N.Y. 10023	12.____
13.	Dr. Alberto Grosso 3475 12th Avenue Brooklyn, N.Y. 11218	Dr. Alberto Grosso 3475 12th Avenue Brooklyn, N.Y. 11218	13.____
14.	Mrs. Ruth Bortias 482 Theresa Ct. Far Rockaway, N.Y. 11691	Ms. Ruth Bortlas 482 Theresa Ct. Far Rockaway, N.Y. 11169	14.____
15.	Mr. & Mrs. Howard Fox 2301 Sedgwick Ave. Bronx, N.Y. 10468	Mr. & Mrs. Howard Fox 231 Sedgwick Ave. Bronx, N.Y. 10468	15.____
16.	Miss Marjorie Black 223 East 23 Street New York, N.Y. 10010	Miss Margorie Black 223 East 23 Street New York, N.Y. 10010	16.____

	COLUMN I	COLUMN II	
17.	Michelle Herman 806 Valley Rd. Old Tappan, N.J. 07675	Michelle Hermann 806 Valley Dr. Old Tappan, N.J. 07675	17.____

KEY (CORRECT ANSWERS)

1.	C	7.	A	13.	D
2.	A	8.	C	14.	C
3.	D	9.	D	15.	B
4.	B	10.	B	16.	A
5.	B	11.	A	17.	C
6.	A	12.	D		

TEST 2

DIRECTIONS: Questions 1 through 15 are to be answered SOLELY on the instructions given below. *PRINT THE LETTER OF THE CORRECT ANSWER IN THE SPACE AT THE RIGHT.*

INSTRUCTIONS

In each of the following questions, the 3-line name and address in Column I is the master-list entry, and the 3-line entry in Column II is the information to be checked against the master list. If there is one line that does not match, mark your answer A; if there are two lines that do not match, mark your answer B; if all three lines do not match, mark your answer C; if the lines all match exactly, mark your answer D.

Sample Question

Column I	Column II
Mark L. Field	Mark L. Field
11-09 Price Park Blvd.	11-99 Prince Park Way
Bronx, N.Y. 11402	Bronx, N.Y. 11401

The first lines in each column match exactly. The second lines do not match since 11-09 does not match 11-99; and Blvd. does not match Way. The third lines do not match either since 11402 does not match 11401. Therefore, there are two lines that do not match, and the CORRECT answer is B.

	COLUMN I	COLUMN II	
1.	Jerome A. Jackson 1243 14th Avenue New York, N.Y. 10023	Jerome A. Johnson 1234 14th Avenue New York, N.Y. 10023	1.____
2.	Sophie Strachtheim 33-28 Connecticut Ave. Far Rockaway, N.Y. 11697	Sophie Strachtheim 33-28 Connecticut Ave. Far Rockaway, N.Y. 11697	2.____
3.	Elisabeth N.T. Gorrell 256 Exchange St. New York, N.Y. 10013	Elizabeth N.T. Gorrell 256 Exchange St. New York, N.Y. 10013	3.____
4.	Maria J. Gonzalez 7516 E. Sheepshead Rd. Brooklyn, N.Y. 11240	Maria J. Gonzalez 7516 N. Shepshead Rd. Brooklyn, N.Y. 11240	4.____
5.	Leslie B. Brautenweiler 21 57A Seiler Terr. Flushing, N.Y. 11367	Leslie B. Brautenwieler 21-75A Seiler Terr. Flushing, N.J. 11367	5.____

	COLUMN I	COLUMN II	
6.	Rigoberto J. Peredes 157 Twin Towers, #18F Tottenville, S. I., N.Y,	Rigoberto J. Peredes 157 Twin Towers, #18F Tottenville, S.I., N.Y.	6.____
7.	Pietro F. Albino P.O. Box 7548 Floral Park, N.Y. 11005	Pietro F. Albina P.O. Box 7458 Floral Park, N.Y. 11005	7.____
8.	Joanne Zimmerman Bldg. SW, Room 314 532-4601	Joanne Zimmermann Bldg. SW, Room 314 532-4601	8.____
9.	Carlyle Whetstone Payroll Div. –A, Room 212A 262-5000, ext. 471	Carlyle Whetstone Payroll Div. –A, Room 212A 262-5000, ext. 417	9.____
10.	Kenneth Chiang Legal Council, Room 9745 (201) 416-9100, ext. 17	Kenneth Chiang Legal Counsel, Room 9745 (201) 416-9100, Ext. 17	10.____
11.	Ethel Koenig Personnel Services Division, Room 433; 635-7572	Ethel Hoenig Personal Services Division, Room 433; 635-7527	11.____
12.	Joyce Ehrhardt Office of the Administrator, Room W56; 387-8706	Joyce Ehrhart Office of the Administrator, Room W56; 387-7806	12.____
13.	Ruth Lang EAM Bldg., Room C101 625-2000, ext. 765	Ruth Lang EAM Bldg., Room C110 625-2000, ext. 765	13.____
14.	Anne Marie Ionozzi Investigations, Room 827 576-4000, ext. 832	Anna Marie Ionozzi Investigation, Room 827 566-4000, ext. 832	14.____
15.	Willard Jameson Fm C Bldg., Room 687 454-3010	Willard Jamieson Fm C Bldg., Room 687 454-3010	15.____

KEY (CORRECT ANSWERS)

1.	B	6.	D	C	C
2.	D	7.	B	12.	B
3.	A	8.	D	13.	A
4.	A	9.	B	14.	C
5.	C	10.	A	15.	A

TEST 3

DIRECTIONS: Questions 1 through 10 are to be answered on the basis of the following instructions. *PRINT THE LETTER OF THE CORRECT ANSWER IN THE SPACE AT THE RIGHT.*

<u>INSTRUCTIONS</u>

For each such set of names, addresses, and numbers listed in Columns I and II, select your answer from the following options:

The names in Columns I and II are different,
The addresses in Columns I and II are different,
The numbers in Columns I and II are different,
The names, addresses, and numbers in Columns I and II are identical.

	<u>COLUMN I</u>	<u>COLUMN II</u>	
1.	Francis Jones 62 Stately Avenue 96-12446	Francis Jones 62 Stately Avenue 96-21446	1.____
2.	Julio Montez 19 Ponderosa Road 56-73161	Julio Montez 19 Ponderosa Road 56-71361	2.____
3.	Mary Mitchell 2314 Melbourne Drive 68-92172	Mary Mitchell 2314 Melbourne Drive 68-92172	3.____
4.	Harry Patterson 25 Dunne Street 14-33430	Harry Patterson 25 Dunne Street 14-34330	4.____
5.	Patrick Murphy 171 West Hosmer Street 93-81214	Patrick Murphy 171 West Hosmer Street 93-18214	5.____
6.	August Schultz 816 St. Clair Avenue 53-40149	August Schultz 816 St. Claire Avenue 53-40149	6.____
7.	George Taft 72 Runnymede Street 47-04033	George Taft 72 Runnymede Street 47-04023	7.____
8.	Angus Henderson 1418 Madison Street 81-76375	Angus Henderson 1318 Madison Street 81-76375	8.____

	COLUMN I	COLUMN II	
9.	Carolyn Mazur 12 Riverview Road 38-99615	Carolyn Mazur 12 Rivervane Road 38-99615	9.____
10.	Adele Russell 1725 Lansing Lane 72-91962	Adela Russell 1725 Lansing Lane 72-91962	10.____

KEY (CORRECT ANSWERS)

1.	C	6.	B
2.	C	7.	C
3.	D	8.	D
4.	C	9.	B
5.	C	10.	A

TEST 4

DIRECTIONS: Questions 1 through 20 test how good you are at catching mistakes in typing or printing. In each question, the name and address in Column II should be an exact copy of the name and address in Column I. Mark your answer
A. If there is no mistake in either name or address;
B. If there is a mistake in both name and address;
C. If there is a mistake only in the name;
D. If there is a mistake only in the address.
PRINT THE LETTER OF THE CORRECT ANSWER IN THE SPACE AT THE RIGHT.

	COLUMN I	COLUMN II	
1.	Milos Yanocek 33-60 14 Street Long Island City, N.Y. 11011	Milos Yanocek 33-60 14 Street Long Island City, N.Y. 11001	1.____
2.	Alphonse Sabattelo 24 Minnetta Lane New York, N.Y. 10006	Alphonse Sabbattelo 24 Minetta Lane New York, N.Y. 10006	2.____
3.	Helen Steam 5 Metropolitan Oval Bronx, N.Y. 10462	Helene Stearn 5 Metropolitan Oval Bronx, N.Y. 10462	3.____
4.	Jacob Weisman 231 Francis Lewis Boulevard Forest Hills, N.Y. 11325	Jacob Weisman 231 Francis Lewis Boulevard Forest Hills, N.Y. 11325	4.____
5.	Riccardo Fuente 134 West 83 Street New York, N.Y. 10024	Riccardo Fuentes 134 West 88 Street New York, N.Y. 10024	5.____
6.	Dennis Lauber 52 Avenue D Brooklyn, N.Y. 11216	Dennis Lauder 52 Avenue D Brooklyn, N.Y. 11216	6.____
7.	Paul Cutter 195 Galloway Avenue Staten Island, N.Y. 10356	Paul Cutter 175 Galloway Avenue Staten Island, N.Y. 10365	7.____
8.	Sean Donnelly 45-58 41 Avenue Woodside, N.Y. 11168	Sean Donnelly 45-58 41 Avenue Woodside, N.Y. 11168	8.____
9.	Clyde Willot 1483 Rockaway Avenue Brooklyn, N.Y. 11238	Clyde Willat 1483 Rockaway Avenue Brooklyn, N.Y. 11238	9.____

	COLUMN I	COLUMN II	
10.	Michael Stanakis 419 Sheriden Avenue Staten Island, N.Y. 10363	Michael Stanakis 419 Sheraden Avenue Staten Island, N.Y. 10363	10.____
11.	Joseph DiSilva 63-84 Saunders Road Rego Park, N.Y. 11431	Joseph Disilva 64-83 Saunders Road Rego Park, N.Y. 11431	11.____
12.	Linda Polansky 2224 Fendon Avenue Bronx, N.Y. 20464	Linda Polansky 2255 Fenton Avenue Bronx, N.Y. 10464	12.____
13.	Alfred Klein 260 Hillside Terrace Staten Island, N.Y. 15545	Alfred Klein 260 Hillside Terrace Staten Island, N.Y. 15545	13.____
14.	William McDonnell 504 E. 55 Street New York, N.Y. 10103	William McConnell 504 E. 55 Street New York, N.Y. 10108	14.____
15.	Angela Cipolla 41-11 Parson Avenue Flushing, N.Y. 11446	Angela Cipola 41-11 Parsons Avenue Flushing, N.Y. 11446	15.____
16.	Julie Sheridan 1212 Ocean Avenue Brooklyn, N.Y. 11237	Julia Sheridan 1212 Ocean Avenue Brooklyn, N.Y. 11237	16.____
17.	Arturo Rodriguez 2156 Cruger Avenue Bronx, N.Y. 10446	Arturo Rodrigues 2156 Cruger Avenue Bronx, N.Y. 10446	17.____
18.	Helen McCabe 2044 East 19 Street Brooklyn, N.Y. 11204	Helen McCabe 2040 East 19 Street Brooklyn, N.Y. 11204	18.____
19.	Charles Martin 526 West 160 Street New York, N.Y. 10022	Charles Martin 526 West 160 Street New York, N.Y. 10022	19.____
20.	Morris Rabinowitz 31 Avenue M Brooklyn, N.Y. 11216	Morris Rabinowitz 31 Avenue N Brooklyn, N.Y. 11216	20.____

KEY (CORRECT ANSWERS)

1.	D	11.	B
2.	B	12.	D
3.	C	13.	A
4.	A	14.	B
5.	B	15.	B
6.	C	16.	C
7.	D	17.	C
8.	A	18.	D
9.	B	19.	A
10.	D	20.	D

TEST 5

DIRECTIONS: In copying the addresses below from Column A to the same line in Column B, an Agent-in-Training made some errors. For Questions 1 through 5, if you find that the agent made an error in
only one line, mark your answer A;
only two lines, mark your answer B;
only three lines, mark your answer C;
all four lines, mark your answer D.

EXAMPLE

COLUMN A	COLUMN B
24 Third Avenue	24 Third Avenue
5 Lincoln Road	5 Lincoln Street
50 Central Park West	6 Central Park West
37-21 Queens Boulevard	21-37 Queens Boulevard

Since errors were made on only three lines, namely the second, third, and fourth, the CORRECT answer is C.

PRINT THE LETTER OF THE CORRECT ANSWER IN THE SPACE AT THE RIGHT.

	COLUMN A	COLUMN B	
1.	57-22 Springfield Boulevard	75-22 Springfield Boulevard	1.____
	94 Gun Hill Road	94 Gun Hill Avenue	
	8 New Dorp Lane	8 New Drop Lane	
	36 Bedford Avenue	36 Bedford Avenue	
2.	538 Castle Hill Avenue	538 Castle Hill Avenue	2.____
	54-15 Beach Channel Drive	54-15 Beach Channel Drive	
	21 Ralph Avenue	21 Ralph Avenue	
	162 Madison Avenue	162 Morrison Avenue	
3.	49 Thomas Street	49 Thomas Street	3.____
	27-21 Northern Blvd.	21-27 Northern Blvd.	
	86 125th Street	86 125th Street	
	872 Atlantic Ave.	872 Baltic Ave,	
4.	261-17 Horace Harding Expwy.	261-17 Horace Harding Pkwy.	4.____
	191 Fordham Road	191 Fordham Road	
	6 Victory Blvd.	6 Victoria Blvd.	
	552 Oceanic Ave.	552 Ocean Ave.	
5.	90-05 38th Avenue	90-05 36th Avenue	5.____
	19 Central Park West	19 Central Park East	
	9281 Avenue X	9281 Avenue X	
	22 West Farms Square	22 West Farms Square	

KEY (CORRECT ANSWERS)

1. C
2. A
3. B
4. C
5. B

TEST 6

DIRECTIONS: For Questions 1 through 10, choose the letter in Column II next to the number which EXACTLY matches the number in Column I. *PRINT THE LETTER OF THE CORRECT ANSWER IN THE SPACE AT THE RIGHT.*

COLUMN I	COLUMN II	
1. 14235	A. 13254 B. 12435 C. 13245 D. 14235	1.____
2. 70698	A. 90768 B. 60978 C. 70698] D. 70968	2.____
3. 11698	A. 11689 B. 11986 C. 11968 D. 11698	3.____
4. 50497	A. 50947 B. 50497 C. 50749 D. 54097	4.____
5. 69635	A. 60653 B. 69630 C. 69365 D. 69635	5.____
6. 1201022011	A. 1201022011 B. 1201020211 C. 1202012011 D. 1021202011	6.____
7. 3893981389	A. 3893891389 B. 3983981389 C. 3983891389 D. 3893981389	7.____
8. 4765476589	A. 4765476598 B. 4765476588 C. 4765476589 D. 4765746589	8.____

9. 8679678938

A. 8679687938
B. 8679678938
C. 8697678938
D. 8678678938

9.____

10. 6834836932

A. 6834386932
B. 6834836923
C. 6843836932
D. 6834836932

10.____

Questions 11-15.

DIRECTIONS: For Questions 11 through 15, determine how many of the symbols in Column Z are exactly the same as the symbol in Column Y.
If none is exactly the same, answer A;
If only one symbol is exactly the same, answer B;
If two symbols are exactly the same, answer C;
If three symbols are exactly the same, answer D.

COLUMN Y	COLUMN Z	
11. A123B1266	A123B1366 A123B1266 A133B1366 A123B1266	11.____
12. CC28D3377	CD22D3377 CC38D3377 CC28C3377 CC28D2277	12.____
13. M21AB201X	M12AB201X M21AB201X M21AB201Y M21BA201X	13.____
14. PA383Y744	AP383Y744 PA338Y744 PA388Y744 PA383Y774	14.____
15. PB2Y8893	PB2Y8893 PB2Y8893 PB3Y8898 PB2Y8893	15.____

KEY (CORRECT ANSWERS)

1.	D	6.	A	11.	C
2.	C	7.	D	12.	A
3.	D	8.	C	13.	B
4.	B	9.	B	14.	A
5.	D	10.	D	15.	D

FILING

EXAMINATION SECTION

TEST 1

Questions 1-9.

DIRECTIONS: An important part of the duties of an office worker in a public agency is to file office records. Questions 1 through 9 are designed to determine whether you can file records correctly. Each of these questions consists of four names. For each question, select the one of the four names that should be FOURTH if the four names were arranged in alphabetical order. *PRINT THE LETTER OF THE CORRECT ANSWER IN THE SPACE AT THE RIGHT.*

1. A. 6th National Bank B. Sexton Lock Co. 1.____
   C. The 69th Street League D. Thomas Saxon Corp.

2. A. 4th Avenue Printing Co. B. The Four Corners Corp. 2.____
   C. Dr. Milton Fournet D. The Martin Fountaine Co.

3. A. Mr. Chas. Le Mond B. Model Express, Inc. 3.____
   C. Lenox Enterprises D. Mobile Supply Co.

4. A. Frank Waller Johnson B. Frank Walter Johnson 4.____
   C. Wilson Johnson D. Frank W. Johnson

5. A. Miss Anne M. Carlsen B. Mrs. Albert S. Carlson 5.____
   C. Mr. Alan Ross Carlsen D. Dr. Anthony Ash Carlson

6. A. Delaware Paper Co. B. William Del Ville 6.____
   C. Ralph A. Delmar D. Wm. K. Del Ville

7. A. The Lloyd Disney Co. B. Mrs. Raymond Norris 7.____
   C. Oklahoma Envelope, Inc. D. Miss Esther O'Neill

8. A. The Olympic Eraser Co. B. Mrs. Raymond Norris 8.____
   C. Oklahoma Envelope, Inc. D. Miss Esther O'Neill

9. A. Patricia MacNamara B. Eleanor McNally 9.____
   C. Robt. MacPherson, Jr. D. Helen McNair

Questions 10-21.

DIRECTIONS: Questions 10 through 21 are to be answered on the basis of the usual rules for alphabetical filing. For each question, indicate in the space at the right the letter preceding the name which should be THIRD in alphabetical order.

10. A. Russell Cohen B. Henry Cohn 10.____
C. Wesley Chambers D. Arthur Connors

11. A. Wanda Jenkins B. Pauline Jennings 11.____
C. Leslie Jantzenberg D. Rudy Jensen

12. A. Arnold Wilson B. Carlton Willson 12.____
C. Duncan Williamson D. Ezra Wilston

13. A. Joseph M. Buchman B. Gustave Bozzerman 13.____
C. Constantino Brunelli D. Armando Buccino

14. A. Barbara Waverly B. Corinne Warterdam 14.____
C. Dennis Waterman D. Harold Wartman

15. A. Jose Mejia B. Bernard Mendelsohn 15.____
C. Antonio Mejias D. Richard Mazzitelli

16. A. Hesselberg, Norman J. B. Hesselman, Nathan B. 16.____
C. Hazel, Robert S. D. Heintz, August J.

17. A. Oshins, Jerome B. Ohsie, Marjorie 17.____
C. O'Shaugn, F.J. D. O'Shea, Frances

18. A. Petrie, Joshua A. B. Pendleton, Oscar 18.____
C. Pertwee, Joshua D. Perkins, Warren G.

19. A. Morganstern, Alfred B. Morganstern, Albert 19.____
C. Monroe, Mildred D. Modesti, Ernest

20. A. More, Stewart B. Moorhead, Jay 20.____
C. Moore, Benjamin D. Moffat, Edith

21. A. Ramirez, Paul B. Revere, Pauline 21.____
C. Ramos, Felix D. Ramazotti, Angelo

KEY (CORRECT ANSWERS)

1.	C	11.	B
2.	A	12.	A
3.	B	13.	D
4.	B	14.	C
5.	D	15.	C
6.	A	16.	A
7.	C	17.	D
8.	D	18.	C
9.	B	19.	B
10.	B	20.	B

21. C

TEST 2

DIRECTIONS: Each question or incomplete statement is followed by several suggested answers or completions. Select the one that BEST answers the question or completes the statement. *PRINT THE LETTER OF THE CORRECT ANSWER IN THE SPACE AT THE RIGHT.*

Questions 1-4.

DIRECTIONS: Questions 1 through 4 are to be answered on the basis of the following alphabetical rules.

RULES FOR ALPHABETICAL FILING

<u>Names of Individuals</u>

The names of individuals are filed in strict alphabetical order, *first* according to the last name, *then* according to first name or initial, and *finally* according to middle name or initial. For example: George Allen precedes Edward Bell and Leonard Reston precedes Lucille Reston.

When last names are the same, for example, A. Green and Agnes Green, the one with the initial comes before the one with the name written out when the first initials are identical.

Prefixes such as De, O', Mac, Mc and Van are filed as written and are treated as part of the names to which they are connected. For example, Gladys McTeaque is filed before Frances Meadows.

1. If the following four names were put into an alphabetical list, what would the FIRST name on the list be? 1.____
   A. Wm. C. Paul
   B. W. Paul
   C. Alice Paul
   D. Alyce Paule

2. If the following four names were put into an alphabetical list, what would the THIRD name on the list be? 2.____
   A. I. MacCarthy
   B. Irene MacKarthy
   C. Ida McCaren
   D. I.A. McCarthy

3. If the following four names were put into an alphabetical list, what would the SECOND name on the list be? 3.____
   A. John Gilhooley
   B. Ramon Gonzalez
   C. Gerald Gilholy
   D. Samuel Gilvecchio

4. If the following four names were put into an alphabetical list, what would the FOURTH name on the list be? 4.____
   A. Michael Edwinn
   B. James Edwards
   C. Mary Edwin
   D. Carlo Edwards

Questions 5-9.

DIRECTIONS: Questions 5 through 9 consist of a group of names which are to be arranged in alphabetical order for filing.

5. Of the following, the name which should be filed FIRST is 5.____
   A. Joseph J. Meadeen
   B. Gerard L. Meader
   C. John F. Madcar
   D. Philip F. Malder

6. Of the following, the name which should be filed LAST is 6.____
   A. Stephen Fischer
   B. Benjamin Fitchmann
   C. Thomas Fishman
   D. Augustus S. Fisher

7. The name which should be filed SECOND is 7.____
   A. Yeatman, Frances
   B. Yeaton, C.S.
   C. Yeatman, R.M.
   D. Yeats, John

8. The name which should be filed THIRD is 8.____
   A. Hauser, Ann
   B. Hauptmann, Jane
   C. Hauster, Mary
   D. Rauprich, Julia

9. The name which should be filed SECOND is 9.____
   A. Flora McDougall
   B. Fred E. MacDowell
   C. Juanita Mendez
   D. James A. Madden

Questions 10-14.

DIRECTIONS: Questions 10 through 14 are to be answered based on an alphabetical arrangement of the following list of names.

Walker, Carol J.	Wacht, Michael	Wade, Ethel
Wall, Fredrick	Wall, Francis	Wall, Frank
Wachs, Paul	Walker, Carol L.	Wagner, Arthur
Walters, Daniel	Wade, Ellen	Wald, William
Wagner, Allen	Walters, David	Walker, Carmen

10. The 4th name on the alphabetized list would be 10.____
   A. Wade, Ellen
   B. Wade, Ethel
   C. Wagner, Allen
   D. Wagner, Arthur

11. The 7th name on the alphabetized list would be 11.____
   A. Walker, Carmen
   B. Walker, Carol J.
   C. Walker, Carol L.
   D. Wald, William

12. The name that would come immediately AFTER Wagner, Arthur on the alphabetized list would be 12.____
   A. Wade, Ethel
   B. Wagner, Allen
   C. Wald, William
   D. Walker, Carol L.

13. The name that would come immediately BEFORE Wall, Frank would be 13.____
    A. Wall, Francis
    B. Wall, Fredrick
    C. Walters, David
    D. Walters, Daniel

14. The 12th name on the alphabetized list would be 14.____
    A. Walker, Carol L.
    B. Wald, William
    C. Wall, Francis
    D. Wall, Frank

KEY (CORRECT ANSWERS)

1.	C	6.	B	11.	D
2.	C	7.	C	12.	C
3.	A	8.	A	13.	A
4.	A	9.	D	14.	D
5.	C	10.	B		

TEST 3

DIRECTIONS: Each question or incomplete statement is followed by several suggested answers or completions. Select the one that BEST answers the question or completes the statement. *PRINT THE LETTER OF THE CORRECT ANSWER IN THE SPACE AT THE RIGHT.*

Questions 1-8.

DIRECTIONS: Questions 1 through 8 are based on the Rules of Alphabetical Filing given below. Read these rules carefully before answering the questions.

Names of People

1. The names of people are filed in strict alphabetical order, first according to the last name, then according to first name or initial, and finally according to middle name or initial. For example: George Allen comes before Edward Bell, and Leonard P. Reston comes before Lucille B. Reston.

2. When last names are the same, for example, A. Green and Agnes Green, the one with the initial comes before the one with the name written out when the first initials are identical.

3. When first and last names are alike and the middle name is given, for example, John David Doe and John Devoe Doe, the names should be filed in alphabetical order of the middle names.

4. When first and last names are the same, a name without a middle initial comes before one with a middle name or initial. For example, John Doe comes before John A. Doe and John Alan Doe.

5. When first and last names are the same, a name with a middle initial comes before one with a middle name beginning with the same initial. For example, Jack R. Hertz comes before Jack Richard Hertz.

6. Prefixes such as De, O', Mac, Mc, and Van are filed as written and are treated as part of the names to which they are connected. For example, Robert O'Dea is filed before David Olsen.

7. Abbreviated names are treated as if they were spelled out. For example: Chas. is filed as Charles and Thos. is filed as Thomas.

8. Titles and designations such as Dr., Mr., and Prof. are disregarded in filing.

Names of Organizations

1. The names of business organizations are filed according to the order in which each word in the name appears. When an organization name bears the name of a person, it is filed according to the rules for filing names of people as given above. For example: William Smith Service Co. comes before Television Distributors, Inc.

2. Where bureau, board, office or department appears as the first part of the title of a governmental agency, that agency should be filed under the word in the title expressing the chief function of the agency. For example, Bureau of Budget would be filed as if written Budget, (Bureau of the). The Department of Personnel would be filed as if written Personnel, (Department of).

3. When the following words are part of an organization, they are disregarded: the, of, and.

4. When there are numbers in a name, they are treated as if they were spelled out. For example: 10th Street Bootery is filed as Tenth Street Bootery.

Each question from 1 through 8 contains four names numbered from 1 through 4 but not necessarily numbered in correct filing order. Answer each question by choosing the letter corresponding to the CORRECT filing order of the four names in accordance with the above rules.

<u>SAMPLE QUESTION:</u>

I. Robert J. Smith
II. R. Jeffrey Smith
III. Dr. A. Smythe
IV. Allen R. Smithers

A. I, II, III, IV B. III, I, II, IV C. II, I, IV, III D. III, II, I, IV

Since the correct filing order, in accordance with the above rules is II I, IV, III, the correct answer is C.

1. I. J. Chester VanClief II. John C. Van Clief 1.____
III. J. VanCleve IV. Mary L. Vance

The CORRECT answer is:
A. IV, III, I, II B. IV, III, II, I C. III, I, II, IV D. III, IV, I, II

2. I. Community Development Agency II. Department of Social Services 2.____
III. Board of Estimate IV. Bureau of Gas and Electricity

The CORRECT answer is:
A. III, IV, I, II B. 1, II, IV, III C. II, I, III, IV D. I, III, IV, II

3. I. Dr. Chas. K. Dahlman II. F. & A. Delivery Service 3.____
III. Department of Water Supply IV. Demano Men's Custom Tailors

The CORRECT answer is:
A. I, II, III, IV B. I, IV, II, III C. IV, I, II, III D. IV, I, III, II

4. I. 48th Street Theater
II. Fourteenth Street Day Care Center
III. Professor A. Cartwright
IV. Albert F. McCarthy
4.____

The CORRECT answer is:
A. IV, II, I, III B. IV, III, I, II C. III, II, I, IV D. III, I, II, IV

5. I. Frances D'Arcy
II. Mario L. DelAmato
III. William R. Diamond
IV. Robert J. DuBarry
5.____

The CORRECT answer is:
A. I, II, IV, III B. II, I, III, IV C. I, II, III, IV D. II, I, III, IV

6. I. Evelyn H. D'Amelio
II. Jane R. Bailey
III. Robert Bailey
IV. Frank Baily
6.____

The CORRECT answer is:
A. I, II, III, IV B. I, III, II, IV C. II, III, IV, I D. III, II, IV, I

7. I. Department of Markets
II. Bureau of Handicapped Children
III. Housing Authority Administration Building
IV. Board of Pharmacy
7.____

The CORRECT answer is:
A. II, I, III, IV B. I, II, IV, III C. I, II, III, IV D. III, II, I, IV

8. I. William A. Shea Stadium
II. Rapid Speed Taxi Co.
III. Harry Stampler's Rotisserie
III. Wilhelm Albert Shea
8.____

The CORRECT answer is:
A. II, III, IV, I B. IV, I, III, II C. II, IV, I, III D. III, IV, I, II

Questions 9-18.

DIRECTIONS: Questions 9 through 18 each show in Column I names written on four ledger cards (lettered w, x, y, z) which have to be filed. You are to choose the option (lettered A, B, C, or D) in Column II which BEST represents the proper order for filing the cards.

SAMPLE

COLUMN I	COLUMN II
w. John Stevens	A. w, y, z, x
x. John D. Stevenson	B. y, w, z, x
y. Joan Stevens	C. x, y, w, z
z. J. Stevenson	D. x, w, y, z

The correct way to file the cards is:
y. Joan Stevens
w. John Stevens
z. J. Stevenson
x. John D. Stevenson

The correct order is shown by the letters y, w, z, x in that sequence. Since, in Column II, B appears in front of the letters y, w, z, x in that sequence, B is the correct answer to the sample question.

Now answer the following questions, using the same procedure.

9. COLUMN I
w. Juan Montoya
x. Manuel Montenegro
y. Victor Matos
z. Victoria Maltos

COLUMN II
A. y, z, x, w
B. z, y, x, w
C. z, y, w, x
D. y, x, z, w

9.____

10. COLUMN I
w. Frank Carlson
x. Robert Carlson
y. George Carlson
z. Frank Carlton

COLUMN II
A. z, x, w, y
B. z, y, x, w
C. w, y, z, x
D. w, z, y, x

10.____

11. COLUMN I
w. Carmine Rivera
x. Jose Rivera
y. Frank River
z. Joan Rivers

COLUMN II
A. y, w, x, z
B. y, x, w, z
C. w, x, y, z
D. w, x, z, y

11.____

12. COLUMN I
w. Jerome Mathews
x. Scott A. Matthew
y. Charles B. Matthew
z. Scott C. Mathewsw

COLUMN II
A. w, y, z, x
B. z, y, x, w
C. z, w, x, y
D. w, z, y, x

12.____

13. COLUMN I
w. John McMahan
x. John P. MacMahan
y. Joseph DeMayo
z. Joseph D. Mayo

COLUMN II
A. w, x, y, z
B. y, x, z, w
C. x, w, y, z
D. y, x, w, z

13.____

14. COLUMN I
w. Raymond Martinez
x. Ramon Martinez
y. Prof. Ray Martinez
z. Dr. Raymond Martin

COLUMN II
A. z, x, y, w
B. z, y, x, w
C. z, w, y, x
D. y, x, w, z

14.____

15. COLUMN I — COLUMN II — 15.____

COLUMN I	COLUMN II
w. Mr. Robert Vincent Mackintosh	A. y, x, z, w
x. Robert Reginald Macintosh	B. x, w, z, y
y. Roger V. McIntosh	C. x, w, y, z
z. Robert R. Mackintosh	D. x, z, w, y

16. COLUMN I — COLUMN II — 16.____

COLUMN I	COLUMN II
w. Dr. D. V. Facsone	A. y, w, z, x
x. Prof. David Fascone	B. w, y, x, z
y. Donald Facsone	C. w, y, z, x
z. Mrs. D. Fascone	D. z, w, x, y

17. COLUMN I — COLUMN II — 17.____

COLUMN I	COLUMN II
w. Johnathan Q. Addams	A. z, x, w, y
x. John Quincy Adams	B. z, x, y, w
y. J. Quincy Addams	C. y, w, x, z
z. Jerimiah Adams	D. x, w, z, y

18. COLUMN I — COLUMN II — 18.____

COLUMN I	COLUMN II
w. Nehimiah Persoff	A. w, z, x, y
x. Newton Pershing	B. x, z, y, w
y. Newman Perring	C. y, x, w, z
z. Nelson Persons	D. z, y, w, x

KEY (CORRECT ANSWERS)

1.	A	6.	D	11.	A	16.	C
2.	D	7.	D	12.	D	17.	B
3.	B	8.	C	13.	B	18.	C
4.	D	9.	B	14.	A		
5.	C	10.	C	15.	D		

TEST 4

Questions 1-13.

DIRECTIONS: Each question from 1 through 13 contains four names. For each question, choose the name that should be FIRST if he four names are to be arranged in alphabetical order in accordance with the Rule for Alphabetical Filing of Names of People given below. Read this rule carefully. Then, for each question, mark your answer space with the letter that is next to the name that should be first in alphabetical order.

RULE FOR ALPHABETICAL FILING OF NAMES OF PEOPLE

The names of people are filed in strict alphabetical order, first according to the last name, then according to the first name. For example; George Allen comes before Edward Bell, and Alice Reston comes before Lucille Reston.

SAMPLE QUESTION
A. Roger Smith (2)
B. Joan Smythe (4)
C. Alan Smith (1)
D. James Smithe (3)

The number in parentheses show the proper alphabetical order in which these names should be filed. Since the name that should be filed FIRST is Alan Smith, the correct answer to the sample question is C.

1. A. William Claremont B. Antonio Clements C. Anthony Clemente D. William Claymont 1.____

2. A. Wayne Fumando B. Sarah Femando C. Susan Fumando D. Wilson Femando 2.____

3. A. Wilbur Hanson B. Wm. Hansen C. Robert Hansen D. Thomas Hanson 3.____

4. A. George St. John B. Thomas Santos C. Frances Starks D. Mary S. Stranum 4.____

5. A. Franklin Carrol B. Timothy Carrol C. Timothy S. Carol D. Frank F. Carroll 5.____

6. A. Christie-Barry Storage B. John Christie-Barry C. The Christie-Barry Company D. Anne Christie-Barrie 6.____

7. A. Inter State Travel Co. A. Interstate Car Rental C. Inter State Trucking D. Interstate Lending Inst. 7.____

8. A. The Los Angeles Tile Co. 8.____
   B. Anita F. Los
   C. The Lost & Found Detective Agency
   D. Jason Los-Brio

9. A. Prince Charles B. Prince Charles Coiffures 9.____
   C. Chas. F. Prince D. Thomas A. Charles

10. A. U.S. Dept. of Agriculture B. United States Aircraft Co. 10.____
    C. U.S. Air Transport, Inc. D. The United Union

11. A. Meyer's Art Shop B. Frank B. Meyer 11.____
    C. Meyers' Paint Store D. Meyer and Goldberg

12. A. David Des Laurier B. Des Moines Flower Shop 12.____
    C. Henry Desanto D. Mary L. Desta

13. A. Jeffrey Van Der Meer B. Jeffrey M. Vander 13.____
    C. Jeffrey Van D. Wallace Meer

KEY (CORRECT ANSWERS)

1.	A	6.	D	11.	A
2.	B	7.	B	12.	C
3.	C	8.	B	13.	D
4.	A	9.	D		
5.	C	10.	C		

TEST 5

Questions 1-10.

DIRECTIONS: Questions 1 through 10 are to be answered on the basis of the usual rules of filing. Column I lists, next to the numbers 1 to 10, the names of 10 clinic patients. Column II lists, next to the letters A to D, the headings of file drawers into which you are to place the records of these patients. For each question, indicate in the space at the right the letter preceding the heading of the file drawer in which the record should be filed.

COLUMN I	COLUMN II	
1. Charles Coughlin	A. Cab-Cep	1.____
2. Mary Carstairs	B. Ceq-Cho	2.____
3. Joseph Collin	C. Chr-Coj	3.____
4. Thomas Chelsey	D. Cok-Czy	4.____
5. Cedric Chalmers		5.____
6. Mae Clarke		6.____
7. Dora Copperhead		7.____
8. Arnold Cohn		8.____
9. Charlotte Crumboldt		9.____
10. Frances Celine		10.____

Questions 11-18.

DIRECTIONS: Questions 11 to 18 are to be answered on the basis of the usual rules of filing. Column I lists, next to the numbers 11 to 18, the names of 8 clinic patients. Column II lists, next to the letters A to O, the headings of file drawers into which you are to place the records of these patients. For each question, indicate in the space at the right the letter preceding the heading of the file drawer in which the record should be filed.

COLUMN I	COLUMN II	
11. Thomas Adams	A. Aab-Abi	11.____
	B. Abj-Ach	
12. Joseph Albert	C. Aci-Aco	12.____
	D. Acp-Ada	
13. Frank Anaster	E. Adb-Afr	13.____
	F. Afs-Ago	
14. Charles Abt	G. Agp-Ahz	14.____
	H. Aia-Ako	
15. John Alfred	I. Akp-Ald	15.____
	J. Ale-Amo	
16. Louis Aron	K. Amp-Aor	16.____
	L. Aos-Apr	
17. Francis Amos	M. Aps-Asi	17.____
	N. Asj-Ati	
18. William Adler	O. Atj-Awz	18.____

Questions 19-28.

DIRECTIONS: Questions 19 through 28 are to be answered on the basis of the usual rules of filing. Column I lists, next to the numbers 19 through 28, the names of 10 clinic patients. Column II lists, next to the letters A to D the headings of file drawers into which you are to place the medical records of these patients. For each question, indicate in the space at the right the letter preceding the heading of the file drawer in which the record should be filed.

COLUMN I	COLUMN II	
19. Frank Shea	A. Sab-Sej	19.____
20. Rose Seaborn	B. Sek-Sio	20.____
21. Samuel Smollin	C. Sip-Soo	21.____
22. Thomas Shur	D. Sop-Syz	22.____
23. Ben Schaefer		23.____
24. Shirley Strauss		24.____
25. Harry Spiro		25.____
26. Dora Skelly		26.____
27. Sylvia Smith		27.____
28. Arnold Selz		28.____

KEY (CORRECT ANSWERS)

1.	D	11.	D	21.	C
2.	A	12.	I	22.	B
3.	D	13.	K	23.	A
4.	B	14.	B	24.	D
5.	B	15.	J	25.	D
6.	C	16.	M	26.	C
7.	D	17.	J	27.	C
8.	C	18.	E	28.	B
9.	D	19.	B		
10.	A	20.	A		

CODING

COMMENTARY

An ingenious question-type called coding, involving elements of alphabetizing, filing, name and number comparison, and evaluative judgment and application, has currently won wide acceptance in testing circles for measuring clerical aptitude and general ability, particularly on the senior (middle) grades (levels).

While the directions for this question usually vary in detail, the candidate is generally asked to consider groups of names, codes, and numbers, and, then, according to a given plan, to arrange codes in alphabetic order; to arrange these in numerical sequence; to re-arrange columns of names and numbers in correct order; to espy errors in coding; to choose the correct coding arrangement in consonance with the given directions and examples, etc.

This question-type appears to have few paramaters in respect to form, substance, or degree of difficulty.

Accordingly, acquaintance with, and practice in, the coding question is recommended for the serious candidate.

EXAMINATION SECTION
TEST 1

DIRECTIONS:

CODE TABLE

Name of Applicant	H	A	N	G	S	B	R	U	K	E
Test Code	c	o	m	p	l	e	x	i	t	y
File Number	0	1	2	3	4	5	6	7	8	9

Assume that each of the above *capital letters* is the first letter of the Name of an Applicant, that the *small letter* directly beneath each capital letter is the Test Code for the Applicant, and that the *number* directly beneath each code letter is the File Number for the Applicant.

In each of the following questions, the test code letters and the file numbers in Columns 2 and 3 should correspond to the capital letters in Column 1. For each question, look at each column carefully and mark your answer as follows:

If there is an error only in Column 2, mark your answer A.
If there is an error only in Column 3, mark your answer B.
If there is an error in both Columns 2 and 3, mark your answer C.
If both Columns 2 and 3 are correct, mark your answer D.

The following sample question is given to help you understand the procedure.

SAMPLE QUESTION

Column 1	Column 2	Column 3
AKEHN	otyci	18902

In Column 2, the final test code letter "i" should be "m." Column 3 is correctly coded to Column 1. Since there is an error only in Column 2, the answer is A

	Column 1	Column 2	Column 3	
1.	NEKKU	mytti	29987	1.____
2.	KRAEB	txlye	86095	2.____
3.	ENAUK	ymoit	92178	3.____
4.	REANA	xeomo	69121	4.____
5.	EKHSE	ytcxy	97049	5.____

KEY (CORRECT ANSWERS)

1. B
2. C
3. D
4. A
5. C

TEST 2

DIRECTIONS: The employee identification codes in Column I begin and end with a capital letter and have an eight-digit number in between. In Questions 1 through 8, employee identification codes in Column I are to be arranged according to the following rules:

First: Arrange in alphabetical order according to the first letter.

Second: When two or more employee identification codes have the same first letter, arrange in alphabetical order according to the last letter.

Third: When two or more employee codes have the same first and last letters, arrange in numerical order beginning with the lowest number.

The employee identification codes in Column I are numbered 1 through 5 in the order in which they are listed. In Column II the numbers 1 through 5 are arranged in four different ways to show different arrangements of the corresponding employee identification numbers. Choose the answer in Column II in which the employee identification numbers are arranged according to the above rules.

SAMPLE QUESTION

Column I	Column II
1. E75044127B	A. 4, 1, 3, 2, 5
2. B96399104A	B. 4, 1, 2, 3, 5
3. B93939086A	C. 4, 3, 2, 5, 1
4. B47064465H	D. 3, 2, 5, 4, 1
5. B99040922A	

In the sample question, the four employee identification codes starting with B should be put before the employee identification code starting with E. The employee identification codes starting with B and ending with A should be put before the employee identification codes starting with B and ending with H. The three employee identification codes starting with B and ending with A should be listed in numerical order, beginning with the lowest number. The correct way to arrange the employee identification codes, therefore, is 3, 2, 5, 4, 1 shown below.

3. B93939086A
2. B96399104A
5. B99040922A
4. B47064465H
1. E75044127B

Therefore, the answer to the sample question is D. Now answer the following questions according to the above rules.

	Column I	Column II	
1.	1. G42786441J	A. 2, 5, 4, 3, 1	1.____
	2. H45665413J	B. 5, 4, 1, 3, 2	
	3. G43117690J	C. 4, 5, 1, 3, 2	
	4. G43546698I	D. 1, 3, 5, 4, 2	
	5. G41679942I		

2. 1. S44556178T
   2. T43457169T
   3. S53321176T
   4. T53317998S
   5. S67673942S

   A. 1, 3, 5, 2, 4
   B. 4, 3, 5, 2, 1
   C. 5, 3, 1, 2, 4
   D. 5, 1, 3, 4, 2

2.____

3. 1. R63394217D
   2. R63931247D
   3. R53931247D
   4. R66874239D
   4. R46799366D

   A. 5, 4, 2, 3, 1
   B. 1, 5, 3, 2, 4
   C. 5, 3, 1, 2, 4
   D. 5, 1, 2, 3, 4

3.____

4. 1. A35671968B
   2. A35421794C
   3. A35466987B
   4. C10435779A
   5. C00634779B

   A. 3, 2, 1, 4, 5
   B. 2, 3, 1, 5, 4
   C. 1, 3, 2, 4, 5
   D. 3, 1, 2, 4, 5

4.____

5. 1. I99746426Q
   2. I10445311Q
   3. J63749877P
   4. J03421739Q
   5. J00765311Q

   A. 2, 1, 3, 5, 4
   B. 5, 4, 2, 1, 3
   C. 4, 5, 3, 2, 1
   D. 2, 1, 4, 5, 3

5.____

6. 1. M33964217N
   2. N33942770N
   3. N06155881M
   4. M00433669M
   5. M79034577N

   A. 4, 1, 5, 2, 3
   B. 5, 1, 4, 3, 2
   C. 4, 1, 5, 3, 2
   D. 1, 4, 5, 2, 3

6.____

7. 1. D77643905C
   2. D44106788C
   3. D13976022F
   4. D97655430E
   5. D00439776F

   A. 1, 2, 5, 3, 4
   B. 5, 3, 2, 1, 4
   C. 2, 1, 5, 3, 4
   D. 2, 1, 4, 5, 3

7.____

8. 1. W22746920A
   2. W22743720A
   3. W32987655A
   4. W43298765A
   5. W30987433A

   A. 2, 1, 3, 4, 5
   B. 2, 1, 5, 3, 4
   C. 1, 2, 3, 4, 5
   D. 1, 2, 5, 3, 4

8.____

KEY (CORRECT ANSWERS)

1. B	5. A
2. D	6. C
3. C	7. D
4. D	8. B

TEST 3

DIRECTIONS: Each of the following equestions consists of three sets of names and name codes. In each question, the two names and name codes on the same line are supposed to be exactly the same.

Look carefully at each set of names and codes and mark your answer:

A. if there are mistakes in all three sets
B. if there are mistakes in two of the sets
C. if there is a mistake in only one set
D. if there are no mistakes in any of the sets

The following sample question is given to help you understand the procedure.

Macabe, John N.	- V	53162	Macade, John N.	- V	53162
Howard, Joan S.	- J	24791	Howard, Joan S.	- J	24791
Ware, Susan B.	- A	45068	Ware, Susan B.	- A	45968

In the above sample question, the names and name codes of the first set are not exactly the same because of the spelling of the last name (Macabe - Macade). The names and name codes of the second set are exactly the same. The names and name codes of the third set are not exactly the same because the two name codes are different (A 45068 - A 45968), Since there are mistakes in only 2 of the sets, the answer to the sample question is B.

1.	Powell, Michael C. - 78537 F Martinez, Pablo, J. - 24435 P MacBane, Eliot M. - 98674 E	Powell, Michael C. - 78537 F Martinez, Pablo J. - 24435 P MacBane, Eliot M. - 98674 E	1.____
2.	Fitz-Kramer Machines Inc. - 259090 Marvel Cleaning Service - 482657 Donate, Carl G. - 637418	Fitz-Kramer Machines Inc. - 259090 Marvel Cleaning Service - 482657 Danato, Carl G. - 687418	2.____
3.	Martin Davison Trading Corp. - 43108 T Cotwald Lighting Fixtures - 76065 L R. Crawford Plumbers - 23157 C	Martin Davidson Trading Corp. - 43108 T Cotwald Lighting Fixtures - 70056 L R. Crawford Plumbers - 23157 G	3.____
4.	Fraiman Engineering Corp. - M4773 Neuman, Walter B. - N7745 Pierce, Eric M. - W6304	Friaman Engineering Corp. -M4773 Neumen, Walter B. - N7745 Pierce, Eric M. - W6304	4.____
5.	Constable, Eugene - B 64837 Derrick, Paul - H 27119 Heller, Karen - S 49606	Comstable, Eugene - B 64837 Derrik, Paul - H 27119 Heller, Karen - S 46906	5.____
6.	Hernando Delivery Service Co. - D 7456 Barettz Electrical Supplies - N 5392 Tanner, Abraham - M 4798	Hernando Delivery Service Co. - D 7456 Barettz Electrical Supplies - N 5392 Tanner, Abraham - M 4798	6.____
7.	Kalin Associates - R 38641 Sealey, Robert E. - P 63533 Scalsi Office Furniture	Kaline Associates - R 38641 Sealey, Robert E. - P 63553 Scalsi Office Furniture	7.____

8.	Janowsky, Philip M.- 742213 Hansen, Thomas H. - 934816 L. Lester and Son Inc. - 294568	Janowsky, Philip M.- 742213 Hanson, Thomas H. - 934816 L. Lester and Son Inc. - 294568	8.____

KEY (CORRECT ANSWERS)

1. D
2. C
3. A
4. B
5. A
6. D
7. B
8. C

TEST 4

DIRECTIONS: The following questions are to be answered on the basis of the following Code Table. In this table, for each number, a corresponding code letter is given. Each of the questions contains three pairs of numbers and code letters. In each pair, the code letters should correspond with the numbers in accordance with the Code Table.

CODE TABLE

Number	1	2	3	4	5	6	7	8	9	0
Corresponding Code Letter	Y	N	Z	X	W	T	U	P	S	R

In some of the pairs below, an error exists in the coding. Examine the pairs in each question carefully. If an error exists in:

Only one of the pairs in the question, mark your answer A.
Any two pairs in the question, mark your answer B.
All three pairs in the question, mark your answer C.
None of the pairs in the question, mark your answer D.

SAMPLE QUESTION

37258 - ZUNWP
948764 - SXPTTX
73196 - UZYSP

In the above sample, the first pair is correct since each number, as listed, has the correct corresponding code letter. In the second pair, an error exists because the number 7 should have the code letter U instead of the letter T. In the third pair, an error exists because the number 6 should have the code letter T instead of the letter P. Since there are errors in two of the three pairs, the correct answer is B.

1. 493785 - XSZUPW
   86398207 - PTUSPNRU
   5943162 - WSXZYTN
   1.____

2. 5413968412 - WXYZSTPXYR
   8763451297 - PUTZXWYZSU
   4781965302 - XUPYSUWZRN
   2.____

3. 79137584 - USYRUWPX
   638247 - TZPNXS
   49679312 - XSTUSZYN
   3.____

4. 37854296 - ZUPWXNST
   09183298 - RSYXZNSP
   91762358 - SYUTNXWP
   4.____

5. 3918762485 - ZSYPUTNXPW
   1578291436 - YWUPNSYXZT
   2791385674 - NUSYZPWTUX
   5.____

6. 197546821 - YSUWSTPNY 6.____
873024867 - PUZRNWPTU
583179246 - WPZYURNXT

7. 510782463 - WYRUSNXTZ 7.____
478192356 - XUPYSNZWT
961728532 - STYUNPWXN

KEY (CORRECT ANSWERS)

1. A
2. C
3. B
4. B
5. D

6. C
7. B

TEST 5

DIRECTIONS: Assume that each of the capital letters is the first letter of the name of a city using EAM equipment. The number directly beneath each capital letter is the code number for the city. The small letter beneath each code number is the code letter for the number of EAM divisions in the city and the + or - symbol directly beneath each code letter is the code symbol which signifies whether or not the city uses third generation computers with the EAM equipment.

The questions that follow show City Letters in Column I, Code Numbers in Column II, Code Letters in Column III, and Code Symbols in Column IV. If correct. each Citv Letter in Column I should correspond by position with each of the three codes shown in the other three columns, in accordance with the coding key shown. *BUT* there are some errors. For each question,

If there is a total of *ONE* error in Columns 2, 3, and 4, mark your answer A.
If there is a total of *TWO* errors in Columns 2, 3, and 4, mark your answer B.
If there is a total of *THREE* errors in Columns 2, 3, and 4, mark your answer C.
If Columns 2, 3, and 4 are correct, mark your answer D.

SAMPLE QUESTION

I City Letter	II Code Numbers	III Code Letters	IV Code Symbols
YJMOS	53798	ebgih	- - + + -

The errors are as follows: In Column 2, the Code Number should be "2" instead of "3" for City Letter "J," and in Column 4 the Code Symbol should be "+" instead of "-" for City Letter "Y." Since there is a total of two errors in Columns 2, 3, and 4, the answer to this sample question is B.

Now answer questions 1 through 9 according to these rules.

CODING KEY

City Letter	P	J	R	T	Y	K	M	S	0
Code Number	1	2	3	4	5	6	7	8	9
Code Letter	a	b	c	d	e	f	g	h	i
Code Symbol	+	-	+	-	+	-	+	-	+

	I City Letters	II Code Numbers	III Code Letters	IV Code Symbols	
1.	KORMP	69371	fiega	- - + + +	1.____
2.	OTPSY	94186	bdahe	+ - - - +	2.____
3.	RSJTM	38147	chbeg	- - - - +	3.____
4.	PMSKJ	17862	aghfb	+ + - - -	4.____
5.	MYTJR	75423	gedfc	+ + - - +	5.____
6.	TPKYO	41679	dafei	- + - + -	6.____
7.	SKORT	86935	hficd	- - + + -	7.____
8.	JRYPK	23519	bdeaf	- + + + -	8.____
9.	ROMPY	49715	cigad	+ + - + +	9.____

KEY (CORRECT ANSWERS)

1. B
2. C
3. C
4. D
5. A
6. B
7. A
8. B
9. C

TEST 6

Assume that each of the capital letters is the first letter of the name of an offense, that the small letter directly beneath each capital letter is the code letter for the offense, and that the number directly beneath each code letter is the file number for the offense.

DIRECTIONS: In each of the following questions, the code letters and file numbers should correspond to the capital letters.

If there is an error only in Column 2, mark your answer A.
If there is an error only in Column 3, mark your answer B.
If there is an error in both Column 2 and Column 3, mark your answer C.
If both Columns 2 and 3 are correct, mark your answer D.

SAMPLE QUESTION

Column 1	Column 2	Column 3
BNARGHSVVU	emoxtylcci	6357905118

The code letters in Column 2 are correct but the first "5" in Column 3 should be "2." Therefore, the answer is B. Now answer the following questions according to the above rules.

CODE TABLE

Name of Offense	V	A	N	D	S	B	R	U	G	H
Code Letter	c	o	m	p	l	e	x	i	t	y
File Number	1	2	3	4	5	6	7	8	9	0

	Column 1	Column 2	Column 3	
1.	HGDSBNBSVR	ytplxmelcx	0945736517	1.____
2.	SDGUUNHVAH	lptiimycoy	5498830120	2.____
3.	BRSNAAVUDU	exlmooctpi	6753221848	3.____
4.	VSRUDNADUS	cleipmopil	1568432485	4.____
5.	NDSHVRBUAG	mplycxeiot	3450175829	5.____
6.	GHUSNVBRDA	tyilmcexpo	9085316742	6.____
7.	DBSHVURANG	pesycixomt	4650187239	7.____
8.	RHNNASBDGU	xymnolepti	7033256398	8.____

KEY (CORRECT ANSWERS)

1. C
2. D
3. A
4. C
5. B

6. D
7. A
8. C

TEST 7

DIRECTIONS: Each of the following questions contains three sets of code letters and code numbers. In each set, the code numbers should correspond with the code letters as given in the Table, but there is a coding error in some of the sets. Examine the sets in each question carefully.

Mark your answer A if there is a coding error in only *ONE* of the sets in the question.
Mark your answer B if there is a coding error in any *TWO* of the sets in the question.
Mark your answer C if there is a coding error in all *THREE* sets in the question.
Mark your answer D if there is a coding error in *NONE* of the sets in the question.

SAMPLE QUESTION

fgzduwaf - 35720843
uabsdgfw - 04262538
hhfaudgs - 99340257

In the above sample question, the first set is right because each code number matches the code letter as in the Code Table. In the second set, the corresponding number for the code letter b is wrong because it should be 1 instead of 2. In the third set, the corresponding number for the last code letter s is wrong because it should be 6 instead of 7. Since there is an error in two of the sets, the answer to the above sample question is B.

In the Code Table below, each code letter has a corresponding code number directly beneath it.

CODE TABLE

Code Letter	b	d	f	a	g	s	z	w	h	u
Code Number	1	2	3	4	5	6	7	8	9	0

1. fsbughwz - 36104987   zwubgasz - 78025467   1.____
   ghgufddb - 59583221

2. hafgdaas - 94351446   ddsfabsd - 22734162   2.____
   wgdbssgf - 85216553

3. abfbssbd - 41316712   ghzfaubs - 59734017   3.____
   sdbzfwza - 62173874

4. whfbdzag - 89412745   daaszuub - 24467001   4.____
   uzhfwssd - 07936623

5. zbadgbuh - 71425109   dzadbbsz - 27421167   5.____
   gazhwaff - 54798433

6. fbfuadsh - 31304265   gzfuwzsb - 57300671   6.____
   bashhgag - 14699535

KEY (CORRECT ANSWERS)

1. B
2. C
3. B
4. B
5. D
6. C

TEST 8

DIRECTIONS: The following questions are to be answered on the basis of the following Code Table. In this table every letter has a corresponding code number to be punched. Each question contains three pairs of letters and code numbers. In each pair, the code numbers should correspond with the letters in accordance with the Code Table.

CODE TABLE

Letter	P	L	A	N	D	C	0	B	U	R
Corresponding Code Number	1	2	3	4	5	6	7	8	9	0

In some of the pairs below, an error exists in the coding. Examine the pairs in each question. Mark your answer

A if there is a mistake in only *one* of the pairs
B if there is a mistake in only *two* of the pairs
C if there is a mistake in *all three* of the pairs
D if there is a mistake in *none* of the pairs

SAMPLE QUESTION

LCBPUPAB - 26819138
ACOABOL - 3683872
NDURONUC - 46901496

In the above sample, the first pair is correct since each letter as listed has the correct corresponding code number. In the second pair, an error exists because the letter 0 should have the code number 7, instead of 8. In the third pair, an error exists because the letter D should have the code number 5, instead of 6. Since there are errors in two of the three pairs, your answer should be B.

1. ADCANPLC - 35635126 DORURBBO - 57090877 1.____
PNACBUCP - 14368061

2. LCOBLRAP - 26782931 UPANUPCD - 91349156 2.____
RLDACLRO - 02536207

3. LCOROPAR - 26707130 BALANRUP - 83234091 3.____
DOPOAULL - 57173922

4. ONCRUBAP - 74609831 DCLANORD - 56243705 4.____
AORPDUR - 3771590

5. PANRBUCD - 13408965 UAOCDPLR - 93765120 5.____
OPDDOBRA - 71556803

6. BAROLDCP - 83072561 PNOCOBLA - 14767823 6.____
BURPDOLA - 89015723

7. ANNCPABO - 34461387 DBALDRCP - 58325061 7.____
ACRPOUL - 3601792

8.	BLAPOUR - 8321790 RODACORD - 07536805	NOACNPL - 4736412	8.____
9.	ADUBURCL- 3598062 PRONDALU - 10754329	NOCOBAPR - 47578310	9.____
10.	UBADCLOR - 98356270 LONDUPRC - 27459106	NBUPPARA - 48911033	10.____

KEY (CORRECT ANSWERS)

1. C
2. B
3. D
4. B
5. A
6. D
7. B
8. B
9. C
10. A

TEST 9

DIRECTIONS: Answer questions 1 through 10 ONLY on the basis of the following information.

Column I consists of serial numbers of dollar bills. Column II shows different ways of arranging the corresponding serial numbers.

The serial numbers of dollar bills in Column I begin and end with a capital letter and have an eight-digit number in between. The serial numbers in Column I are to be arranged according to the following rules:

FIRST: In alphabetical order according to the first letter.

SECOND: When two or more serial numbers have the same first letter, in alphabetical order according to the last letter.

THIRD: When two or more serial numbers have the same first and last letters, in numerical order, beginning with the lowest number.

The serial numbers in Column I are numbered (1) through (5) in the order in which they are listed. In Column II the numbers (1) through (5) are arranged in four different ways to show different arrangements of the corresponding serial numbers. Choose the answer in Column II in which the serial numbers are arranged according to the above rules.

SAMPLE QUESTION

	COLUMN I	COLUMN II
(1)	E75044127B	(A) 4, 1, 3, 2, 5
(2)	B96399104A	(B) 4, 1, 2, 3, 5
(3)	B93939086A	(C) 4, 3, 2, 5, 1
(4)	B47064465H	(D) 3, 2, 5, 4, 1
(5)	B99040922A	

In the sample question, the four serial numbers starting with B should be put before the serial number starting with E. The serial numbers starting with B and ending with A should be put before the serial number starting with B and ending with H. The three serial numbers starting with B and ending with A should be listed in numerical order, beginning with the lowest number. The correct way to arrange the serial numbers, therefore, is:

(3) B93939086A
(2) B96399104A
(5) B99040922A
(4) B47064465H
(1) E75044127B

Since the order of arrangement is 3, 2, 5, 4, 1, the answer to the sample question is (D).

		COLUMN I		COLUMN II
1.	(1)	P44343314Y	A.	2, 3, 1, 4, 5
	(2)	P44141341S	B.	1, 5, 3, 2, 4
	(3)	P44141431L	C.	4, 2, 3, 5, 1
	(4)	P41143413W	D.	5, 3, 2, 4, 1
	(5)	P44313433H		
2.	(1)	D89077275M	A.	3, 2, 5, 4, 1
	(2)	D98073724N	B.	1, 4, 3, 2, 5
	(3)	D90877274N	C.	4, 1, 5, 2, 3
	(4)	D98877275M	D.	1, 3, 2, 5, 4
	(5)	D98873725N		

3. (1) H32548137E
(2) H35243178A
(3) H35284378F
(4) H35288337A
(5) H32883173B

A. 2, 4, 5, 1, 3
B. 1, 5, 2, 3, 4
C. 1, 5, 2, 4, 3
D. 2, 1, 5, 3, 4

4. (1) K24165039H
(2) F24106599A
(3) L21406639G
(4) C24156093A
(5) K24165593D

A. 4, 2, 5, 3, 1
B. 2, 3, 4, 1, 5
C. 4, 2, 5, 1, 3
D. 1, 3, 4, 5, 2

5. (1) H79110642E
(2) H79101928E
(3) A79111567F
(4) H79111796E
(5) A79111618F

A. 2, 1, 3, 5, 4
B. 2, 1, 4, 5, 3
C. 3, 5, 2, 1, 4
D. 4, 3, 5, 1, 2

6. (1) P16388385W
(2) R16388335V
(3) P16383835W
(4) R18386865V
(5) P18686865W

A. 3, 4, 5, 2, 1
B. 2, 3, 4, 5, 1
C. 2, 4, 3, 1, 5
D. 3, 1, 5, 2, 4

7. (1) B42271749G
(2) B42271779G
(3) E43217779G
(4) B42874119C
(5) E42817749G

A. 4, 1, 5, 2, 3
B. 4, 1, 2, 5, 3
C. 1, 2, 4, 5, 3
D. 5, 3, 1, 2, 4

8. (1) M57906455S
(2) N87077758S
(3) N87707757B
(4) M57877759B
(5) M57906555S

A. 4, 1, 5, 3, 2
B. 3, 4, 1, 5, 2
C. 4, 1, 5, 2, 3
D. 1, 5, 3, 2, 4

9. (1) C69336894Y
(2) C69336684V
(3) C69366887W
(4) C69366994Y
(5) C69336865V

A. 2, 5, 3, 1, 4
B. 3, 2, 5, 1, 4
C. 3, 1, 4, 5, 2
D. 2, 5, 1, 3, 4

10. (1) A56247181D
(2) A56272128P
(3) H56247128D
(4) H56272288P
(5) A56247188D

A. 1, 5, 3, 2, 4
B. 3, 1, 5, 2, 4
C. 3, 2, 1, 5, 4
D. 1, 5, 2, 3, 4

KEY (CORRECT ANSWERS)

1. D	6. D
2. B	7. B
3. A	8. A
4. C	9. A
5. C	10. D

TEST 10

DIRECTIONS: Answer the following questions on the basis of the instructions, the code, and the sample questions given below. Assume that an officer at a certain location is equipped with a two-way radio to keep him in constant touch with his security headquarters. Radio messages and replies are given in code form, as follows:

CODE TABLE

Radio Code for Situation	J	P	M	F	B
Radio Code for Action to be Taken	o	r	a	z	q
Radio Response for Action Being Taken	1	2	3	4	5

Assume that each of the above capital letters is the radio code for a particular type of situation, that the small letter below each capital letter is the radio code for the action an officer is directed to take, and that the number directly below each small letter is the radio response an officer should make to indicate what action was actually taken.

In each of the following questions, the code letter for the action directed (Column 2) and the code number for the action taken (Column 3) should correspond to the capital letters in Column 1.

INSTRUCTIONS: If only Column 2 is different from Column 1, mark your answer I.
If only Column 3 is different from Column 1, mark your answer II.
If both Column 2 and Column 3 are different from Column I, mark your answer III.
If both Columns 2 and 3 are the same as Column 1, mark your answer IV.

SAMPLE QUESTION

Column 1	Column 2	Column 3
JPFMB	orzaq	12453

The CORRECT answer is: A. I B. II C. III D. IV

The code letters in Column 2 are correct, but the numbers "53" in Column 3 should be "35." Therefore, the answer is B. Now answe the following questions according to the above rules.

	Column 1	Column 2	Column 3	
1.	PBFJM	rqzoa	25413	1.____
2.	MPFBJ	zrqao	32541	2.____
3.	JBFPM	oqzra	15432	3.____
4.	BJPMF	qaroz	51234	4.____
5.	PJFMB	rozaq	21435	5.____
6.	FJBMP	zoqra	41532	6.____

KEY (CORRECT ANSWERS)

1. D
2. C
3. B
4. A
5. D
6. A

ARITHMETIC

EXAMINATION SECTION
TEST 1

DIRECTIONS: Each question or incomplete statement is followed by several suggested answers or completions. Select the one that BEST answers the question or completes the statement. *PRINT THE LETTER OF THE CORRECT ANSWER IN THE SPACE AT THE RIGHT.*

1. The sum of 76342 + 49050 + 21206 + 59989 is 1.____
   A. 196586 B. 206087 C. 206587 D. 234487

2. The sum of $452.13 + $963.83 + $621.25 is 2.____
   A. $1936.83 B. $2037.21 C. $2095.73 D. $2135.73

3. The sum of 36392 + 42156 + 98765 is 3.____
   A. 167214 B. 177203 C. 177313 D. 178213

4. The sum of 40125 + 87123 + 24689 is 4.____
   A. 141827 B. 151827 C. 151937 D. 161947

5. The sum of 2379 + 4015 + 6521 + 9986 is 5.____
   A. 22901 B. 22819 C. 21801 D. 21791

6. From 50962 subtract 36197. The answer should be 6.____
   A. 14675 B. 14765 C. 14865 D. 24765

7. From 90000 subtract 31928. The answer should be 7.____
   A. 58072 B. 59062 C. 68172 D. 69182

8. From 63764 subtract 21548. The answer should be 8.____
   A. 42216 B. 43122 C. 45126 D. 85312

9. From $9605.13 subtract $2715.96. The answer should be 9.____
   A. $12,321.09 B. $8,690.16
   C. $6,990.07 D. $6,889.17

10. From 76421 subtract 73101. The answer should be 10.____
    A. 3642 B. 3540 C. 3320 D. 3242

11. From $8.25 subtract $6.50. The answer should be 11.____
    A. $1.25 B. $1.50 C. $1.75 D. $2.25

12. Multiply 563 by 0.50. The answer should be 12.____
    A. 281.50 B. 28.15 C. 2.815 D. 0.2815

13. Multiply 0.35 by 1045. The answer should be 13.____

A. 0.36575 B. 3.6575 C. 36.575 D. 365.75

14. Multiply 25 by 2513. The answer should be 14.____

A. 62825 B. 62725 C. 60825 D. 52825

15. Multiply 423 by 0.01. The answer should be 15.____

A. 0.0423 B. 0.423 C. 4.23 D. 42.3

16. Multiply 6.70 by 3.2. The answer should be 16.____

A. 2.1440 B. 21.440 C. 214.40 D. 2144.0

17. Multiply 630 by 517. The answer should be 17.____

A. 325,710 B. 345,720 C. 362,425 D. 385,660

18. Multiply 35 by 846. The answer should be 18.____

A. 4050 B. 9450 C. 18740 D. 29610

19. Multiply 823 by 0.05. The answer should be 19.____

A. 0.4115 B. 4.115 C. 41.15 D. 411.50

20. Multiply 1690 by 0.10. The answer should be 20.____

A. 0.169 B. 1.69 C. 16.90 D. 169.0

21. Divide 2765 by 35. The answer should be 21.____

A. 71 B. 79 C. 87 D. 93

22. From $18.55 subtract $6.80. The answer should be 22.____

A. $9.75 B. $10.95 C. $11.75 D. $25.35

23. The sum of 2.75 + 4.50 + 3.60 is 23.____

A. 9.75 B. 10.85 C. 11.15 D. 11.95

24. The sum of 9.63 + 11.21 + 17.25 is 24.____

A. 36.09 B. 38.09 C. 39.92 D. 41.22

25. The sum of 112.0 + 16.9 + 3.84 is 25.____

A. 129.3 B. 132.74 C. 136.48 D. 167.3

KEY (CORRECT ANSWERS)

1. C
2. B
3. C
4. C
5. A
6. B
7. A
8. A
9. D
10. C
11. C
12. A
13. D
14. A
15. C
16. B
17. A
18. D
19. C
20. D
21. B
22. C
23. B
24. B
25. B

SOLUTIONS TO PROBLEMS

1. 76,342 + 49,050 + 21,206 + 59,989 = 206,587
2. $452.13 + $963.83 + $621.25 = $2037.21
3. 36,392 + 42,156 + 98,765 = 177,313
4. 40,125 + 87,123 + 24,689 = 151,937
5. 2379 + 4015 + 6521 + 9986 = 22901
6. 50,962 - 36,197 = 14,765
7. 90,000 - 31,928 = 58,072
8. 63,764 - 21,548 = 42,216
9. $9605.13 - $2715.96 = $6889.17
10. 76,421 - 73,101 = 3320
11. $8.25 - $6.50 = $1.75
12. (563)(.50) = 281.50
13. (.35)(1045) = 365.75
14. (25)(2513) = 62,825
15. (423)(.01) = 4.23
16. (6.70)(3.2) = 21.44
17. (630)(517) = 325,710
18. (35)(846) = 29,610
19. (823)(.05) = 41.15
20. (1690)(.10) = 169
21. 2765 ÷ 35 = 79
22. $18.55 - $6.80 = $11.75
23. 2.75 + 4.50 + 3.60 = 10.85
24. 9.63 + 11.21 + 17.25 = 38.09
25. 112.0 + 16.9 + 3.84 = 132.74

TEST 2

Questions 1-10.

DIRECTIONS: Questions 1 through 10 refer to the arithmetic examples shown in the boxes below. Be sure to refer to the proper box when answering each question.

23.3 - 5.72	$491.26 -127.47	$7.95 ÷ $0.15	4758 1639 2075 864 23	27.6 179.47 8.73 46.5
BOX 1	BOX 2	BOX 3	BOX 4	BOX 5
243 x57	57697 -9748	23.65 x 9.7	3/4 260	25/1975
BOX 6	BOX 7	BOX 8	BOX 9	BOX 10

1. The difference between the two numbers in Box 1 is 1.____

   A. 17.42 B. 17.58 C. 23.35 D. 29.02

2. The difference between the two numbers in Box 2 is 2.____

   A. $274.73 B. $363.79 C. $374.89 D. $618.73

3. The result of the division indicated in Box 3 is 3.____

   A. $0.53 B. $5.30 C. 5.3 D. 53

4. The sum of the five numbers in Box 4 is 4.____

   A. 8355 B. 9359 C. 9534 D. 10359

5. The sum of the four numbers in Box 5 is 5.____

   A. 262.30 B. 272.03 C. 372.23 D. 372.30

6. The product of the two numbers in Box 6 is 6.____

   A. 138.51 B. 1385.1 C. 13851 D. 138510

7. The difference between the two numbers in Box 7 is 7.____

   A. 67445 B. 48949 C. 47949 D. 40945

8. The product of the two numbers in Box 8 is 8.____

   A. 22.9405 B. 229.405 C. 2294.05 D. 229405

9. The product of the two numbers in Box 9 is 9.____

   A. 65 B. 120 C. 195 D. 240

10. The result of the division indicated in Box 10 is 10.____

A. 790 B. 379 C. 179 D. 79

Questions 11-20.

DIRECTIONS: Questions 11 through 20 refer to the arithmetic examples shown in the boxes below. Be sure to refer to the proper box when answering each question.

3849 728 3164 773 32 BOX 1	18.70 268.38 17.64 9.40 BOX 2	66788 -8639 BOX 3	154 x48 BOX 4	32.56 x 8.6 BOX 5
34/2890 BOX 6	32.49 - 8.7 BOX 7	$582.17 -38.58 BOX 8	$6.72 ÷ $0.24 BOX 9	3/8 x 264 BOX 10

11. The sum of the five numbers in Box 1 is 11.____

A. 7465 B. 7566 C. 8465 D. 8546

12. The sum of the four numbers in Box 2 is 12.____

A. 341.21 B. 341.12 C. 314.21 D. 314.12

13. The difference between the two numbers in Box 3 is 13.____

A. 75427 B. 74527 C. 58149 D. 57149

14. The product of the two numbers in Box 4 is 14.____

A. 1232 B. 6160 C. 7392 D. 8392

15. The product of the two numbers in Box 5 is 15.____

A. 28.016 B. 280.016 C. 280.16 D. 2800.16

16. The result of the division indicated in Box 6 is 16.____

A. 85 B. 850 C. 8.5 D. 185

17. The difference between the two numbers in Box 7 is 17.____

A. 23.79 B. 21.53 C. 19.97 D. 18.79

18. The difference between the two numbers in Box 8 is 18.____

A. $620.75 B. $602.59 C. $554.75 D. $543.59

19. The result of the division indicated in Box 9 is 19.____

A. .0357 B. 28.0 C. 280 D. 35.7

20. The product of the two numbers in Box 10 is 20.____

A. 9.90 B. 89.0 C. 99.0 D. 199.

21. When 2597 is added to the result of 257 multiplied by 65, the answer is 21.____

A. 16705 B. 19302 C. 19392 D. 19402

22. When 948 is subtracted from the sum of 6527 + 324, the answer is 22.____

A. 5255 B. 5903 C. 7151 D. 7799

23. When 736 is subtracted from the sum of 3191 + 1253, the answer is 23.____

A. 2674 B. 3708 C. 4444 D. 5180

24. Divide 6 2/3 by 2 1/2. 24.____

A. 2 2/3 B. 16 2/3 C. 3 1/3 D. 2 1/2

25. Add: 1/2 + 2 1/4 + 2/3 25.____

A. 3 1/4 B. 2 7/8 C. 4 1/4 D. 3 5/12

KEY (CORRECT ANSWERS)

1. B
2. B
3. D
4. B
5. A

6. C
7. C
8. B
9. C
10. D

11. D
12. D
13. C
14. C
15. B

16. A
17. A
18. D
19. B
20. C

21. B
22. B
23. B
24. A
25. D

SOLUTIONS TO PROBLEMS

1. 23.3 - 5.72 = 17.58

2. $491.26 - $127.47 = $363.79

3. $7.95 $.15 = 53

4. 4758 + 1639 + 2075 + 864 + 23 = 9359

5. 27.6 + 179.47 + 8.73 + 46.5 = 262.3

6. (243)(57) = 13,851

7. 57,697 - 9748 = 47,949

8. (23.65X9.7) = 229.405

9. $(\frac{3}{4})(260)=195$

10. 1975 ÷ 25 = 79

11. 3849 + 728 + 3164 + 773 + 32 = 8546

12. 18.70 + 268.38 + 17.64 + 9.40 = 314.12

13. 66,788 - 8639 = 58,149

14. (154)(48) = 7392

15. (32.56)(8.6) = 280.016

16. 2890 34 = 85

17. 32.49 - 8.7 = 23.79

18. $582.17 - $38.58 = $543.59

19. $6.72 ÷ $.24 = 28

20. $(\frac{3}{8})(264)=99$

21. 2597 + (257)(65) = 2597 + 16,705 = 19,302

22. (6527 + 324) - 948 = 6851 - 948 = 5903

23. (3191 + 1253) - 736 = 4444 - 736 = 3708

24. $6\frac{2}{3} \div 2\frac{1}{2} = (\frac{20}{3})(\frac{2}{5}) = \frac{40}{15} = 2\frac{2}{3}$

25. $\frac{1}{2} + 2\frac{1}{4} + \frac{2}{3} = \frac{6}{12} + 2\frac{3}{12} + \frac{8}{12} = 2\frac{17}{12} = 3\frac{5}{12}$

TEST 3

Questions 1-10.

DIRECTIONS: Questions 1 through 10 refer to the arithmetic examples shown in the boxes below. Be sure to refer to the proper box when answering each item.

8462 2974 5109 763 47 BOX 1	14/1890 BOX 2	182 x63 BOX 3	27412 -8426 BOX 4	$275.15 -162.28 BOX 5
2/3 x 246 BOX 6	14.36 x 7.2 BOX 7	14.6 9.22 143.18 27.1 BOX 8	$6.45 ÷ $0.15 BOX 9	16.6 - 7.91 BOX 10

1. The sum of the five numbers in Box 1 is — 1.____

   A. 16245 B. 16355 C. 17245 D. 17355

2. The result of the division indicated in Box 2 is — 2.____

   A. 140 B. 135 C. 127 6/7 D. 125

3. The product of the two numbers in Box 3 is — 3.____

   A. 55692 B. 16552 C. 11466 D. 1638

4. The difference between the two numbers in Box 4 is — 4.____

   A. 18986 B. 19096 C. 35838 D. 38986

5. The difference between the two numbers in Box 5 is — 5.____

   A. $103.87 B. $112.87 C. $113.97 D. $212.87

6. The product of the two numbers in Box 6 is — 6.____

   A. 82 B. 123 C. 164 D. 369

7. The product of the two numbers in Box 7 is — 7.____

   A. 103.492 B. 103.392 C. 102.392 D. 102.292

8. The sum of the four numbers in Box 8 is — 8.____

   A. 183.00 B. 183.10 C. 194.10 D. 204.00

9. The result of the division indicated in Box 9 is — 9.____

   A. $0.43 B. 4.3 C. 43 D. $4.30

10. The difference between the two numbers in Box 10 is 10.____

A. 8.69 B. 8.11 C. 6.25 D. 3.75

11. Add $4.34, $34.50, $6.00, $101.76, and $90.67. From the result, subtract $60.54 and $10.56. 11.____

A. $76.17 B. $156.37 C. $166.17 D. $300.37

12. Add 2,200, 2,600, 252, and 47.96. From the result, subtract 202.70, 1,200, 2,150, and 434.43. 12.____

A. 1,112.83 B. 1,213.46 C. 1,341.51 D. 1,348.91

13. Multiply 1850 by .05 and multiply 3300 by .08. Then, add both results. 13.____

A. 242.50 B. 264.00 C. 333.25 D. 356.50

14. Multiply 312.77 by .04. Round off the result to the nearest hundredth. 14.____

A. 12.52 B. 12.511 C. 12.518 D. 12.51

15. Add 362.05, 91.13, 347.81, and 17.46. Then, divide the result by 6. The answer rounded off to the nearest hundredth is 15.____

A. 138.409 B. 137.409 C. 136.41 D. 136.40

16. Add 66.25 and 15.06. Then, multiply the result by 2 1/6. The answer is MOST NEARLY 16.____

A. 176.18 B. 176.17 C. 162.66 D. 162.62

17. Each of the following options contains three decimals. In which case do all three decimals have the same value? 17.____

A. .3; .30; .03
B. .25; .250; .2500
C. 1.9; 1.90; 1.09
D. .35; .350; .035

18. Add 1/2 the sum of (539.84 and 479.26) to 1/3 the sum of (1461.93 and 927.27). Round off the result to the nearest whole number. 18.____

A. 3408 B. 2899 C. 1816 D. 1306

19. Multiply $5,906.09 by 15%. Then, divide the result by 3. 19.____

A. $295.30 B. $885.91 C. $8,859.14 D. $29,530.45

20. A team has won 10 games, lost 4, and has 6 games yet to play. How many of these remaining games MUST be won if the team is to win 65% of its games for the season? 20.____

A. One
B. Two
C. Four
D. None of the above

21. If a certain candy sells at the rate of $1 for 2 1/2 ounces, what is the price per pound? (Do not include tax.) 21.____

A. $2.50 B. $6.40 C. $8.50 D. $4.00

22. Which is the SMALLEST of the following numbers? 22.___

A. .3980 B. .3976 C. .39752 D. .399

23. A tank can be filled by one pipe in 10 minutes and by another in 15 minutes. How long will it take to fill the tank if both pipes are opened? 23.___
_______ min.

A. 4 B. 5 C. 6 D. 7.5

24. If $17.60 is to be divided between two people so that one person receives one and three-fourths as much as the other, how much should each receive? 24.___

A. $6.40 and $11.20
B. $5.50 and $12.10
C. $6.60 and $11.20
D. $6.00 and $11.60

25. Mr. Burns owns a block of land which is exactly 320 ft. long and 140 ft. wide. At 40¢ per square foot, how much will it cost to build a 4 foot cement walk around this land, bound by its outer edge? 25.___

A. $1420.80 B. $1472 C. $368 D. $1446.40

KEY (CORRECT ANSWERS)

1. D	11. C
2. B	12. A
3. C	13. D
4. A	14. D
5. B	15. C
6. C	16. B
7. B	17. B
8. C	18. D
9. C	19. A
10. A	20. D

21. B
22. C
23. C
24. A
25. D

SOLUTIONS TO PROBLEMS

1. 8462 + 2974 + 5109 + 763 + 47 = 17,355

2. 1890 ÷ 14 = 135

3. (182)(63) = 11,466

4. 27,412 - 8426 = 18,986

5. $275.15 - $162.28 = $112.87

6. $(\frac{2}{3})(246) = 164$

7. (14.36)(7.2) = 103.392

8. 14.6 + 9.22 + 143.18 + 27.1 = 194.1

9. $6.45 $.15 = 43

10. 16.6 - 7.91 = 8.69

11. ($4.34 + $34.50 + $6.00 + $101.76 + $90.67) - ($60.54 + $10.56) = $237.27 - $71.10 = $166.17

12. (2200 + 2600 + 252 + 47.96) - (202.70 + 1200 + 2150 + 434.43) = 5099.96 - 3987.13 = 1112.83

13. (1850)(.05) + (3300X.08) = 92.5 + 264 = 356.5

14. (312.77)(.04) = 12.5108 = 12.51 rounded off to nearest hundredth

15. (362.05 + 91.13 + 347.81 + 17.46) 6 = 818.45 6 = 136.4083" = 136.41 rounded off to nearest hundredth

16. $(66.25+15.06)(2\frac{1}{6}) = (81.31)(2\frac{1}{6}) \approx 176.17$

17. .25 = .250 = .2500

18. 1/2(539.84 + 479.26) + 1/3(1461.93 + 927.27) = 509.55 + 796.4 = 1305.95 = 1306 rou-naed off to nearest whole number

19. $(\$5906.09)(.15)(\frac{1}{3})$ = $295.3045 = $295.30 rounded off to 2 places

20. (.65)(20) = 13 games won. Thus, the team must win 3 more games.

21. Let x = price per pound. Then, $\frac{1.00}{x} = \frac{2\frac{1}{2}}{16}$. Solving, x = 6.40

22. .39752 is the smallest of the numbers.

23. Let x = required minutes. Then, $\frac{x}{10} + \frac{x}{15} = 1$. So, 3x + 2x = 30. Solving, x = 6.

24. Let x, 1.75x represent the two amounts. Then, x + 1.75x = $17.60. Solving, x = $6.40 and 1.75x = $11.20.

25. Area of cement walk = (320)(140) - (312)(132) = 3616 sq.ft. Then, (3616)(.40) = $1446.40.

TEST 4

DIRECTIONS: Each question or incomplete statement is followed by several suggested answers or completions. Select the one that BEST answers the question or completes the statement. *PRINT THE LETTER OF THE CORRECT ANSWER IN THE SPACE AT THE RIGHT.*

1. Subtract: 10,376
   -8,492 1.____

   A. 1834 B. 1884 C. 1924 D. 2084

2. Subtract: $155.22
   - 93.75 2.____

   A. $61.47 B. $59.33 C. $59.17 D. $58.53

3. Subtract: $22.50
   -13.78 3.____

   A. $9.32 B. $9.18 C. $8.92 D. $8.72

4. Multiply: 485
   x32 4.____

   A. 13,350 B. 15,520 C. 16,510 D. 17,630

5. Multiply: $3.29
   x 14 5.____

   A. $41.16 B. $42.46 C. $44.76 D. $46.06

6. Multiply: 106
   x318 6.____

   A. 33,708 B. 33,632 C. 33,614 D. 33,548

7. Multiply: 119
   x1.15 7.____

   A. 136.85 B. 136.94 C. 137.15 D. 137.34

8. Divide: 432 by 16 8.____

   A. 37 B. 32 C. 27 D. 24

9. Divide: $115.65 by 5 9.____

   A. $24.25 B. $23.13 C. $22.83 D. $22.55

10. Divide: 18,711 by 63 10.____

    A. 267 B. 273 C. 283 D. 297

11. Divide: 327.45 by .15 11.____

    A. 1,218 B. 2,183 C. 2,243 D. 2,285

12. The sum of 637.894, 8352.16, 4.8673, and 301.5 is MOST NEARLY 12.____

A. 8989.5 B. 9021.35 C. 9294.9 D. 9296.4

13. If 30 is divided by .06, the result is 13.____

A. 5 B. 50 C. 500 D. 5000

14. The sum of the fractions 1/3, 4/6, 3/4, 1/2, and 1/12 is 14.____

A. 3 1/4 B. 2 1/3 C. 2 1/6 D. 1 11/12

15. If 96934.42 is divided by 53.496, the result is MOST NEARLY 15.____

A. 181 B. 552 C. 1812 D. 5520

16. If 25% of a number is 48, the number is 16.____

A. 12 B. 60 C. 144 D. 192

17. The average number of reports filed per day by a clerk during a five-day week was 720. He filed 610 reports the first day, 720 reports the second day, 740 reports the third day, and 755 reports the fourth day. 17.____
The number of reports he filed the fifth day was

A. 748 B. 165 C. 775 D. 565

18. The number 88 is 2/5 of 18.____

A. 123 B. 141 C. 220 D. 440

19. If the product of 8.3 multiplied by .42 is subtracted from the product of 156 multiplied by .09, the result is MOST NEARLY 19.____

A. 10.6 B. 13.7 C. 17.5 D. 20.8

20. The sum of 284.5, 3016.24, 8.9736, and 94.15 is MOST NEARLY 20.____

A. 3402.9 B. 3403.0 C. 3403.9 D. 4036.1

21. If 8394.6 is divided by 29.17, the result is MOST NEARLY 21.____

A. 288 B. 347 C. 2880 D. 3470

22. If two numbers are multiplied together, the result is 3752. If one of the two numbers is 56, the other number is 22.____

A. 41 B. 15 C. 109 D. 67

23. The sum of the fractions 1/4, 2/3, 3/8, 5/6, and 3/4 is 23.____

A. 20/33 B. 1 19/24 C. 2 1/4 D. 2 7/8

24. The fraction 7/16 expressed as a decimal is 24.____

A. .1120 B. .2286 C. .4375 D. .4850

25. If .10 is divided by 50, the result is 25.____

A. .002 B. .02 C. .2 D. 2

KEY (CORRECT ANSWERS)

1. B
2. A
3. D
4. B
5. D

6. A
7. A
8. C
9. B
10. D

11. B
12. D
13. C
14. B
15. C

16. D
17. C
18. C
19. A
20. C

21. A
22. D
23. D
24. C
25. A

SOLUTIONS TO PROBLEMS

1. 10,376 - 8492 = 1884

2. \$155.22 - \$93.75 = \$61.47

3. \$22.50 - \$13.78 = \$8.72

4. (485)(32) = 15,520

5. (\$3.29)(14) = \$46.06

6. (106)(318) = 33,708

7. (119)(1.15) = 136.85

8. $432 \div 16 = 27$

9. \$115.65÷5=\$23.13

10. $18{,}711 \div 63 = 297$

11. $327.45 \div .15 = 2183$

12. $637.894 + 8352.16 + 4.8673 + 301.5 = 9296.4213 \approx 9296.4$

13. $30 \div .06 = 500$

14. $\frac{1}{3}+\frac{4}{6}+\frac{3}{4}+\frac{1}{2}+\frac{1}{12}=\frac{4}{12}+\frac{8}{12}+\frac{9}{12}+\frac{6}{12}+\frac{1}{12}=\frac{28}{12}=2\frac{1}{3}$

15. $96{,}934.42 \div 53.496 \approx 1811.99 \approx 1812$

16. Let x = number. Then, .25x = 48. Solving, x = 192.

17. Let x = number of reports on 5th day. Then, (610 + 720 + 740 + 755 + x)/5 = 720. Simplifying, 2825 + x = 3600, so x = 775.

18. $88 \div \frac{2}{5} = 220$

19. $(156)(.09) - (8.3)(.42) = 10.554 \approx 10.6$

20. $284.5 + 3016.24 + 8.9736 + 94.15 = 3403.8636 \approx 3403.9$

21. $8394.6 \div 29.17 \approx 287.78 \approx 288$

22. The other number = $3752 \div 56 = 67$

23. $\frac{1}{4}+\frac{2}{3}+\frac{3}{8}+\frac{5}{6}+\frac{3}{4}=\frac{6}{24}+\frac{16}{24}+\frac{9}{24}+\frac{20}{24}+\frac{18}{24}=\frac{69}{24}=2\frac{7}{8}$

24. $\frac{7}{16}=.4375$

25. $.10 \div 50 = .002$

EXAMINATION SECTION

TEST 1

DIRECTIONS: Each question or incomplete statement is followed by several suggested answers or completions. Select the one that BEST answers the question or completes the statement. *PRINT THE LETTER OF THE CORRECT ANSWER IN THE SPACE AT THE RIGHT.*

Questions 1-25.

DIRECTIONS: Select the word with the MOST appropriate meaning for the italicized word in each of Questions 1 through 25.

1. The directions were *explicit*. 1.____
   A. petulant B. satiric C. awkward
   D. unequivocal E. foreign

2. The teacher explained *mutability*. 2.____
   A. change B. harmony C. annihilation
   D. ethics E. candor

3. He was a *secular* man. 3.____
   A. holy B. evil C. worldly
   D. superior E. small

4. They submitted a list of their *progeny*. 4.____
   A. experiments B. books C. holdings
   D. theories E. offspring

5. She admired his *sententious* replies. 5.____
   A. simple B. pithy C. coherent
   D. lucid E. inane

6. He believed in the ancient *dogma*. 6.____
   A. priest B. prophet C. seer
   D. doctrine E. ruler

7. They studied a Grecian *archetype*. 7.____
   A. model B. urn C. epic D. ode E. play

8. The *insurrection* was described on the front page. 8.____
   A. surgery B. pageant C. ceremony
   D. game E. revolt

9. He was known for his *procrastination*. 9.____
   A. justification B. learning C. delay
   D. ambition E. background

10. The doctor analyzed the *toxic* ingredients. 10.____
    A. poisonous B. anemic C. trivial
    D. obscure E. distinct

11. It was a *portentous* occurrence. 11.____
    A. pleasant B. decisive C. ominous
    D. monetary E. hearty

12. His *espousal* of the plan was applauded. 12.____
    A. explanation B. rejection C. ridicule
    D. adoption E. revision

13. Her condition was *lachrymose*. 13.____
    A. improved B. tearful C. hopeful
    D. precocious E. tenuous

14. It was a *precarious* situation. 14.____
    A. uncomplicated B. peaceful C. precise
    D. uncertain E. precipitous

15. He was lost in a *reverie*. 15.____
    A. chancery B. dream C. forest
    D. cavern E. tarn

16. The hero was a young *gallant*. 16.____
    A. suitor B. fool C. gull
    D. lawyer E. executive

17. Their practices were *nefarious*. 17.____
    A. unprofitable B. ignorant C. multifarious
    D. wicked E. wishful

18. He insisted upon the *proviso*. 18.____
    A. stipulation B. pronunciation C. examination
    D. supply E. equipment

19. The spirit came from the *nether* regions. 19.____
    A. frozen B. lower C. lost
    D. bright E. mysterious

20. His actions were *malevolent*. 20.____
    A. unassuming B. silent C. evil
    D. peaceful E. constructive

21. He had a *florid* complexion. 21.____
    A. sanguine B. pallid C. fair
    D. sickly E. normal

22. The lawyer explained the legal *parlance*. 22.____
    A. action
    B. maneuver
    C. situation
    D. language
    E. procedure

23. They were present at the *interment*. 23.____
    A. concert
    B. trial
    C. embarkation
    D. burial
    E. performance

24. He made a *moot* point. 24.____
    A. definite
    B. sensible
    C. debatable
    D. strong
    E. correct

25. They carefully examined the *cryptic* message. 25.____
    A. occult
    B. legible
    C. valid
    D. familiar
    E. warning

Questions 26-40.

DIRECTIONS: Indicate the number of syllables in each of the following words.

26. vicissitude 26.____
27. blown 27.____
28. maintenance 28.____
29. symbolization 29.____
30. athletics 30.____
31. actually 31.____
32. friend 32.____
33. perseverance 33.____
34. physiology 34.____
35. pronunciation 35.____
36. vacuum 36.____
37. sophomore 37.____
38. opportunity 38.____
39. hungry 39.____
40. temperament 40.____

Questions 41-60.

DIRECTIONS: Indicate the one misspelled work in each of the following Questions 41 through 60 by indicating the letter of the misspelled word in the space at the right.

41. A. holiday B. noticeable C. fourty D. miniature E. yeast 41.____

42. A. grievance B. murmur C. occurance D. business E. captain 42.____

43. A. succeed B. vegatable C. pleasant D. picnicking E. shepherd 43.____

44. A. psychology B. plebian C. exercise D. fiery E. concise 44.____

45. A. ninety B. optimistic C. professor D. repitition E. siege 45.____

46. A. tarriff B. absence C. grammar D. license E. balloon 46.____

47. A. dissipation B. ecstasy C. prarie D. marriage E. consistent 47.____

48. A. supersede B. twelfth C. vacillate D. playright E. expense 48.____

49. A. fundamental B. government C. accomodate D. cafeteria E. surely 49.____

50. A. cemetary B. indispensable C. dormitory D. environment E. divine 50.____

51. A. irritible B. permissible C. irresistible D. rhythmical E. source 51.____

52. A. interprete B. opinion C. guard D. familiar E. possible 52.____

53. A. conscience B. existence C. loneliness D. leisure E. exhileration 53.____

54. A. villian B. weird C. seize D. tragedy E. crystal 54.____

55. A. develop B. bachelor C. dilemma D. operate E. synonym 55.____

56. A. university B. connoiseur C. aisle 56.____
D. transferred E. division

57. A. zoology B. conscious C. aptitude 57.____
D. restaurant E. sacriligious

58. A. tendency B. vital C. analyze 58.____
D. consistant E. proceed

59. A. proceedure B. surround C. disastrous 59.____
D. beginning E. arrival

60. A. encrease B. pursuing C. necessary 50.____
D. tyranny E. strength

Questions 61-80.

DIRECTIONS: Indicate the part of speech for each italicized word in the following sentences by selecting the letter of the part of speech from the key above each set of questions.

A. Noun
B. Pronoun
C. Verb
D. Adjective
E. Adverb

61. You are entirely *wrong*. 61.____

62. On *Sunday*, we will attend church. 62.____

63. *That* is the main problem. 63.____

64. He was invited to the party, *Saturday*. 64.____

65. I shall introduce a *technical* term. 65.____

66. It was a *novel* turn of events. 66.____

67. He wanted *that* gift for himself. 67.____

68. A few definitions will help *us* to understand. 68.____

69. He let them reach their own *conclusions*. 69.____

70. I must ask *you* to remain silent. 70.____

A. Preposition
B. Conjunction
C. Pronoun
D. Adverb
E. Adjective

71. *This* is a stupid answer. 71.____

72. He solved the mystery *without* the police. 72.____

73. She felt *secure* in his protection, 73.____

74. He believed in the *scientific* method. 74.____

75. Do not destroy their *traditional* beliefs. 75.____

76. They chartered the bus, *but* they did not go. 76.____

77. The young men are *quiet* with fear. 77.____

78. She talked *cheerfully* to the visitors. 78.____

79. The candidate was *certain* of victory. 79.____

80. I hope you will take *that* with you. 80.____

Questions 81-100.

DIRECTIONS: Indicate the use of each italicized word in the following sentences by choosing the letter of the CORRECT usage from the key above each set of questions.

A. Subject of Verb
B. Predicate Nominative or Subjective Complement
C. Predicate Adjective
D. Direct Object of Verb
E. Indirect Object of Verb

81. They made *him* president of the club. 81.____

82. There was nothing *odd* about the situation. 82.____

83. Give them *time* enough for thought. 83.____

84. He supervised the *work* himself. 84.____

85. Will you do *me* a favor? 85.____

86. The salad dressing tasted *good*. 86.____

87. In the crash, the *body* was thrown forward. 87.____

88. On a bench in the park was a single *man.* 88.____

89. There were two *men* who carried the trunk. 89.____

90. I am older than *you.* 90.____

A. Object of Preposition
B. Subject of Infinitive
C. Direct Object of Verb
D. Indirect Object of Verb
E. Predicate Nominative or Subjective Complement

91. Let *them* suffer the consequences. 91.____

92. Offer *them* the key to the apartment. 92.____

93. He heard the *bell* ring. 93.____

94. Let *us* try another solution. 94.____

95. No one except *John* had volunteered. 95.____

96. Show *us* one example of your style. 96.____

97. Will you send *her* the flowers? 97.____

98. I want *you* to take her home. 98.____

99. He told his *father* that he would obey. 99.____

100. Do not write on the second *page.* 100.____

Questions 101-115.

DIRECTIONS: Indicate the kind of verbal italicized in the following sentences by choosing the appropriate letter from the key below.

A. Gerund
B. Participle
C. Infinitive

101. The manuscript, *corrected* and typed, was on the desk. 101.____

102. He heard the bullet *ricochet.* 102.____

103. *Finding* the answer is a difficult task. 103.____

104. The animal, *hidden* from view, was trembling. 104.____

105. *Pretending* to be asleep, he listened attentively. 105.____

106. The professor, a *qualified* lecturer, entered the room. 106.____

107. They enjoyed *camping* at the lake. 107.____

108. Let them *come* to me. 108.____

109. He was annoyed by the *buzzing* sound. 109.____

110. It was a *stimulating* performance. 110.____

111. He had an accident while *returning* to the city. 111.____

112. *Encouraged* to study, the class opened the books. 112.____

113. He heard the gun *explode*. 113.____

114. They called him the *forgotten* man. 114.____

115. *Realizing* his mistake, he apologized. 115.____

Questions 116-130.

DIRECTIONS: Indicate the CORRECT punctuation for the following sentences by choosing the letter of the correct punctuation from the key below where brackets appear.

A. Comma
B. Semicolon
C. Colon
D. Dash
E. No punctuation

116. He explained [ ] that he could not attend. 116.____

117. The executive [ ] prepared for the interview and entered the room. 117.____

118. She admitted [ ] that the suggestion was wrong. 118.____

119. He did not object [ ] to dealing with him. 119.____

120. The chairman disagreed [ ] the members did not. 120.____

121. You must report to duty on November 10 [ ] 2022. 121.____

122. The father [ ] and two sons went fishing. 122.____

123. Act on the following problems [ ] administration, supervision, and policy. 123.____

124. This is excellent [ ] it has insight. 124.____

125. "I will take the car [ ]" he said. 125.____

126. I will do it [ ] however, you must help me. 126.____

127. When the show ended [ ] he returned home. 127.____

128. Stop [ ] making all of that noise. 128.____

129. Be firm [ ] exercise your authority. 129.____

130. The first example is poor [ ] the second is good. 130.____

Questions 131-150.

DIRECTIONS: Place a *C* in the space at the right if the sentence is correctly punctuated and a *W* in the space at the right if the sentence is incorrectly punctuated.

131. Its later than you think. 131.____

132. While I was eating the toast burned. 132.____

133. The fire started at ten o'clock in the morning. 133.____

134. She asked, "Did you say, 'I will go?" 134.____

135. Richards handling of the question warranted praise. 135.____

136. July 4 is a holiday. 136.____

137. Oh perhaps you are right. 137.____

138. Will you answer the door, John? 138.____

139. While he was bathing the dog came in. 139.____

140. He was a calm gentle person. 140.____

141. He wore a new bow tie. 141.____

142. The shout "Block that kick" echoed upon the field. 142.____

143. Ladies and gentlemen take your seats. 143.____

144. However you must do your work. 144.____

145. My brothers are: John, Bill, and Charles. 145.____

146. While I was painting the neighbor opened the door. 146.____

147. One should fight for honor: not fame. 147.____

148. "Will you sing" he asked? 148.____

149. He played tennis, and then bowled. 149.____

150. On Monday April 5, we leave for Europe. 150.____

KEY (CORRECT ANSWERS)

1.	D	31.	4	61.	D	91.	C	121.	A
2.	A	32.	1	62.	A	92.	D	122.	E
3.	C	33.	4	63.	B	93.	C	123.	C
4.	E	34.	5	64.	A	94.	C	124.	D
5.	B	35.	5	65.	D	95.	A	125.	A
6.	D	36.	2	66.	D	96.	C	126.	B
7.	A	37.	3	67.	D	97.	C	127.	A
8.	E	38.	5	68.	B	98.	C	128.	E
9.	C	39.	2	69.	A	99.	C	129.	B
10.	A	40.	3	70.	B	100.	A	130.	B
11.	C	41.	C	71.	C	101.	B	131.	W
12.	D	42.	C	72.	A	102.	B	132.	W
13.	B	43.	B	73.	D	103.	A	133.	C
14.	D	44.	B	74.	E	104.	B	134.	W
15.	B	45.	D	75.	E	105.	A	135.	W
16.	A	46.	A	76.	B	106.	B	136.	C
17.	D	47.	C	77.	E	107.	A	137.	W
18.	A	48.	D	78.	D	108.	C	138.	C
19.	B	49.	C	79.	E	109.	B	139.	W
20.	C	50.	A	80.	C	110.	B	140.	W
21.	A	51.	A	81.	D	111.	A	141.	C
22.	D	52.	A	82.	C	112.	B	142.	W
23.	D	53.	E	83.	D	113.	C	143.	W
24.	C	54.	A	84.	D	114.	B	144.	W
25.	A	55.	C	85.	E	115.	A	145.	W
26.	3	56.	B	86.	C	116.	E	143.	W
27.	1	57.	E	87.	A	117.	E	147.	W
28.	3	58.	D	88.	B	118.	E	148.	W
29.	5	59.	A	89.	A	119.	E	149.	W
30.	3	60.	A	90.	C	120.	B	150.	W

EXAMINATION SECTION

TEST 1

DIRECTIONS: Each question or incomplete statement is followed by several suggested answers or completions. Select the one that BEST answers the question or completes the statement. *PRINT THE LETTER OF THE CORRECT ANSWER IN THE SPACE AT THE RIGHT.*

Questions 1-22.

DIRECTIONS: Read through each group of words. Indicate in the space at the right the letter of the misspelled word.

1. A. miniature B. recession C. accommodate D. supress 1.____

2. A. mortgage B. illogical C. fasinate D. pronounce 2.____

3. A. calendar B. heros C. ecstasy D. librarian 3.____

4. A. initiative B. extraordinary C. villian D. exaggerate 4.____

5. A. absence B. sense C. dosn't D. height 5.____

6. A. curiosity B. ninety C. truely D. grammar 6.____

7. A. amateur B. definate C. meant D. changeable 7.____

8. A. excellent B. studioes C. achievement D. weird 8.____

9. A. goverment B. description C. sergeant D. desirable 9.____

10. A. proceed B. anxious C. neice D. precede 10.____

11. A. environment B. omitted C. apparant D. misconstrue 11.____

12. A. comparative B. hindrance C. benefited D. unamimous 12.____

13. A. embarrass B. recommend 13.____
C. desciple D. argument

14. A. sophomore B. suprintendent 14.____
C. concievable D. disastrous

15. A. agressive B. questionnaire 15.____
C. occurred D. rhythm

16. A. peaceable B. conscientious 16.____
C. redicule D. deterrent

17. A. mischievious B. writing 17.____
C. competition D. athletics

18. A. auxiliary B. synonymous 18.____
C. maneuver D. repitition

19. A. existence B. optomistic 19.____
C. acquitted D. tragedy

20. A. hypocrisy B. parrallel 20.____
C. exhilaration D. prevalent

21. A. convalesence B. infallible 21.____
C. destitute D. grotesque

22. A. magnanimity B. asassination 22.____
C. incorrigible D. pestilence

Questions 23-40.

DIRECTIONS: In Questions 23 through 40, one sentence fragment contains an error in punctuation or capitalization. Indicate the letter of the INCORRECT sentence fragment and place it in the space at the right.

23. A. Despite a year's work 23.____
B. in a well-equipped laboratory
C. my Uncle failed to complete his research
D. now he will never graduate.

24. A. Gene, if you are going to sleep 24.____
B. all afternoon I will enter
C. that ladies' golf tournament
D. sponsored by the Chamber of Commerce.

25. A. Seeing the cat slink toward the barn, 25.____
B. the farmer's wife jumped off the
C. ladder picked up a broom, and began
D. shouting at the top of her voice.

26. A. Extending over southeast Idaho and 26.____
B. northwest Wyoming, the Tetons
C. are noted for their height; however the
D. highest peak is actually under 14,000 feet.

27. A. "Sarah, can you recall the name 27.____
B. of the English queen
C. who supposedly said, 'We are not
D. amused?"

28. A. My aunt's graduation present to me 28.____
B. cost, I imagine more than she could
C. actually afford. It's a
D. Swiss watch with numerous features.

29. A. On the left are examples of buildings 29.____
B. from the Classical Period; two temples
C. one of which was dedicated to Zeus; the
D. Agora, a marketplace; and a large arch.

30. A. Tired of sonic booms, the people who 30.____
B. live near Springfield's Municipal Airport
C. formed an anti noise organization
D. with the amusing name of Sound Off.

31. A. "Joe, Mrs. Sweeney said, "your family 31.____
B. arrives Sunday. Since you'll be in
C. the Labor Day parade, we could ask Mr.
D. Krohn, who has a big car, to meet them."

32. A. The plumber emerged from the basement and 32.____
B. said, "Mr. Cohen I found the trouble in
C. your water heater. Could you move those
D. Schwinn bikes out of my way?"

33. A. The President walked slowly to the 33.____
B. podium, bowed to Edward Everett Hale
C. the other speaker, and began his formal address:
D. "Fourscore and seven years ago...."

34. A. Mr. Fontana, I hope, will arrive before 34.____
B. the beginning of the ceremonies; however,
C. if his plane is delayed, I have a substitute
D. speaker who can be here at a moments' notice.

35. A. Gladys wedding dress, a satin creation, 35.____
B. lay crumpled on the floor; her veil,
C. torn and streaked, lay nearby. "Jilted!"
D. shrieked Gladys. She was clearly annoyed.

36. A. Although it is poor grammar, the word 36.____
B. hopefully has become television's newest
C. pet expression; I hope (to use the correct
D. form) that it will soon pass from favor.

37. A. Plaza Apartment Hotel 37.____
B. 103 Tower road
C. Hampstead, Iowa 52025
D. March 13, 2021

38. A. Circulation Department 38.____
B. British History Illustrated
C. 3000 Walnut Street
D. Boulder Colorado 80302

39. A. Dear Sirs: 39.____
B. Last spring I ordered a subscription to your
C. magazine. I had read and enjoyed the May
D. issue containing the article titled "kings."

40. A. I have not however, received a 40.____
B. single issue. Will you check this?
C. Sincerely,
D. Maria Herrera

Questions 41-70.

DIRECTIONS: Questions 41 through 70 represent common grammatical concerns: subject-verb agreement, appropriate use of pronouns, and appropriate use of verbs. Read each sentence and indicate the letter of the grammatically CORRECT answer in the space at the right.

41. THE REIVERS, one of William Faulkner's last works, _____ made into a movie starring Steve McQueen. 41.____
A. has been B. have been C. are being D. were

42. He _____ on the ground, his eyes fastened on an ant slowly pushing a morsel of food toward the ant hill. 42.____
A. layed B. laid C. had laid D. lay

43. Nobody in the tri-cities _____ to admit that a flood could be disastrous. 43.____
A. are willing B. have been willing
C. is willing D. were willing

44. "_____," the senator asked, "have you convinced to run against the incumbent?" 44._____
A. Who B. Whom C. Whomever D. Womsoever

45. Of all the psychology courses that I took, Statistics 101 _____ the most demanding. 45._____
A. was B. are C. is D. were

46. Neither the conductor nor the orchestra members _____ the music to be applauded so enthusiastically. 46._____
A. were expecting
B. was expecting
C. is expected
D. has been expecting

47. The requirements for admission to the Lettermen's Club _____ posted outside the athletic director's office for months. 47._____
A. was B. was being C. has been D. have been

48. Please give me a list of the people _____ to compete in the kayak race. 48._____
A. whom you think have planned
B. who you think has planned
C. who you think is planning
D. who you think are planning

49. I saw Eloise and Abelard earlier today; _____ were riding around in a fancy 1956 MG. 49._____
A. she and him B. her and him C. she and he D. her and he

50. If you _____ the trunk in the attic, I'll unpack it later today. 50._____
A. can sit
B. are able to sit
C. can set
D. have sat

51. _____ all of the flour been used, or may I borrow three cups? 51._____
A. Have B. Has C. Is D. Could

52. In exasperation, the cycle shop's owner suggested that _____ there too long. 52._____
A. us boys were
B. we boys were
C. us boys had been
D. we boys had been

53. Idleness as well as money _____ the root of all evil. 53._____
A. have been
B. were to have been
C. is
D. are

54. Only the string players from the quartet—Gregory, Isaac, _____—remained after the concert to answer questions. 54._____
A. him, and I
B. he, and I
C. him, and me
D. he, and me

55. Of all the antiques that _____ for sale, Gertrude chose to buy a stupid glass thimble. 55._____
A. was
B. is
C. would have
D. were

56. The detective snapped, "Don't confuse me with theories about _____ you believe committed the crime!" 56.____
A. who B. whom C. whomever D. which

57. _____ when we first called, we might have avoided our present predicament. 57.____
A. The plumber's coming
B. If the plumber would have come
C. If the plumber had come
D. If the plumber was to have come

58. We thought the sun _____ in the north until we discovered that our compass was defective. 58.____
A. had rose
B. had risen
C. had rised
D. had raised

59. Each play of Shakespeare's _____ more than _____ share of memorable characters. 59.____
A. contain its
B. contains; its
C. contains; it's
D. contain; their

60. Our English teacher suggested to _____ seniors that either Tolstoy or Dickens _____ the outstanding novelist of the nineteenth century. 60.____
A. we; was considered
B. we; were considered
C. us; was considered
D. us; were considered

61. Sherlock Holmes, together with his great friend and companion Dr. Watson, _____ to aid the woman _____ had stumbled into the room. 61.____
A. has agreed; who
B. have agreed; whom
C. has agreed; whom
D. have agreed; who

62. Several of the deer _____ when they spotted my backpack _____ open in the meadow. 62.____
A. was frightened; laying
B. were frightened; lying
C. were frightened; laying
D. was frightened; lying

63. After the Scholarship Committee announces _____ selection, hysterics often _____. 63.____
A. it's; occur
B. its; occur
C. their; occur
D. their; occurs

64. I _____ the key on the table last night so you and _____ could find it. 64.____
A. layed; her
B. lay; she
C. laid; she
D. laid; her

65. Some of the antelope _____ wandered away from the meadow where the rancher _____ the block of salt. 65.____
A. has; sat
B. has; set
C. have; had set
D. has; sets

66. Macaroni and cheese _____ best to us (that is, to Andy and _____) when Mother adds extra cheddar cheese. 66._____
   A. tastes; I
   B. tastes; me
   C. taste; me
   D. taste; I

67. Frank said, "It must have been _____ called the phone company." 67._____
   A. she who
   B. she whom
   C. her who
   D. her whom

68. The herd _____ moving restlessly at every bolt of lightning; it was either Ted or _____ who saw the beginning of the stampede. 68._____
   A. was; me
   B. were; I
   C. was; I
   D. have been; me

69. The foreman _____ his lateness by saying that his alarm clock _____ until six minutes before eight. 69._____
   A. explains; had not rang
   B. explained; has not rung
   C. has explained; rung
   D. explained; hadn't rung

70. Of all the coaches, Ms. Cox is the only one who _____ that Sherry dives more gracefully than _____. 70._____
   A. is always saying; I
   B. is always saying; me
   C. are always saying; I
   D. were always saying; me

Questions 71-90.

DIRECTIONS: Choose the word in Questions 71 through 90 that is MOST opposite in meaning to the italicized word.

71. *fact* 71._____
   A. statistic
   B. statement
   C. incredible
   D. conjecture

72. *stiff* 72._____
   A. fastidious
   B. babble
   C. supple
   D. apprehensive

73. *blunt* 73._____
   A. concise B. tactful C. artistic D. humble

74. *foreign* 74._____
   A. pertinent B. comely C. strange D. scrupulous

75. *anger* 75._____
   A. infer B. pacify C. taint D. revile

76. *frank* 76._____
   A. earnest B. reticent C. post D. expensive

77. *secure* 77.____
A. precarious B. acquire C. moderate D. frenzied

78. *petty* 78.____
A. harmonious B. careful
C. forthright D. momentous

79. *concede* 79.____
A. dispute B. reciprocate
C. subvert D. propagate

80. *benefit* 80.____
A. liquidation B. bazaar
C. detriment D. profit

81. *capricious* 81.____
A. preposterous B. constant
C. diabolical D. careless

82. *boisterous* 82.____
A. devious B. valiant C. girlish D. taciturn

83. *harmony* 83.____
A. congruence B. discord C. chagrin D. melody

84. *laudable* 84.____
A. auspicious B. despicable
C. acclaimed D. doubtful

85. *adherent* 85.____
A. partisan B. stoic C. renegade D. recluse

86. *exuberant* 86.____
A. frail B. corpulent C. austere D. bigot

87. *spurn* 87.____
A. accede B. flail C. efface D. annihilate

88. *spontaneous* 88.____
A. hapless B. corrosive
C. intentional D. willful

89. *disparage* 89.____
A. abolish B. exude C. incriminate D. extol

90. *timorous* 90.____
A. succinct B. chaste C. audacious D. insouciant

KEY (CORRECT ANSWERS)

1.	D	21.	A	41.	A	61.	A	81.	B
2.	C	22.	B	42.	D	62.		82.	D
3.	B	23.	C	43.	C	63.	B	83.	B
4.	C	24.	B	44.	B	64.	C	84.	B
5.	C	25.	C	45.	A	65.	C	85.	C
6.	C	26.	C	46.	A	66.	B	86.	C
7.	B	27.	D	47.	D	67.	A	87.	A
8.	B	28.	B	48.	A	68.	C	88.	C
9.	A	29.	B	49.	C	69.	D	89.	D
10.	C	30.	C	50.	C	70.	A	90.	C
11.	C	31.	A	51.	B	71.	D		
12.	D	32.	B	52.	D	72.	C		
13.	C	33.	B	53.	C	73.	B		
14.	C	34.	D	54.	B	74.	A		
15.	A	35.	A	55.	D	75.	B		
16.	C	36.	B	56.	B	76.	B		
17.	A	37.	B	57.	C	77.	A		
18.	D	38.	D	58.	B	78.	D		
19.	B	39.	D	59.	B	79.	A		
20.	B	40.	A	60.	C	80.	C		

WORD MEANING
COMMENTARY

DESCRIPTION OF THE TEST

On many examinations, you will have questions about the meaning of words or vocabulary.

In this type of question, you have to state what a word or phrase means. (A phrase is a group of words.) This word or phrase is in capital letters in a sentence. You are also given for each question five other words or groups of words—lettered A, B, C, D, and E—as possible answers. One of these words or groups of words means the same as the word or group of words in CAPITAL letters. Only one is right. You are to pick out the one that is right and select the letter of your answer.

HINTS FOR ANSWERING WORD-MEANING QUESTIONS

Read each question carefully.

Choose the best answer of the five choices even though it is not the word you might use yourself.

Answer first those that you know. Then do the others.

If you know that some of the suggested answers are not right, pay no more attention to them.

Be sure that you have selected an answer for every question, even if you have to guess.

SAMPLE QUESTIONS

DIRECTIONS: For the following questions, select the word or group of words lettered A, B, C, D, or E that means MOST NEARLY the same as the word in capital letters. Indicate the letter of the CORRECT answer for each question.

SAMPLE QUESTIONS 1 AND 2

1. The letter was SHORT. SHORT means MOST NEARLY 1.____
   A. tall B. wide C. brief D. heavy E. dark

EXPLANATION

SHORT is a word you have used to describe something that is small, or not long, or little, etc. Therefore, you would not have to spend much time figuring out the right answer. You would choose C. brief.

2. The young man is VIGOROUS. VIGOROUS means MOST NEARLY 2.____
   A. serious B. reliable C. courageous
   D. strong E. talented

EXPLANATION

VIGOROUS is a word that you have probably used yourself or read somewhere. It carries with it the idea of being active, full of pep, etc. Which one of the five choices comes closest to meaning that? Certainly not A. serious, B. reliable, or E. talented; C. courageous—maybe, D. strong—maybe. But between courageous or strong, you would have to agree that strong is the better choice. Therefore, you would choose D.

WORD MEANING

EXAMINATION SECTION

TEST 1

DIRECTIONS: For the following questions, select the word or group of words lettered A, B, C, D, or E that means MOST NEARLY the same as the word in capital letters. *PRINT THE LETTER OF THE CORRECT ANSWER IN THE SPACE AT THE RIGHT.*

1. To SULK means MOST NEARLY to 1.____
   A. cry B. annoy C. lament D. be sullen E. scorn

2. To FLOUNDER means MOST NEARLY to 2.____
   A. investigate B. label C. struggle
   D. consent E. escape

3. PARLEY means MOST NEARLY 3.____
   A. discussion B. thoroughfare C. salon
   D. surrender E. division

4. MAESTRO means MOST NEARLY 4.____
   A. official B. ancestor C. teacher
   D. watchman E. alien

5. MEANDERING means MOST NEARLY 5.____
   A. cruel B. adjusting C. winding
   D. smooth E. combining

6. GNARLED means MOST NEARLY 6.____
   A. angry B. bitter C. twisted
   D. ancient E. embroidered

7. TEMPERANCE means MOST NEARLY 7.____
   A. moderation B. climate C. carelessness
   D. disagreeableness E. rigidity

8. A PRECARIOUS position is one that is 8.____
   A. foresighted B. careful C. modest
   D. headstrong E. uncertain

9. COVETOUS means MOST NEARLY 9.____
   A. undisciplined B. grasping C. timid
   D. insincere E. secretive

10. PRIVATION means MOST NEARLY 10.____
    A. reward B. superiority in rank
    C. hardship D. suitability of behavior
    E. solitude

TEST 2

DIRECTIONS: For the following questions, select the word or group of words lettered A, B, C, D, or E that means MOST NEARLY the same as the word in capital letters. *PRINT THE LETTER OF THE CORRECT ANSWER IN THE SPACE AT THE RIGHT.*

1. To INFILTRATE means MOST NEARLY to 1.____
   A. pass through B. stop C. consider
   D. challenge openly E. meet secretly

2. REVOCATION means MOST NEARLY 2.____
   A. certificate B. repeal C. animation
   D. license E. plea

3. LOQUACIOUS means MOST NEARLY 3.____
   A. grim B. stern C. talkative
   D. lighthearted E. liberty-loving

4. APERTURE means MOST NEARLY 4.____
   A. basement B. opening C. phantom
   D. protective coloring E. light refreshment

5. A PUNGENT odor is one that is 5.____
   A. biting B. smooth C. quarrelsome
   D. wrong E. proud

6. To CORROBORATE means MOST NEARLY to 6.____
   A. deny B. elaborate C. confirm
   D. gnaw E. state

7. BENEVOLENCE means MOST NEARLY 7.____
   A. good fortune B. well-being C. inheritance
   D. violence E. charitableness

8. PETULANT means MOST NEARLY 8.____
   A. rotten B. fretful C. unrelated
   D. weird E. throbbing

9. DERELICT means MOST NEARLY 9.____
   A. abandoned B. widowed C. faithful
   D. insincere E. hysterical

10. INCISIVE means MOST NEARLY 10.____
    A. stimulating B. accidental C. brief
    D. penetrating E. final

TEST 3

DIRECTIONS: For the following questions, select the word or group of words lettered A, B, C, D, or E that means MOST NEARLY the same as the word in capital letters. *PRINT THE LETTER OF THE CORRECT ANSWER IN THE SPACE AT THE RIGHT.*

1. To LAUD means MOST NEARLY to 1.____
   A. praise B. cleanse C. replace
   D. squander E. frown upon

2. To TAUNT means MOST NEARLY to 2.____
   A. jeer at B. tighten C. rescue
   D. interest E. ward off

3. DEITY means MOST NEARLY 3.____
   A. renown B. divinity C. delicacy
   D. destiny E. futility

4. GRAVITY means MOST NEARLY 4.____
   A. displeasure B. thankfulness C. suffering
   D. roughness E. seriousness

5. A CONTEMPTUOUS author is one that is 5.____
   A. thoughtful B. soiled C. dishonorable
   D. scornful E. self-satisfied

6. To WAIVE means MOST NEARLY to 6.____
   A. exercise B. swing C. claim
   D. give up E. wear out

7. To ASPIRE means MOST NEARLY to 7.____
   A. fade away B. excite C. desire earnestly
   D. breathe heavily E. roughen

8. PERTINENT means MOST NEARLY 8.____
   A. related B. saucy C. quick
   D. impatient E. excited

9. DEVASTATION means MOST NEARLY 9.____
   A. desolation B. displeasure C. dishonor
   D. neglect E. religious fervor

10. IMMINENT means MOST NEARLY 10.____
    A. sudden B. important C. delayed
    D. threatening E. forceful

TEST 4

DIRECTIONS: For the following questions, select the word or group of words lettered A, B, C, D, or E that means MOST NEARLY the same as the word in capital letters. *PRINT THE LETTER OF THE CORRECT ANSWER IN THE SPACE AT THE RIGHT.*

1. CONTROVERSAL means MOST NEARLY 1.____
   A. faultfinding B. pleasant C. debatable
   D. ugly E. talkative

2. GHASTLY means MOST NEARLY 2.____
   A. hasty B. furious C. breathless
   D. deathlike E. spiritual

3. A BELLIGERENT attitude is one that is 3.____
   A. worldly B. warlike C. loudmouthed
   D. furious E. artistic

4. PROFICIENCY means MOST NEARLY 4.____
   A. wisdom B. oversupply C. expertness
   D. advancement E. sincerity

5. COMPASSION means MOST NEARLY 5.____
   A. rage B. strength of character
   C. forcefulness D. sympathy
   E. uniformity

6. DISSENSION means MOST NEARLY 6.____
   A. treatise B. pretense C. fear
   D. lineage E. discord

7. To INTIMATE means MOST NEARLY to 7.____
   A. charm B. hint C. disguise
   D. frighten E. hum

8. To BERATE means MOST NEARLY to 8.____
   A. classify B. scold C. underestimate
   D. take one's time E. evaluate

9. DEARTH means MOST NEARLY 9.____
   A. scarcity B. width C. affection
   D. wealth E. warmth

10. To MEDITATE means MOST NEARLY to 10.____
    A. rest B. stare C. doze
    D. make peace E. reflect

TEST 5

DIRECTIONS: For the following questions, select the word or group of words lettered A, B, C, D, or E that means MOST NEARLY the same as the word in capital letters. *PRINT THE LETTER OF THE CORRECT ANSWER IN THE SPACE AT THE RIGHT.*

1. BONDAGE means MOST NEARLY 1.____
   A. poverty B. redemption C. slavery
   D. retirement E. complaint

2. AGILITY means MOST NEARLY 2.____
   A. wisdom B. nimbleness C. agreeable
   D. simplicity E. excitement

3. To ABDICATE means MOST NEARLY to 3.____
   A. achieve B. protest C. renounce
   D. demand E. steal

4. To STIFLE means MOST NEARLY to 4.____
   A. talk nonsense B. sidestep C. depress
   D. smother E. stick

5. EDICT means MOST NEARLY 5.____
   A. abbreviation B. lie C. carbon copy
   D. correction E. decree

6. AMITY means MOST NEARLY 6.____
   A. ill will B. hope C. pity
   D. friendship E. pleasure

7. COERCION means MOST NEARLY 7.____
   A. force B. disgust C. suspicion
   D. pleasure E. criticism

8. To ABASH means MOST NEARLY to 8.____
   A. embarrass B. encourage C. punish
   D. surrender E. overthrow

9. TACITURN means MOST NEARLY 9.____
   A. weak B. evil C. tender
   D. silent E. sensitive

10. REMISS means MOST NEARLY 10.____
    A. memorable B. neglectful C. useless
    D. prompt E. exact

TEST 6

DIRECTIONS: For the following questions, select the word or group of words lettered A, B, C, D, or E that means MOST NEARLY the same as the word in capital letters. *PRINT THE LETTER OF THE CORRECT ANSWER IN THE SPACE AT THE RIGHT.*

1. STAGNANT means MOST NEARLY 1.____
   A. inactive B. alert C. selfish
   D. difficult E. scornful

2. MANDATORY means MOST NEARLY 2.____
   A. instant B. obligatory C. evident
   D. strategic E. unequaled

3. INFERNAL means MOST NEARLY 3.____
   A. immodest B. incomplete C. domestic
   D. second-rate E. fiendish

4. To EXONERATE means MOST NEARLY to 4.____
   A. free from blame B. warn C. drive out
   D. overcharge E. plead

5. ARBITER means MOST NEARLY 5.____
   A. friend B. judge C. drug
   D. tree surgeon E. truant

6. ENMITY means MOST NEARLY 6.____
   A. boredom B. puzzle C. ill will
   D. offensive language E. entanglement

7. To DISCRIMINATE means MOST NEARLY to 7.____
   A. fail B. delay C. accuses
   D. distinguish E. reject

8. DERISION means MOST NEARLY 8.____
   A. disgust B. ridicule C. fear
   D. anger E. heredity

9. EXULTANT means MOST NEARLY 9.____
   A. essential B. elated C. praiseworthy
   D. plentiful E. high-priced

10. OSTENSIBLE 10.____
    A. vibrating B. odd C. apparent
    D. standard E. ornate

TEST 7

DIRECTIONS: For the following questions, select the word or group of words lettered A, B, C, D, or E that means MOST NEARLY the same as the word in capital letters. *PRINT THE LETTER OF THE CORRECT ANSWER IN THE SPACE AT THE RIGHT.*

1. To ABHOR means MOST NEARLY 1.____
   A. hate B. admire C. taste
   D. skip E. resign

2. DUTIFUL means MOST NEARLY 2.____
   A. lasting B. sluggish C. required
   D. soothing E. obedient

3. ZEALOT means MOST NEARLY 3.____
   A. breeze B. enthusiast C. vault
   D. wild animal E. musical instrument

4. A MAGNANIMOUS attitude is one that is 4.____
   A. high-minded B. faithful C. concerned
   D. individual E. small

5. To CITE means MOST NEARLY to 5.____
   A. protest B. depart C. quote
   D. agitate E. perform

6. OBLIVION means MOST NEARLY 6.____
   A. hindrance B. accident C. courtesy
   D. forgetfulness E. old age

7. CARDINAL means MOST NEARLY 7.____
   A. independent B. well-organized C. subordinate
   D. dignified E. chief

8. To DEPLETE means MOST NEARLY to 8.____
   A. restrain B. corrupt C. despair
   D. exhaust E. spread out

9. To SUPERSEDE means MOST NEARLY to 9.____
   A. retire B. replace C. overflow
   D. bless E. oversee

10. SPORADIC means MOST NEARLY 10.____
    A. bad-tempered B. infrequent C. radical
    D. reckless E. humble

TEST 8

DIRECTIONS: For the following questions, select the word or group of words lettered A, B, C, D, or E that means MOST NEARLY the same as the word in capital letters. *PRINT THE LETTER OF THE CORRECT ANSWER IN THE SPACE AT THE RIGHT.*

1. To NEUTRALIZE means MOST NEARLY to 1.____
   A. entangle B. strengthen C. counteract
   D. combat E. converse

2. To INSINUATE means MOST NEARLY to 2.____
   A. destroy B. hint C. do wrong
   D. accuse E. release

3. DIMINUTIVE means MOST NEARLY 3.____
   A. proud B. slow C. small
   D. watery E. puzzling

4. PLIGHT means MOST NEARLY 4.____
   A. departure B. weight C. conspiracy
   D. predicament E. stamp

5. An ILLICIT relationship is one that is 5.____
   A. unlawful B. overpowering C. ill-advised
   D. small-scale E. unreadable

6. A BENIGN manner is one that is 6.____
   A. contagious B. fatal C. ignorant
   D. kindly E. decorative

7. REVERIE means MOST NEARLY 7.____
   A. abusive language B. love song C. backward step
   D. daydream E. holy man

8. APPREHENSIVE means MOST NEARLY 8.____
   A. quiet B. firm C. curious
   D. sincere E. fearful

9. To RECOIL means MOST NEARLY to 9.____
   A. shrink B. attract C. electrify
   D. adjust E. fear

10. GUISE means MOST NEARLY 10.____
   A. trickery B. request C. innocence
   D. misdeed E. appearance

TEST 9

DIRECTIONS: For the following questions, select the word or group of words lettered A, B, C, D, or E that means MOST NEARLY the same as the word in capital letters. *PRINT THE LETTER OF THE CORRECT ANSWER IN THE SPACE AT THE RIGHT.*

1. To RELINQUISH means MOST NEARLY to 1.____
   A. regret B. abandon C. pursue
   D. secure E. penetrate

2. INJUNCTION means MOST NEARLY 2.____
   A. error B. attack C. injustice
   D. suggestion E. order

3. ADVENT means MOST NEARLY 3.____
   A. attachment B. reference C. arrival
   D. excitement E. vent

4. BICAMERAL means MOST NEARLY 4.____
   A. dealing with life forms B. meeting on alternate years
   C. over-sweet D. having two legislative branches
   E. having two meanings

5. A PERVERSE attitude is one that is 5.____
   A. contrary B. stingy C. unfortunate
   D. hereditary E. easygoing

6. To THWART means MOST NEARLY to 6.____
   A. assist B. whimper C. slice
   D. escape E. block

7. DEVOID means MOST NEARLY 7.____
   A. empty B. illegal C. affectionate
   D. pious E. annoying

8. A BLAND manner is one that is 8.____
   A. gentle B. guilty C. salty
   D. unfinished E. majestic

9. To OSTRACIZE means MOST NEARLY to 9.____
   A. flatter B. scold C. show off
   D. banish E. vibrate

10. CANDOR means MOST NEARLY 10.____
    A. sociability B. outspokenness C. grief
    D. light E. flattery

TEST 10

DIRECTIONS: For the following questions, select the word or group of words lettered A, B, C, D, or E that means MOST NEARLY the same as the word in capital letters. *PRINT THE LETTER OF THE CORRECT ANSWER IN THE SPACE AT THE RIGHT.*

1. ACQUIT means MOST NEARLY 1.____
   A. increase B. harden C. clear
   D. sharpen E. sentence

2. DEXTERITY means MOST NEARLY 2.____
   A. conceit B. skill C. insistence
   D. embarrassment E. guidance

3. ASSIMILATE means MOST NEARLY 3.____
   A. absorb B. imitate C. maintain
   D. outrun E. curb

4. DESPONDENCY means MOST NEARLY 4.____
   A. relief B. gratitude C. dejection
   D. hatred E. poverty

5. A BUOYANT manner is one that is 5.____
   A. conceited B. cautioning C. youthful
   D. musical E. cheerful

6. CULINARY means MOST NEARLY 6.____
   A. having to do with cooking B. pertaining to dressmaking
   C. fond of eating D. loving money
   E. tending to be secretive

7. CAPRICE means MOST NEARLY 7.____
   A. wisdom B. ornament C. pillar
   D. whim E. energy

8. DETERRENT means MOST NEARLY 8.____
   A. restraining B. cleansing C. deciding
   D. concluding E. crumbling

9. A PUGNACIOUS attitude is one that is 9.____
   A. sticky B. cowardly C. precise
   D. vigorous E. quarrelsome

10. ABSCOND means MOST NEARLY 10.____
    A. detest B. reduce C. swallow up
    D. dismiss E. flee

TEST 11

DIRECTIONS: For the following questions, select the word or group of words lettered A, B, C, D, or E that means MOST NEARLY the same as the word in capital letters. *PRINT THE LETTER OF THE CORRECT ANSWER IN THE SPACE AT THE RIGHT.*

1. DOLDRUMS means MOST NEARLY 1.____
   A. delirium B. rage C. saturation
   D. incarceration E. listlessness

2. DOUR means MOST NEARLY 2.____
   A. gloomy B. cowardly C. untidy
   D. stingy E. doubtful

3. DRAGOON means MOST NEARLY 3.____
   A. defy B. enlist C. surrender
   D. lead E. persecute

4. EMPIRICAL means MOST NEARLY 4.____
   A. experiential B. undeniable C. melancholy
   D. territorial E. traditional

5. ENCOMIUM means MOST NEARLY 5.____
   A. antidote B. adage C. anteroom
   D. eulogy E. bombast

6. ENTOMOLOGIST means MOST NEARLY student of 6.____
   A. insects B. fish C. words
   D. fossils E. reptiles

7. EPHEMERAL means MOST NEARLY 7.____
   A. persistent B. useless C. effete
   D. visionary E. short-lived

8. ETIOLOGY means MOST NEARLY 8.____
   A. epitome B. inertia C. astronomy
   D. disease E. cause

9. FETISH means MOST NEARLY 9.____
   A. tuft of hair above horse's foot B. embryo of an animal
   C. object of excessive devotion D. spirit of a festival
   E. feast of the Haitians

10. GAMUT means MOST NEARLY 10.____
   A. gamble B. alphabet C. keys
   D. chess move E. range

TEST 12

DIRECTIONS: For the following questions, select the word or group of words lettered A, B, C, D, or E that means MOST NEARLY the same as the word in capital letters. *PRINT THE LETTER OF THE CORRECT ANSWER IN THE SPACE AT THE RIGHT.*

1. HALLOW means MOST NEARLY 1.____
   A. shout aloud B. make sacred C. haunt
   D. reveal E. hole out

2. HEGEMONY means MOST NEARLY 2.____
   A. flight B. restraint C. nationalism
   D. autonomy E. leadership

3. HERMETIC means MOST NEARLY 3.____
   A. air-tight B. protruding C. sequestered
   D. briskly E. ascetic

4. IBID means MOST NEARLY 4.____
   A. that is B. as an example C. the same
   D. see above E. and so forth

5. IMPUGN means MOST NEARLY 5.____
   A. enhance B. attribute C. assail
   D. compromise E. defend

6. INCIPIENT means MOST NEARLY 6.____
   A. tasteless B. annoying C. unyielding
   D. ultimate E. commencing

7. INEXORABLE means MOST NEARLY 7.____
   A. hateful B. conciliatory C. unresponsive
   D. relentless E. pliant

8. INTREPID means MOST NEARLY 8.____
   A. awesome B. bellicose C. undisciplined
   D. courageous E. pacific

9. INVECTIVE means MOST NEARLY 9.____
   A. self study B. geometrical analysis C. verbal abuse
   D. hard-won victory E. indecision

10. INVEIGLED means MOST NEARLY 10.____
    A. ensnared B. terrified C. coerced
    D. corrupted E. incarcerated

TEST 13

DIRECTIONS: For the following questions, select the word or group of words lettered A, B, C, D, or E that means MOST NEARLY the same as the word in capital letters. *PRINT THE LETTER OF THE CORRECT ANSWER IN THE SPACE AT THE RIGHT.*

1. ITERANT means MOST NEARLY 1.____
   A. distant B. repeating C. directed
   D. wandering E. errant

2. LAMPOON means MOST NEARLY 2.____
   A. magazine B. satire C. clown
   D. lament E. shade

3. LAPIDARY means MOST NEARLY one who 3.____
   A. collects butterflies B. breaks up large estates
   C. indulges the senses D. judges the quality of beverages
   E. cuts precious stones

4. MERETRICIOUS means MOST NEARLY 4.____
   A. according to the metric system B. deserving
   C. scholarly D. indigent
   E. tawdry

5. MITIGATE means MOST NEARLY 5.____
   A. exonerate B. handicap C. aggravate
   D. appease E. defile

6. MORES means MOST NEARLY 6.____
   A. beginnings B. conglomerations C. curses
   D. mutations E. customs

7. NOSTRUM means MOST NEARLY 7.____
   A. ocean sea B. paternity C. remedy
   D. pungency E. family

8. OBJURGATE means MOST NEARLY 8.____
   A. chide B. sacrifice C. oppose
   D. purge E. repeat

9. OSSIFY means MOST NEARLY 9.____
   A. vacillate B. harden C. categorize
   D. tipple E. abstain

10. PARLOUS means MOST NEARLY 10.____
    A. wise B. bargaining C. talkative
    D. dangerous E. partial

TEST 14

DIRECTIONS: For the following questions, select the word or group of words lettered A, B, C, D, or E that means MOST NEARLY the same as the word in capital letters. *PRINT THE LETTER OF THE CORRECT ANSWER IN THE SPACE AT THE RIGHT.*

1. ADVENTITIOUS means MOST NEARLY 1.____
   A. opportunistic B. daring C. helpful
   D. deceptive E. extrinsic

2. AMBIVALENT means MOST NEARLY 2.____
   A. helpful in walking B. equally skillful with both hands
   C. simultaneously hating and loving D. ambiguous in origin
   E. equivalent

3. AMORPHOUS means MOST NEARLY 3.____
   A. inelegant B. clamorous C. quiescent
   D. ardent E. formless

4. ANATHEMA means MOST NEARLY 4.____
   A. despair B. benevolence C. disputation
   D. anomaly E. curse

5. APIARY means MOST NEARLY 5.____
   A. bee house B. pear-shaped figure C. main-traveled road
   D. monkey cage E. bird house

6. APORYPHAL means MOST NEARLY of 6.____
   A. scholarly pursuits B. sacred origin C. ancient beginnings
   D. ecclesiastical power E. doubtful authenticity

7. APOSTASY means MOST NEARLY 7.____
   A. confirmation B. detection C. supposition
   D. canonization E. deification

8. ASCETIC means MOST NEARLY 8.____
   A. exclusive B. sharp C. fragrant
   D. austere E. authentic

9. BADINAGE means MOST NEARLY 9.____
   A. indifference B. song C. banter
   D. mucilage E. autarchy

10. BOGGLE means MOST NEARLY 10.____
    A. dampen B. hesitate C. undermine
    D. disarrange E. haggle

TEST 15

DIRECTIONS: For the following questions, select the word or group of words lettered A, B, C, D, or E that means MOST NEARLY the same as the word in capital letters. *PRINT THE LETTER OF THE CORRECT ANSWER IN THE SPACE AT THE RIGHT.*

1. BUCOLIC means MOST NEARLY 1.____
   A. rustic B. flatulent C. angry
   D. loud E. bureaucratic

2. CAESURA means MOST NEARLY 2.____
   A. genesis B. referring to Caesar C. tyranny
   D. domain E. break

3. CAREEN means MOST NEARLY 3.____
   A. lurch B. wail C. pour
   D. contain E. corrode

4. CARET means MOST NEARLY 4.____
   A. measure of weight B. sign of omission C. technique in ballet
   D. growth of root E. notice for caution

5. CARIES means MOST NEARLY 5.____
   A. treatment B. convalescent C. decay
   D. chemicals E. roots

6. CASIOST means MOST NEARLY 6.____
   A. sophistical reasoner B. careless worker C. innocent victim
   D. habitual late-comer E. frenzied lawyer

7. CHIMERICAL means MOST NEARLY 7.____
   A. scientific B. debasing C. well-ordered
   D. maniacal E. fanciful

8. CLABBER means MOST NEARLY 8.____
   A. gossip B. climb C. crop
   D. entwine E. curdle

9. COMME IL FAUT means MOST NEARLY 9.____
   A. unnecessary B. erroneous C. proper
   D. mixed E. illegal

10. CRYPTIC means MOST NEARLY 10.____
    A. succinct B. astringent C. death-like
    D. crotchety E. occult

TEST 16

DIRECTIONS: For the following questions, select the word or group of words lettered A, B, C, D, or E that means MOST NEARLY the same as the word in capital letters. *PRINT THE LETTER OF THE CORRECT ANSWER IN THE SPACE AT THE RIGHT.*

1. CYNOSURE means MOST NEARLY 1.____
   A. act of completion B. occupation of ease C. attitude of doubt
   D. center of attraction E. cynical statement

2. DEBENTURE means MOST NEARLY 2.____
   A. written acknowledgment of debt B. sale of preferred stock
   C. illegal sale of securities D. dividend on stocks or bonds
   E. disclaimer in a prospectus

3. DEMURRER means MOST NEARLY 3.____
   A. promotion B. objection C. interrogation
   D. retainer E. demerit

4. DERELICTION means MOST NEARLY 4.____
   A. general decline B. damaging criticism C. probable cause
   D. abandoned vessel E. failure in duty

5. DESCRIED means MOST NEARLY 5.____
   A. delimned B. defined C. rejected
   D. erred E. discerned

6. DESIDERATUM means MOST NEARLY 6.____
   A. final outcome B. hearty approval C. last remnant
   D. desired object E. prescribed treatment

7. DISCRETE means MOST NEARLY 7.____
   A. separate B. reserved C. foresighted
   D. unbounded E. tactful

8. DISINGENUOUS means MOST NEARLY 8.____
   A. unsophisticated B. skillful C. apathetic
   D. naïve E. insincere

9. DISSIDENT means MOST NEARLY 9.____
   A. malodorous B. amoral C. discordant
   D. unfeeling E. divisive

10. EGREGIOUS means MOST NEARLY 10.____
    A. debased B. inconsequential C. incorrigible
    D. egotistical E. prominent

TEST 17

DIRECTIONS: For the following questions, select the word or group of words lettered A, B, C, D, or E that means MOST NEARLY the same as the word in capital letters. *PRINT THE LETTER OF THE CORRECT ANSWER IN THE SPACE AT THE RIGHT.*

1. EMPATHY means MOST NEARLY 1.____
   A. comatose condition
   B. sympathetic understanding
   C. depressed feeling
   D. political subdivision
   E. patriotic devotion

2. ESOTERIC means MOST NEARLY 2.____
   A. abstruse
   B. intestinal
   C. lively
   D. joining
   E. essential

3. ESPERANTO means MOST NEARLY 3.____
   A. fabled country
   B. artificial language
   C. European peace manifesto
   D. place of abandoned hope
   E. pertaining to the Elysian Fields

4. EUPHEMISM means MOST NEARLY 4.____
   A. pleasant sight
   B. right direction
   C. verbal platitude
   D. buoyant feeling
   E. inoffensive expression

5. FINICAL means MOST NEARLY 5.____
   A. blundering
   B. fastidious
   C. conclusive
   D. maniacal
   E. extravagant

6. GUERDON means MOST NEARLY 6.____
   A. debacle
   B. shield
   C. fruit
   D. obstacle
   E. recompense

7. GYVES means MOST NEARLY 7.____
   A. gallows
   B. chains
   C. barbs
   D. vegetables
   E. jives

8. HEDONIST means MOST NEARLY 8.____
   A. reviler
   B. recluse
   C. pleasure-seeker
   D. savage
   E. hermit

9. HIATUS means MOST NEARLY 9.____
   A. flower
   B. gap
   C. mistake
   D. digression
   E. hearsay

10. IMBROGLIO means MOST NEARLY 10.____
    A. secluded dwelling
    B. impassioned plea
    C. rampant destruction
    D. petit point
    E. complicated situation

TEST 18

DIRECTIONS: For the following questions, select the word or group of words lettered A, B, C, D, or E that means MOST NEARLY the same as the word in capital letters. *PRINT THE LETTER OF THE CORRECT ANSWER IN THE SPACE AT THE RIGHT.*

1. IMPALPABLE means MOST NEARLY not 1.____
   A. truthful B. concrete C. throbbing
   D. deviating E. suggestive

2. IMPECUNIOUS means MOST NEARLY 2.____
   A. poor B. wayward C. troublesome
   D. inordinate E. ingenuous

3. IMPORTUNATE means MOST NEARLY 3.____
   A. critical B. empty-handed C. disastrous
   D. pusillanimous E. pressing

4. IMPRIMIS means MOST NEARLY 4.____
   A. church dignitary B. sanction C. manuscript
   D. sacred song E. in the first place

5. INURED means MOST NEARLY 5.____
   A. belligerent B. hardened C. apprehensive
   D. irreverent E. injured

6. INVIDIOUS means MOST NEARLY 6.____
   A. obscure B. unconquerable C. offensive
   D. niggardly E. invariable

7. JOCOSE means MOST NEARLY 7.____
   A. intemperate B. contemptuous C. morose
   D. nugatory E. facetious

8. LACHRYMOSE means MOST NEARLY 8.____
   A. milky B. disdainful C. comic
   D. tearful E. comatose

9. LISSOME means MOST NEARLY 9.____
   A. nimble B. comely C. laughable
   D. lackadaisical E. aggressive

10. MERCURIAL means MOST NEARLY 10.____
   A. thermal B. coy C. volatile
   D. ponderous E. unchangeable

KEYS (CORRECT ANSWERS)

TEST 1

1. D 6. C
2. C 7. A
3. A 8. E
4. C 9. B
5. C 10. C

TEST 2

1. A 6. C
2. B 7. E
3. C 8. B
4. B 9. A
5. A 10. D

TEST 3

1. A 6 D
2. A 7. C
3. B 8. A
4. E 9. A
5. D 10. D

TEST 4

1. C 6. E
2. D 7. B
3. B 8. B
4. C 9. A
5. D 10. E

TEST 5

1. C 6. D
2. B 7. A
3. C 8. A
4. D 9. D
5. E 10. B

TEST 6

1. A 6. D
2. B 7. D
3. E 8. B
4. A 9. B
5. B 10. C

TEST 7

1. A 6. D
2. E 7. E
3. B 8. D
4. A 9. B
5. C 10. B

TEST 8

1. C 6. D
2. B 7. D
3. C 8. E
4. D 9. A
5. A 10. E

TEST 9

1. B 6. E
2. E 7. A
3. C 8. A
4. D 9. D
5. A 10. B

TEST 10

1. C 6. A
2. B 7. D
3. A 8. A
4. C 9. E
5. E 10. E

TEST 11

1. E 6. A
2. A 7. E
3. E 8. E
4. A 9. C
5. D 10. E

TEST 12

1. B 6. E
2. E 7. D
3. A 8. D
4. C 9. C
5. C 10. A

TEST 13

1. B 6. E
2. B 7. C
3. E 8. A
4. E 9. B
5. D 10. D

TEST 14

1. E 6. E
2. C 7. B
3. E 8. D
4. E 9. C
5. A 10. B

TEST 15

1. A 6. A
2. E 7. E
3. A 8. E
4. B 9. C
5. C 10. E

TEST 16

1. D 6. D
2. A 7. A
3. B 8. E
4. E 9. C
5. E 10. E

TEST 17

1. B 6. E
2. A 7. B
3. B 8. C
4. E 9. B
5. B 10. E

TEST 18

1. B 6. C
2. A 7. E
3. E 8. D
4. E 9. A
5. B 10. C

EXAMINATION SECTION
TEST 1

DIRECTIONS: In each of the following tests in this part, select the letter of the one MISSPELLED word in each of the following groups of words. If no word is misspelled, select the last item, letter E (none misspelled). *PRINT THE LETTER OF THE CORRECT ANSWER IN THE SPACE AT THE RIGHT.*

1. A. grateful B. fundimental C. census D. analysis E. *NONE MISSPELLED* 1.____

2. A. installment B. retrieve C. concede D. dissapear E. *NONE MISSPELLED* 2.____

3. A. accidentaly B. dismissal C. conscientious D. indelible E. *NONE MISSPELLED* 3.____

4. A. perceive B. carreer C. anticipate D. acquire E. *NONE MISSPELLED* 4.____

5. A. facility B. reimburse C. assortment D. guidance E. *NONE MISSPELLED* 5.____

6. A. plentiful B. across C. advantagous D. similar E. *NONE MISSPELLED* 6.____

7. A. omission B. pamphlet C. guarrantee D. repel E. *NONE MISSPELLED* 7.____

8. A. maintenance B. always C. liable D. anouncement E. *NONE MISSPELLED* 8.____

9. A. exaggerate B. sieze C. condemn D. commit E. *NONE MISSPELLED* 9.____

10. A. pospone B. altogether C. grievance D. excessive E. *NONE MISSPELLED* 10.____

11. A. arguing B. correspondance C. forfeit D. dissension E. *NONE MISSPELLED* 11.____

12. A. occasion B. description C. prejudice D. elegible E. *NONE MISSPELLED* 12.____

13. A. accomodate B. initiative C. changeable D. enroll E. *NONE MISSPELLED* 13.____

14. A. temporary B. insistent C. benificial D. separate E. *NONE MISSPELLED* 14.____

15. A. achieve B. dissapoint C. unanimous D. judgment E. *NONE MISSPELLED* 15.____

16. A. proceed B. publicly C. sincerity D. successful E. *NONE MISSPELLED* 16.____

17. A. deceive B. goverment C. preferable
D. repetitive E. *NONE MISSPELLED* 17.____

18. A. emphasis B. skillful C. advisible
D. optimistic E. *NONE MISSPELLED* 18.____

19. A. tendency B. rescind C. crucial
D. noticable E. *NONE MISSPELLED* 19.____

20. A. privelege B. abbreviate C. simplify
D. divisible E. *NONE MISSPELLED* 20.____

KEY (CORRECT ANSWERS)

1. B. fundamental
2. D. disappear
3. A. accidentally
4. B. career
5. E. None Misspelled
6. C. advantageous
7. C. guarantee
8. D. announcement
9. B. seize
10. A. postpone
11. B. correspondence
12. D. eligible
13. A. accommodate
14. C. beneficial
15. B. disappoint
16. E. None Misspelled
17. B. government
18. C. advisable
19. D. noticeable
20. A. privilege

TEST 2

DIRECTIONS: In each of the following tests in this part, select the letter of the one MISSPELLED word in each of the following groups of words. If no word is misspelled, select the last item, letter E (none misspelled). *PRINT THE LETTER OF THE CORRECT ANSWER IN THE SPACE AT THE RIGHT.*

1. A. typical B. descend C. summarize D. continuel E. *NONE MISSPELLED* 1.____

2. A. courageous B. recomend C. omission D. eliminate E. *NONE MISSPELLED* 2.____

3. A. compliment B. illuminate C. auxilary D. installation E. *NONE MISSPELLED* 3.____

4. A. preliminary B. aquainted C. syllable D. analysis E. *NONE MISSPELLED* 4.____

5. A. accustomed B. negligible C. interupted D. bulletin E. *NONE MISSPELLED* 5.____

6. A. summoned B. managment C. mechanism D. sequence E. *NONE MISSPELLED* 6.____

7. A. commitee B. surprise C. noticeable D. emphasize E. *NONE MISSPELLED* 7.____

8. A. occurrance B. likely C. accumulate D. grievance E. grievance 8.____

9. A. obstacle B. particuliar C. baggage D. fascinating E. *NONE MISSPELLED* 9.____

10. A. innumerable B. seize C. applicant D. dicionery E. *NONE MISSPELLED* 10.____

11. A. primary B. mechanic C. referred D. admissible E. *NONE MISSPELLED* 11.____

12. A. cessation B. beleif C. aggressive D. allowance E. *NONE MISSPELLED* 12.____

13. A. leisure B. authentic C. familiar D. contemptable E. *NONE MISSPELLED* 13.____

14. A. volume B. forty C. dilemma D. seldum E. *NONE MISSPELLED* 14.____

15. A. discrepancy B. aquisition C. exorbitant D. lenient E. *NONE MISSPELLED* 15.____

16. A. simultanous B. penetrate C. revision D. conspicuous E. *NONE MISSPELLED* 16.____

17. A. ilegible B. gracious C. profitable D. obedience E. *NONE MISSPELLED* 17.____

18. A. manufacturer B. authorize C. compelling 18.____
D. pecular E. *NONE MISSPELLED*

19. A. anxious B. rehearsal C. handicaped 19.____
D. tendency E. *NONE MISSPELLED*

20. A. meticulous B. accompaning C. initiative 20.____
D. shelves E. *NONE MISSPELLED*

KEY (CORRECT ANSWERS)

1. D. continual
2. B. recommend
3. C. auxiliary
4. B. acquainted
5. C. interrupted
6. B. management
7. A. committee
8. A. occurrence
9. B. particular
10. D. dictionary
11. E. None Misspelled
12. B. belief
13. D. contemptible
14. D. seldom
15. B. acquisition
16. A. simultaneous
17. A. illegible
18. D. peculiar
19. C. handicapped
20. B. accompanying

TEST 3

DIRECTIONS: In each of the following tests in this part, select the letter of the one MISSPELLED word in each of the following groups of words. If no word is misspelled, select the last item, letter E (none misspelled). *PRINT THE LETTER OF THE CORRECT ANSWER IN THE SPACE AT THE RIGHT.*

1. A. grievous B. dilettante C. gibberish D. upbraid E. *NONE MISSPELLED* 1.____

2. A. embarrassing B. playright C. unmanageable D. symmetrical E. *NONE MISSPELLED* 2.____

3. A. sestet B. denouement C. liaison D. tattooing E. *NONE MISSPELLED* 3.____

4. A. prophesied B. soliliquy C. supersede D. hemorrhage E. *NONE MISSPELLED* 4.____

5. A. colossal B. renascent C. parallel D. omnivorous E. *NONE MISSPELLED* 5.____

6. A. passable B. dispensable C. deductable D. irreducible E. *NONE MISSPELLED* 6.____

7. A. guerrila B. carousal C. maneuver D. staid E. *NONE MISSPELLED* 7.____

8. A. maintenance B. mountainous C. sustenance D. gluttinous E. *NONE MISSPELLED* 8.____

9. A. holocaust B. irascible C. buccanneer D. mischievous E. *NONE MISSPELLED* 9.____

10. A. diphthong B. rhododendron C. inviegle D. shellacked E. *NONE MISSPELLED* 10.____

11. A. Phillipines B. currant C. dietitian D. coercion E. *NONE MISSPELLED* 11.____

12. A. courtesey B. buoyancy C. fiery D. shepherd E. *NONE MISSPELLED* 12.____

13. A. censor B. queue C. obbligato D. antartic E. *NONE MISSPELLED* 13.____

14. A. chrystal B. chrysanthemum C. chrysalis D. chrome E. *NONE MISSPELLED* 14.____

15. A. shreik B. siege C. sheik D. sieve E. *NONE MISSPELLED* 15.____

16. A. leisure B. gladioluses C. kindergarden D. tonnage E. *NONE MISSPELLED* 16.____

17. A. emminent B. imminent C. blatant D. privilege E. *NONE MISSPELLED* 17.____

18. A. diphtheria B. collander C. seize 18.____
    D. sleight E. *NONE MISSPELLED*

19. A. frolicking B. caramel C. germaine 19.____
    D. kohlrabi E. *NONE MISSPELLED*

20. A. dispensable B. compatable C. recommend 20.____
    D. feasible E. *NONE MISSPELLED*

KEY (CORRECT ANSWERS)

1. E. None Misspelled
2. B. playwright
3. E. None Misspelled
4. B. soliloquy
5. E. None Misspelled
6. C. deductible
7. A. guerrilla
8. D. gluttonous
9. C. buccaneer
10. C. inveigle
11. A. Philippines
12. A. courtesy
13. D. antarctic
14. A. crystal
15. A. shriek
16. C. kindergarten
17. A. eminent
18. B. colander
19. C. germane
20. B. compatible

TEST 4

DIRECTIONS: In each of the following tests in this part, select the letter of the one MISSPELLED word in each of the following groups of words. If no word is misspelled, select the last item, letter E (none misspelled). *PRINT THE LETTER OF THE CORRECT ANSWER IN THE SPACE AT THE RIGHT.*

1. A. coercion B. rescission C. license D. prophecied E. *NONE MISSPELLED* 1.____

2. A. calcimine B. seive C. procedure D. poinsettia E. *NONE MISSPELLED* 2.____

3. A. entymology B. echoing C. subtly D. stupefy E. *NONE MISSPELLED* 3.____

4. A. mocassin B. assassin C. battalion D. despicable E. *NONE MISSPELLED* 4.____

5. A. moustache B. sovereignty C. drunkeness D. staccato E. *NONE MISSPELLED* 5.____

6. A. notoriety B. stereotype C. trellis D. Uraguay E. *NONE MISSPELLED* 6.____

7. A. hummock B. idiosyncrasy C. licentiate D. plagiarism E. *NONE MISSPELLED* 7.____

8. A. denim B. hyssop C. innoculate D. malevolent E. *NONE MISSPELLED* 8.____

9. A. boundaries B. corpulency C. gauge D. jingoes E. *NONE MISSPELLED* 9.____

10. A. assassin B. refulgeant C. sorghum D. suture E. *NONE MISSPELLED* 10.____

11. A. dormatory B. glimpse C. mediocre D. repetition E. *NONE MISSPELLED* 11.____

12. A. ambergris B. docility C. loquacious D. Pharoah E. *NONE MISSPELLED* 12.____

13. A. curriculum B. ninety-eighth C. occurrence D. repertoire E. *NONE MISSPELLED* 13.____

14. A. belladonna B. equable C. immersion D. naphtha E. *NONE MISSPELLED* 14.____

15. A. itinerary B. ptomaine C. similar D. solicetous E. *NONE MISSPELLED* 15.____

16. A. liquify B. mausoleum C. Philippines D. singeing E. *NONE MISSPELLED* 16.____

17. A. descendant B. harrassed C. implausible D. irreverence E. *NONE MISSPELLED* 17.____

18. A. crystallize B. imperceptible C. isinglass 18.___
D. precede E. *NONE MISSPELLED*

19. A. accommodate B. deferential C. gazeteer 19.___
D. plenteous E. *NONE MISSPELLED*

20. A. aching B. buttress C. indigenous 20.___
D. mischievous E. *NONE MISSPELLED*

KEY (CORRECT ANSWERS)

1.	D.	prophesied
2.	B.	sieve
3.	A.	entomology
4.	A.	moccasin
5.	C.	drunkenness
6.	D.	Uruguay
7.	E.	None Misspelled
8.	C.	inoculate
9.	E.	None Misspelled
10.	B.	refulgent
11.	A.	dormitory
12.	D.	Pharaoh
13.	E.	None Misspelled
14.	E.	None misspelled
15.	D.	solicitous
16.	A.	liquefy
17.	B.	harassed
18.	E.	None Misspelled
19.	C.	gazetteer
20.	E.	None Misspelled

TEST 5

DIRECTIONS: In each of the following tests in this part, select the letter of the one MISSPELLED word in each of the following groups of words. If no word is misspelled, select the last item, letter E (none misspelled). *PRINT THE LETTER OF THE CORRECT ANSWER IN THE SPACE AT THE RIGHT.*

1. A. comensurable B. fracas C. obeisance D. remittent E. *NONE MISSPELLED* 1.____

2. A. defiance B. delapidated C. motley D. rueful E. *NONE MISSPELLED* 2.____

3. A. demeanor B. epoch C. furtive D. parley E. *NONE MISSPELLED* 3.____

4. A. disciples B. influencial C. nemesis D. poultry E. *NONE MISSPELLED* 4.____

5. A. decision B. encourage C. incidental D. satyr E. *NONE MISSPELLED* 5.____

6. A. collate B. connivance C. luxurient D. manageable E. *NONE MISSPELLED* 6.____

7. A. constituencies B. crocheted C. foreclosure D. scintillating E. *NONE MISSPELLED* 7.____

8. A. arraignment B. assassination C. carburator D. irrationally E. *NONE MISSPELLED* 8.____

9. A. livelihood B. noticeable C. optomiatic D. psychology E. *NONE MISSPELLED* 9.____

10. A. daub B. massacre C. repitition D. requiem E. *NONE MISSPELLED* 10.____

11. A. adversary B. beneficiary C. cemetery D. desultory E. *NONE MISSPELLED* 11.____

12. A. criterion B. elicit C. incredulity D. omnishient E. *NONE MISSPELLED* 12.____

13. A. dining B. fiery C. incidentally D. rheumatism E. *NONE MISSPELLED* 13.____

14. A. collaborator B. gaudey C. habilitation D. logician E. *NONE MISSPELLED* 14.____

15. A. dirge B. ogle C. recumbent D. reminiscence E. *NONE MISSPELLED* 15.____

16. A. conscientious B. renunciation C. inconvenient D. inoculate E. *NONE MISSPELLED* 16.____

17. A. crystalline B. scimitar C. ecstacy D. vestigial E. *NONE MISSPELLED* 17.____

18. A. phlegmatic B. rhythm C. plebescite D. refectory E. *NONE MISSPELLED* 18.____

19. A. resilient B. resevoir C. recipient D. sobriety E. *NONE MISSPELLED* 19.____

20. A. privilege B. leige C. leisure D. basilisk E. *NONE MISSPELLED* 20.____

KEY (CORRECT ANSWERS)

1. A. commensurable
2. B. dilapidated
3. E. None Misspelled
4. B. influential
5. E. None Misspelled
6. C. luxuriant
7. E. None Misspelled
8. C. carburetor
9. C. optimistic
10. C. repetition
11. E. None Misspelled
12. D. omniscient
13. E. None Misspelled
14. B. gaudy
15. E. None Misspelled
16. E. None Misspelled
17. C. ecstasy
18. C. plebiscite
19. B. reservoir
20. B. liege

TEST 6

DIRECTIONS: In each of the following tests in this part, select the letter of the one MISSPELLED word in each of the following groups of words. If no word is misspelled, select the last item, letter E (none misspelled). *PRINT THE LETTER OF THE CORRECT ANSWER IN THE SPACE AT THE RIGHT.*

1. A. repellent B. elliptical C. paralelling D. colossal E. *NONE MISSPELLED* 1.____

2. A. uproarious B. grievous C. armature D. tabular E. *NONE MISSPELLED* 2.____

3. A. ammassed B. embarrassed C. promissory D. asymmetrical E. *NONE MISSPELLED* 3.____

4. A. maintenance B. correspondence C. benificence D. miasmic E. *NONE MISSPELLED* 4.____

5. A. demurred B. occurrence C. temperament D. abhorrance E. *NONE MISSPELLED* 5.____

6. A. proboscis B. lucious C. mischievous D. vilify E. *NONE MISSPELLED* 6.____

7. A. feasable B. divisible C. permeable D. forcible E. *NONE MISSPELLED* 7.____

8. A. courteous B. venemous C. heterogeneous D. lustrous E. *NONE MISSPELLED* 8.____

9. A. millionaire B. mayonnaise C. questionaire D. silhouette E. *NONE MISSPELLED* 9.____

10. A. contemptible B. irreverent C. illimitable D. inveigled E. *NONE MISSPELLED* 10.____

11. A. prevalent B. irrelavent C. ecstasy D. auxiliary E. *NONE MISSPELLED* 11.____

12. A. impeccable B. raillery C. precede D. occurrence E. *NONE MISSPELLED* 12.____

13. A. patrolling B. vignette C. ninety D. surveilance E. *NONE MISSPELLED* 13.____

14. A. holocaust B. incidently C. weird D. canceled E. *NONE MISSPELLED* 14.____

15. A. emmendation B. gratuitous C. fissionable D. dilemma E. *NONE MISSPELLED* 15.____

16. A. harass B. innuendo C. capilary D. pachyderm E. *NONE MISSPELLED* 16.____

17. A. concomitant B. Lilliputian C. sarcophagus D. melifluous E. *NONE MISSPELLED* 17.____

18.	A. interpolate D. inveigh	B. disident E. *NONE MISSPELLED*	C. venal	18.___
19.	A. supercillious D. irresistible	B. biennial E. *NONE MISSPELLED*	C. gargantuan	19.___
20.	A. conniving D. incorruptible	B. expedite E. *NONE MISSPELLED*	C. inflammible	20.___

KEY (CORRECT ANSWERS)

1. C. paralleling
2. E. None Misspelled
3. A. amassed
4. C. beneficence
5. D. abhorrence
6. B. luscious
7. A. feasible
8. B. venomous
9. C. questionnaire
10. E. None Misspelled
11. B. irrelevant
12. E. None Misspelled
13. D. surveillance
14. B. incidentally
15. A. emendation
16. C. capillary
17. D. mellifluous
18. B. dissident
19. A. supercilious
20. C. inflammable

TEST 7

DIRECTIONS: In each of the following tests in this part, select the letter of the one MISSPELLED word in each of the following groups of words. If no word is misspelled, select the last item, letter E (none misspelled). *PRINT THE LETTER OF THE CORRECT ANSWER IN THE SPACE AT THE RIGHT.*

1. A. torturous B. omniscient C. hymenial D. flaccid E. *NONE MISSPELLED* 1.____

2. A. seige B. seize C. frieze D. grieve E. *NONE MISSPELLED* 2.____

3. A. indispensible B. euphony C. victuals D. receptacle E. *NONE MISSPELLED* 3.____

4. A. schism B. fortissimo C. innocuous D. epicurian E. *NONE MISSPELLED* 4.____

5. A. sustenance B. vilefy C. maintenance D. rarefy E. *NONE MISSPELLED* 5.____

6. A. desiccated B. alleviate C. beneficence D. preponderance E. *NONE MISSPELLED* 6.____

7. A. battalion B. incubus C. sacrilegious D. innert E. *NONE MISSPELLED* 7.____

8. A. shiboleth B. connoisseur C. potpourri D. dichotomy E. *NONE MISSPELLED* 8.____

9. A. pamphlet B. similar C. parlament D. benefited E. *NONE MISSPELLED* 9.____

10. A. genealogy B. tyrannical C. diletante D. abhorrence E. *NONE MISSPELLED* 10.____

11. A. effeminate B. concensus C. agglomeration D. fission E. *NONE MISSPELLED* 11.____

12. A. narcissus B. lyceum C. odissey D. peccadillo E. *NONE MISSPELLED* 12.____

13. A. stupefied B. psychiatry C. onerous D. frieze E. *NONE MISSPELLED* 13.____

14. A. intelligible B. semaphore C. pronounciation D. albumen E. *NONE MISSPELLED* 14.____

15. A. annihilate B. tyrannical C. occurence D. allergy E. *NONE MISSPELLED* 15.____

16. A. gauging B. probossis C. specimen D. its E. *NONE MISSPELLED* 16.____

17. A. diphthong B. connoisseur C. iresistible D. dilemma E. *NONE MISSPELLED* 17.____

18. A. affect B. baccillus C. beige 18.____
D. seize E. *NONE MISSPELLED*

19. A. apostasy B. sustenance C. synonym 19.____
D. epigrammatic E. *NONE MISSPELLED*

20. A. discernable B. consul C. efflorescence 20.____
D. complement E. *NONE MISSPELLED*

KEY (CORRECT ANSWERS)

1.	C.	hymeneal
2.	A.	siege
3.	A.	indispensable
4.	D.	epicurean
5.	B.	vilify
6.	E.	None Misspelled
7.	D.	inert
8.	A.	shibboleth
9.	C.	parliament
10.	C.	dilettante
11.	B.	consensus
12.	C.	odyssey
13.	E.	None Misspelled
14.	C.	pronunciation
15.	C.	occurrence
16.	B.	proboscis
17.	C.	irresistible
18.	B.	bacillus
19.	E.	None Misspelled
20.	A.	discernible

TEST 8

DIRECTIONS: In each of the following tests in this part, select the letter of the one MISSPELLED word in each of the following groups of words. If no word is misspelled, select the last item, letter E (none misspelled). *PRINT THE LETTER OF THE CORRECT ANSWER IN THE SPACE AT THE RIGHT.*

1. A. righteous B. seafareing C. colloquial D. contumely E. *NONE MISSPELLED* 1.____

2. A. sanitarium B. vicissitude C. mischievious D. chlorophyll E. *NONE MISSPELLED* 2.____

3. A. captain B. theirs C. asceticism D. acquiesced E. *NONE MISSPELLED* 3.____

4. A. across B. her's C. democracy D. signature E. *NONE MISSPELLED* 4.____

5. A. villain B. vacillate C. imposter D. temperament E. *NONE MISSPELLED* 5.____

6. A. idyllic B. volitile C. obloquy D. emendation E. *NONE MISSPELLED* 6.____

7. A. heinous B. sattelite C. dissident D. ephemeral E. *NONE MISSPELLED* 7.____

8. A. ennoble B. shellacked C. vilify D. indissoluble E. *NONE MISSPELLED* 8.____

9. A. argueing B. intrepid C. papyrus D. foulard E. *NONE MISSPELLED* 9.____

10. A. guttural B. acknowleging C. isosceles D. assonance E. *NONE MISSPELLED* 10.____

11. A. shoeing B. exorcise C. development D. irreperable E. *NONE MISSPELLED* 11.____

12. A. counseling B. cancellation C. kidnapped D. repellant E. *NONE MISSPELLED* 12.____

13. A. disatisfy B. misstep C. usually D. gregarious E. *NONE MISSPELLED* 13.____

14. A. unparalleled B. beggar C. embarrass D. ecstacy E. *NONE MISSPELLED* 14.____

15. A. descendant B. poliomyelitis C. privilege D. tragedy E. *NONE MISSPELLED* 15.____

16. A. nullify B. siderial C. salability D. irrelevant E. *NONE MISSPELLED* 16.____

17. A. paraphenalia B. apothecaries C. occurrence D. plagiarize E. *NONE MISSPELLED* 17.____

18. A. asinine B. dissonent C. opossum 18.____
D. indispensable E. *NONE MISSPELLED*

19. A. orifice B. deferrment C. harass 19.____
D. accommodate E. *NONE MISSPELLED*

20. A. changeable B. therefor C. incidently 20.____
D. dissatisfy E. *NONE MISSPELLED*

KEY (CORRECT ANSWERS)

1. B. seafaring
2. C. mischievous
3. E. None Misspelled
4. B. hers
5. C. impostor
6. B. volatile
7. B. satellite
8. E. None Misspelled
9. A. arguing
10. B. acknowledging
11. D. irreparable
12. D. repellent
13. A. dissatisfy
14. D. ecstasy
15. E. None Misspelled
16. B. sidereal
17. A. paraphernalia
18. B. dissonant
19. B. deferment
20. C. incidentally

TEST 9

DIRECTIONS: In each of the following tests in this part, select the letter of the one MISSPELLED word in each of the following groups of words. If no word is misspelled, select the last item, letter E (none misspelled). *PRINT THE LETTER OF THE CORRECT ANSWER IN THE SPACE AT THE RIGHT.*

1.	A. irreparably D. audible	B. lovable E. *NONE MISSPELLED*	C. comparitively	1.____
2.	A. vilify D. sacreligious	B. efflorescence E. *NONE MISSPELLED*	C. sarcophagus	2.____
3.	A. picnicking D. seize	B. proceedure E. *NONE MISSPELLED*	C. hypocrisy	3.____
4.	A. discomfit D. sarsaparilla	B. sapient E. *NONE MISSPELLED*	C. exascerbate	4.____
5.	A. valleys D. reticence	B. maintainance E. *NONE MISSPELLED*	C. abridgment	5.____
6.	A. idylic D. asterisk	B. beneficent E. *NONE MISSPELLED*	C. singeing	6.____
7.	A. appropos D. mucilage	B. violoncello E. *NONE MISSPELLED*	C. peony	7.____
8.	A. caterpillar D. frieze	B. silhouette E. *NONE MISSPELLED*	C. rhapsody	8.____
9.	A. appendicitis D. tortuous	B. vestigeal E. *NONE MISSPELLED*	C. colonnade	9.____
10.	A. omlet D. miniature	B. diphtheria E. *NONE MISSPELLED*	C. highfalutin	10.____
11.	A. diorama D. conscious	B. sustanance E. *NONE MISSPELLED*	C. disastrous	11.____
12.	A. inelegible D. procedural	B. irreplaceable E. *NONE MISSPELLED*	C. dissatisfied	12.____
13.	A. contemptible D. privilege	B. sacrilegious E. *NONE MISSPELLED*	C. proffessor	13.____
14.	A. inoculate D. hypocrisy	B. diptheria E. *NONE MISSPELLED*	C. gladioli	14.____
15.	A. pessimism D. vulnerible	B. ecstasy E. *NONE MISSPELLED*	C. furlough	15.____
16.	A. supersede D. rhythmical	B. moccasin E. *NONE MISSPELLED*	C. recondite	16.____
17.	A. Adirondack D. Cincinnati	B. Phillipines E. *NONE MISSPELLED*	C. Czechoslovakia	17.____

18. A. weird B. impromptu C. guerrila
D. spontaneously E. *NONE MISSPELLED* 18.____

19. A. newstand B. accidentally C. tangible
D. reservoir E. *NONE MISSPELLED* 19.____

20. A. macaroni B. mackerel C. ukulele
D. giutar E. *NONE MISSPELLED* 20.____

KEY (CORRECT ANSWERS)

1.	C.	comparatively
2.	D.	sacrilegious
3.	B.	procedure
4.	C.	exacerbate
5.	B.	maintenance
6.	A.	idyllic
7.	A.	apropos
8.	E.	None Misspelled
9.	B.	vestigial
10.	A.	omelet
11.	B.	sustenance
12.	A.	ineligible
13.	C.	professor
14.	B.	diphtheria
15.	D.	vulnerable
16.	E.	None Misspelled
17.	B.	Philippines
18.	C.	guerrilla
19.	A.	newsstand
20.	D.	guitar

TEST 10

DIRECTIONS: In each of the following tests in this part, select the letter of the one MISSPELLED word in each of the following groups of words. If no word is misspelled, select the last item, letter E (none misspelled). *PRINT THE LETTER OF THE CORRECT ANSWER IN THE SPACE AT THE RIGHT.*

1. A. rescission B. sacrament C. hypocricy D. salable E. *NONE MISSPELLED* 1.____

2. A. rhythm B. foreboding C. withal D. consciousness E. *NONE MISSPELLED* 2.____

3. A. noticeable B. drunkenness C. frolicked D. abcess E. *NONE MISSPELLED* 3.____

4. A. supersede B. canoeing C. exorbitant D. vigilance E. *NONE MISSPELLED* 4.____

5. A. idiosyncrasy B. pantomine C. isosceles D. wintry E. *NONE MISSPELLED* 5.____

6. A. numbskull B. indispensable C. fatiguing D. gluey E. *NONE MISSPELLED* 6.____

7. A. dryly B. egregious C. recommend D. irresistable' E. *NONE MISSPELLED* 7.____

8. A. unforgettable B. mackeral C. perseverance D. rococo E. *NONE MISSPELLED* 8.____

9. A. mischievous B. tyranical C. desiccate D. battalion E. *NONE MISSPELLED* 9.____

10. A. accede B. ninth C. abyssmal D. commonalty E. *NONE MISSPELLED* 10.____

11. A. resplendent B. colonnade C. harass D. mimicking E. *NONE MISSPELLED* 11.____

12. A. dilletante B. pusillanimous C. grievance D. cataclysm E. *NONE MISSPELLED* 12.____

13. A. anomaly B. connoisseur C. feasable D. stationery E. *NONE MISSPELLED* 13.____

14. A. ennervated B. rescission C. vacillate D. raucous E. *NONE MISSPELLED* 14.____

15. A. liquefy B. poniard C. truculant D. weird E. *NONE MISSPELLED* 15.____

16. A. existance B. lieutenant C. asinine D. parallelogram E. *NONE MISSPELLED* 16.____

17. A. protuberant B. nuisance C. instrumental D. resevoir E. *NONE MISSPELLED* 17.____

18.	A. sustenance D. clairvoyant	B. pedigree E. *NONE MISSPELLED*	C. supercillious	18.____
19.	A. commingle D. priviledge	B. bizarre E. *NONE MISSPELLED*	C. gauge	19.____
20.	A. analagous D. hindrance	B. irresistible E. *NONE MISSPELLED*	C. apparel	20.____

KEY (CORRECT ANSWERS)

1.	C.	hypocrisy
2.	E.	None Misspelled
3.	D.	abscess
4.	E.	None Misspelled
5.	B.	pantomime
6.	A.	numskull
7.	D.	irresistible
8.	B.	mackerel
9.	B.	tyrannical
10.	C.	abysmal
11.	E.	None Misspelled
12.	A.	dilettante
13.	C.	feasible
14.	A.	enervated
15.	C.	truculent
16.	A.	existence
17.	D.	reservoir
18.	C.	supercilious
19.	D.	privilege
20.	A.	analogous

TEST 11

DIRECTIONS: In each of the following tests in this part, select the letter of the one MISSPELLED word in each of the following groups of words. If no word is misspelled, select the last item, letter E (none misspelled). *PRINT THE LETTER OF THE CORRECT ANSWER IN THE SPACE AT THE RIGHT.*

1. A. impute B. imparshal C. immodest D. imminent E. *NONE MISSPELLED* 1.____

2. A. cover B. audit C. adege D. adder E. *NONE MISSPELLED* 2.____

3. A. promissory B. maturity C. severally D. accomodation E. *NONE MISSPELLED* 3.____

4. A. superintendant B. dependence C. dependents D. entrance E. *NONE MISSPELLED* 4.____

5. A. managable B. navigable C. passable D. laughable E. *NONE MISSPELLED* 5.____

6. A. tolerance B. circumference C. insurance D. dominance E. *NONE MISSPELLED* 6.____

7. A. diameter B. tangent C. paralell D. perimeter E. *NONE MISSPELLED* 7.____

8. A. providential B. personal C. accidental D. diagonel E. *NONE MISSPELLED* 8.____

9. A. ballast B. ballustrade C. allotment D. bourgeois E. *NONE MISSPELLED* 9.____

10. A. diverse B. pedantic C. mishapen D. transient E. *NONE MISSPELLED* 10.____

11. A. surgeon B. sturgeon C. luncheon D. stancheon E. *NONE MISSPELLED* 11.____

12. A. pariah B. estrang C. conceive D. puncilious E. *NONE MISSPELLED* 12.____

13. A. camouflage B. serviceable C. mischievious D. menace E. *NONE MISSPELLED* 13.____

14. A. forefeit B. halve C. hundredth D. illusion E. *NONE MISSPELLED* 14.____

15. A. filial B. arras C. pantomine D. filament E. *NONE MISSPELLED* 15.____

16. A. llama B. madrigal C. martinet D. laxitive E. *NONE MISSPELLED* 16.____

17. A. symtom B. serum C. antiseptic D. aromatic E. *NONE MISSPELLED* 17.____

18. A. erasable B. irascible C. audable 18.____
D. laudable E. *NONE MISSPELLED*

19. A. heroes B. folios C. sopranos 19.____
D. cargos E. *NONE MISSPELLED*

20. A. latent B. goddess C. aisle 20.____
D. whose E. *NONE MISSPELLED*

KEY (CORRECT ANSWERS)

1. B. impartial
2. C. adage
3. D. accommodation
4. A. superintendent
5. A. manageable
6. E. None Misspelled
7. C. parallel
8. D. diagonal
9. B. balustrade
10. C. misshapen
11. D. stanchion
12. B. estrange
13. C. mischievous
14. A. forfeit
15. C. pantomime
16. D. laxative
17. A. symptom
18. C. audible
19. D. cargoes
20. E. None Misspelled

TEST 12

DIRECTIONS: In each of the following tests in this part, select the letter of the one MISSPELLED word in each of the following groups of words. If no word is misspelled, select the last item, letter E (none misspelled). *PRINT THE LETTER OF THE CORRECT ANSWER IN THE SPACE AT THE RIGHT.*

1. A. coconut B. bustling C. abducter D. naphtha E. *NONE MISSPELLED* 1.____

2. A. seriatim B. quadruped C. diphthong D. concensus E. *NONE MISSPELLED* 2.____

3. A. sanction B. propencity C. parabola D. despotic E. *NONE MISSPELLED* 3.____

4. A. circumstantial B. imbroglio C. coalesce D. ductill E. *NONE MISSPELLED* 4.____

5. A. spontaneous B. superlitive C. telepathy D. thesis E. *NONE MISSPELLED* 5.____

6. A. adobe B. apellate C. billion D. chiropody E. *NONE MISSPELLED* 6.____

7. A. combatant B. helium C. esprit de corps D. debillity E. *NONE MISSPELLED* 7.____

8. A. iota B. gopher C. demoralize D. culvert E. *NONE MISSPELLED* 8.____

9. A. invideous B. gourmand C. embryo D. despicable E. *NONE MISSPELLED* 9.____

10. A. dispeptic B. dromedary C. dormant D. duress E. *NONE MISSPELLED* 10.____

11. A. spiggot B. suffrage C. technology D. thermostat E. *NONE MISSPELLED* 11.____

12. A. aberration B. antropology C. bayou D. cashew E. *NONE MISSPELLED* 12.____

13. A. ricochet B. poncho C. oposum D. melee E. *NONE MISSPELLED* 13.____

14. A. semester B. quadrent C. penchant D. mustang E. *NONE MISSPELLED* 14.____

15. A. rhetoric B. polygimy C. optimum D. mendicant E. *NONE MISSPELLED* 15.____

16. A. labyrint B. hegira C. ergot D. debenture E. *NONE MISSPELLED* 16.____

17. A. solvant B. radioactive C. photostat D. nominative E. *NONE MISSPELLED* 17.____

18. A. sporadic B. excelsior C. tenible 18.____
D. thorax E. *NONE MISSPELLED*

19. A. mischievous B. bouillon C. asinine 19.____
D. alien E. *NONE MISSPELLED*

20. A. sanguinery B. prolix C. harangue 20.____
D. minutia E. *NONE MISSPELLED*

KEY (CORRECT ANSWERS)

1. C. abductor
2. D. consensus
3. B. propensity
4. D. ductile
5. B. superlative
6. B. appellate
7. D. debility
8. E. None Misspelled
9. A. invidious
10. A. dyspeptic
11. A. spigot
12. B. anthropology
13. C. opossum
14. B. quadrant
15. B. polygamy
16. A. labyrinth
17. A. solvent
18. C. tenable
19. E. None Misspelled
20. A. sanguinary

TEST 13

DIRECTIONS: In each of the following tests in this part, select the letter of the one MISSPELLED word in each of the following groups of words. If no word is misspelled, select the last item, letter E (none misspelled). *PRINT THE LETTER OF THE CORRECT ANSWER IN THE SPACE AT THE RIGHT.*

1. A. controvert B. cache C. auricle D. impromptu E. *NONE MISSPELLED* 1.____

2. A. labial B. heffer C. intrigue D. decagon E. *NONE MISSPELLED* 2.____

3. A. statistics B. syllable C. tenon D. tituler E. *NONE MISSPELLED* 3.____

4. A. lenient B. migraine C. embarras D. nepotism E. *NONE MISSPELLED* 4.____

5. A. lichen B. horoscope C. orthadox D. pageant E. *NONE MISSPELLED* 5.____

6. A. libretto B. humis C. fallacy D. dextrose E. *NONE MISSPELLED* 6.____

7. A. clinical B. alimoney C. bourgeois D. proverbial E. *NONE MISSPELLED* 7.____

8. A. dictator B. clipper C. braggadoccio D. assuage E. *NONE MISSPELLED* 8.____

9. A. reverence B. hydraulic C. felon D. diaphram E. *NONE MISSPELLED* 9.____

10. A. retrobution B. polyp C. optician D. mentor E. *NONE MISSPELLED* 10.____

11. A. resonant B. helicopter C. rejoicing D. decisive E. *NONE MISSPELLED* 11.____

12. A. renigade B. restitution C. faculty D. devise E. *NONE MISSPELLED* 12.____

13. A. solicitors B. gratuitous C. spherical D. crusible E. *NONE MISSPELLED* 13.____

14. A. spongy B. ramify C. pica D. noxtious E. *NONE MISSPELLED* 14.____

15. A. automaton B. cadence C. consummate D. ancillery E. *NONE MISSPELLED* 15.____

16. A. magnanimous B. iminent C. tonsillitis D. dowager E. *NONE MISSPELLED* 16.____

17. A. aerial B. apprehend C. bilinear D. transum E. *NONE MISSPELLED* 17.____

18.	A. vacuum D. warbler	B. idiom E. *NONE MISSPELLED*	C. veriety	18.____
19.	A. zephyr D. nonpareil	B. rarify E. *NONE MISSPELLED*	C. physiology	19.____
20.	A. risque D. meridian	B. posterity E. *NONE MISSPELLED*	C. opus	20.____

KEY (CORRECT ANSWERS)

1. E. None Misspelled
2. B. heifer
3. D. titular
4. C. embarrass
5. C. orthodox
6. B. humus
7. B. alimony
8. C. braggadocio
9. D. diaphragm
10. A. retribution
11. E. None Misspelled
12. A. renegade
13. D. crucible
14. D. noxious
15. D. ancillary
16. B. imminent
17. D. transom
18. C. variety
19. B. rarefy
20. D. meridian

TEST 14

DIRECTIONS: In each of the following tests in this part, select the letter of the one MISSPELLED word in each of the following groups of words. If no word is misspelled, select the last item, letter E (none misspelled). *PRINT THE LETTER OF THE CORRECT ANSWER IN THE SPACE AT THE RIGHT.*

1. A. pygmy B. seggregation C. clayey D. homogeneous E. *NONE MISSPELLED* 1.____

2. A. homeopathy B. predelection C. hindrance D. guillotine E. *NONE MISSPELLED* 2.____

3. A. cumulative B. dandelion C. incission D. malpractice E. *NONE MISSPELLED* 3.____

4. A. paradise B. allegiance C. frustrate D. impecunious E. *NONE MISSPELLED* 4.____

5. A. licquor B. mousse C. exclamatory D. disciple E. *NONE MISSPELLED* 5.____

6. A. lame B. winesome C. valvular D. unadvised E. *NONE MISSPELLED* 6.____

7. A. Terre Haute B. Cyrano de Bergerac C. Stamboul D. Roosvelt E. *NONE MISSPELLED* 7.____

8. A. perambulator B. ruminate C. litturgy D. staple E. *NONE MISSPELLED* 8.____

9. A. hectic B. inpregnate C. otter D. muscat E. *NONE MISSPELLED* 9.____

10. A. lighterage B. lumbar C. insurence D. monsoon E. *NONE MISSPELLED* 10.____

11. A. lethal B. iliterateness C. manifold D. minuet E. *NONE MISSPELLED* 11.____

12. A. forfeit B. halve C. hundredth D. illusion E. *NONE MISSPELLED* 12.____

13. A. dissolute B. conundrum C. fallacious D. descrimination E. *NONE MISSPELLED* 13.____

14. A. diva B. codicile C. expedient D. garrison E. *NONE MISSPELLED* 14.____

15. A. filial B. arras C. pantomine D. filament E. *NONE MISSPELLED* 15.____

16. A. inveigle B. paraphenalia C. archivist D. complexion E. *NONE MISSPELLED* 16.____

17. A. dessicate B. ambidextrous C. meritorious D. revocable E. *NONE MISSPELLED* 17.____

18.	A. queue D. binnocular	B. isthmus E. *NONE MISSPELLED*	C. committal	18.____
19.	A. changeable D. japanned	B. abbreviating E. *NONE MISSPELLED*	C. regretable	19.____
20.	A. Saskechewan D. Apennines	B. Bismarck E. *NONE MISSPELLED*	C. Albuquerque	20.____

KEY (CORRECT ANSWERS)

1.	B.	segregation
2.	B.	predilection
3.	C.	incision
4.	E.	None Misspelled
5.	A.	liquor
6.	B.	winsome
7.	D.	Roosevelt
8.	C.	liturgy
9.	B.	impregnate
10.	C.	insurance
11.	B.	illiterateness
12.	E.	None Misspelled
13.	D.	discrimination
14.	B.	codicil
15.	C.	pantomime
16.	B.	paraphernalia
17.	A.	desiccate
18.	D.	binocular
19.	C.	regrettable
20.	A.	Saskatchewan

TEST 15

DIRECTIONS: In each of the following tests in this part, select the letter of the one MISSPELLED word in each of the following groups of words. If no word is misspelled, select the last item, letter E (none misspelled). *PRINT THE LETTER OF THE CORRECT ANSWER IN THE SPACE AT THE RIGHT.*

1. A. culinery B. millinery C. humpbacked D. improvise E. *NONE MISSPELLED* 1.____

2. A. Brittany B. embarrassment C. coifure D. leveled E. *NONE MISSPELLED* 2.____

3. A. minnion B. aborgine C. antagonism D. arabesque E. *NONE MISSPELLED* 3.____

4. A. tractible B. camouflage C. permanent D. dextrous E. *NONE MISSPELLED* 4.____

5. A. inequitous B. kilowatt C. weasel D. lunging E. *NONE MISSPELLED* 5.____

6. A. palatable B. odious C. motif D. Maltese E. *NONE MISSPELLED* 6.____

7. A. Beau Brummel B. Febuary C. Bedouin D. Damascus E. *NONE MISSPELLED* 7.____

8. A. llama B. madrigal C. illitive D. marlin E. *NONE MISSPELLED* 8.____

9. A. babboon B. dossier C. esplanade D. frontispiece E. *NONE MISSPELLED* 9.____

10. A. thrashing B. threshing C. atavism D. artifect E. *NONE MISSPELLED* 10.____

11. A. ballast B. ballustrade C. allotment D. bourgeois E. *NONE MISSPELLED* 11.____

12. A. amenuensis B. saccharine C. hippopotamus D. rhinoceros E. *NONE MISSPELLED* 12.____

13. A. maintenance B. bullion C. khaki D. libarian E. *NONE MISSPELLED* 13.____

14. A. diverse B. pedantic C. mishapen D. transient E. *NONE MISSPELLED* 14.____

15. A. exhilirate B. avaunt C. avocado D. avocation E. *NONE MISSPELLED* 15.____

16. A. narcotic B. flippancy C. daffodil D. narcisus E. *NONE MISSPELLED* 16.____

17. A. inflamation B. disfranchisement C. surmise D. adviser E. *NONE MISSPELLED* 17.____

18. A. syphon B. inquiry C. shanghaied D. collapsible E. *NONE MISSPELLED* 18.____

19. A. occassionally B. antecedence C. reprehensible D. inveigh E. *NONE MISSPELLED* 19.____

20. A. crescendos B. indispensible C. mosquitoes D. impeccable E. *NONE MISSPELLED* 20.____

KEY (CORRECT ANSWERS)

1.	A.	culinary
2.	C.	coiffure
3.	A.	minion
4.	A.	tractable
5.	A.	iniquitous
6.	E.	None Misspelled
7.	B.	February
8.	D.	illative
9.	A.	baboon
10.	D.	artifact
11.	B.	balustrade
12.	A.	amanuensis
13.	D.	librarian
14.	C.	misshapen
15.	A.	exhilarate
16.	D.	narcissus
17.	A.	inflammation
18.	E.	None Misspelled
19.	A.	occasionally
20.	B.	indispensable

EXAMINATION SECTION

TEST 1

DIRECTIONS: In each of the following questions, only one of the four sentences conforms to standards of correct usage. The other three contain errors in grammar, diction, or punctuation. Select the choice in each question which BEST conforms to standards of correct usage. Consider a choice correct if it contains none of the errors mentioned above, even though there may be other ways of expressing the same thought. *PRINT THE LETTER OF THE CORRECT ANSWER IN THE SPACE AT THE RIGHT.*

1. A. Because he was ill was no excuse for his behavior 1.____
   B. I insist that he see a lawyer before he goes to trial.
   C. He said "that he had not intended to go."
   D. He wasn't out of the office only three days.

2. A. He came to the station and pays a porter to carry his bags into the train. 2.____
   B. I should have liked to live in medieval times.
   C. My father was born in Linville. A little country town where everybody knows everyone else.
   D. The car, which is parked across the street, is disabled.

3. A. He asked the desk clerk for a clean, quiet, room. 3.____
   B. I expected James to be lonesome and that he would want to go home.
   C. I have stopped worrying because I have heard nothing further on the subject.
   D. If the board of directors controls the company, they may take actions which are disapproved by the stockholders.

4. A. Each of the players knew their place. 4.____
   B. He whom you saw on the stage is the son of an actor.
   C. Susan is the smartest of the twin sisters.
   D. Who ever thought of him winning both prizes?

5. A. An outstanding trait of early man was their reliance on omens. 5.____
   B. Because I had never been there before.
   C. Neither Mr. Jones nor Mr. Smith has completed his work.
   D. While eating my dinner, a dog came to the window.

6. A. A copy of the lease, in addition to the Rules and Regulations, are to be given to each tenant. 6.____
   B. The Rules and Regulations and a copy of the lease is being given to each tenant.
   C. A copy of the lease, in addition to the Rules and Regulations, is to be given to each tenant.
   D. A copy of the lease, in addition to the Rules and Regulations, are being given to each tenant.

7. A. Although we understood that for him music was a passion, we were disturbed by the fact that he was addicted to sing along with the soloists. 7.____
   B. Do you believe that Steven is liable to win a scholarship?
   C. Give the picture to whomever is a connoisseur of art.
   D. Whom do you believe to be the most efficient worker in the office?

8. A. Each adult who is sure they know all the answers will some day realize their mistake. 8.____
   B. Even the most hardhearted villain would have to feel bad about so horrible a tragedy.
   C. Neither being licensed teachers, both aspirants had to pass rigorous tests before being appointed.
   D. The principal reason why he wanted to be designated was because he had never before been to a convention.

9. A. Being that the weather was so inclement, the party has been postponed for at least a month. 9.____
   B. He is in New York City only three weeks and he has already seen all the thrilling sights in Manhattan and in the other four boroughs.
   C. If you will look it up in the official directory, which can be consulted in the library during specified hours, you will discover that the chairman and director are Mr. T. Henry Long.
   D. Working hard at college during the day and at the post office during the night, he appeared to his family to be indefatigable.

10. A. I would have been happy to oblige you if you only asked me to do it. 10.____
    B. The cold weather, as well as the unceasing wind and rain, have made us decide to spend the winter in Florida.
    C. The politician would have been more successful in winning office if he would have been less dogmatic.
    D. These trousers are expensive; however, they will wear well.

11. A. All except him wore formal attire at the reception for the ambassador. 11.____
    B. If that chair were to be blown off of the balcony, it might injure someone below.
    C. Not a passenger, who was in the crash, survived the impact.
    D. To borrow money off friends is the best way to lose them.

12. A. Approaching Manhattan on the ferry boat from Staten Island, an unforgettable sight of the skyscrapers is seen. 12.____
    B. Did you see the exhibit of modernistic paintings as yet?
    C. Gesticulating wildly and ranting in stentorian tones, the speaker was the sinecure of all eyes.
    D. The airplane with crew and passengers was lost somewhere in the Pacific Ocean.

13. A. If one has consistently had that kind of training, it is certainly too late to change your entire method of swimming long distances. 13.____
    B. The captain would have been more impressed if you would have been more conscientious in evacuation drills.
    C. The passengers on the stricken ship were all ready to abandon it at the signal.
    D. The villainous shark lashed at the lifeboat with it's tail, trying to upset the rocking boat in order to partake of it's contents.

14. A. As one whose been certified as a professional engineer, I believe that the decision to build a bridge over that harbor is unsound. 14.____
    B. Between you and me, this project ought to be completed long before winter arrives.
    C. He fervently hoped that the men would be back at camp and to find them busy at their usual chores.
    D. Much to his surprise, he discovered that the climate of Korea was like his home town.

15. A. An industrious executive is aided, not impeded, by having a hobby which gives him a fresh point of view on life and its problems. 15.____
    B. Frequent absence during the calendar year will surely mitigate against the chances of promotion.
    C. He was unable to go to the committee meeting because he was very ill.
    D. Mr. Brown expressed his disapproval so emphatically that his associates were embarassed

16. A. At our next session, the office manager will have told you something about his duties and responsibilities. 16.____
    B. In general, the book is absorbing and original and have no hesitation about recommending it.
    C. The procedures followed by private industry in dealing with lateness and absence are different from ours.
    D We shall treat confidentially any information about Mr. Doe, to whom we understand you have sent reports to for many years.

17. A. I talked to one official, whom I knew was fully impartial. 17.____
    B. Everyone signed the petition but him.
    C. He proved not only to be a good student but also a good athlete.
    D. All are incorrect.

18. A. Every year a large amount of tenants are admitted to housing projects. 18.____
    B. Henry Ford owned around a billion dollars in industrial equipment.
    C. He was aggravated by the child's poor behavior.
    D. All are incorrect.

19. A. Before he was committed to the asylum he suffered from the illusion that he was Napoleon. 19.____
B. Besides stocks, there were also bonds in the safe.
C. We bet the other team easily.
D. All are incorrect.

20. A. Bring this report to your supervisory. 20.____
B. He set the chair down near the table.
C. The capitol of New York is Albany.
D. All are incorrect.

21. A. He was chosen to arbitrate the dispute because everyone knew he would be disinterested. 21.____
B. It is advisable to obtain the best council before making an important decision.
C. Less college students are interested in teaching than ever before.
D. All are incorrect.

22. A. She, hearing a signal, the source lamp flashed. 22.____
B. While hearing a signal, the source lamp flashed.
C. In hearing a signal, the source lamp flashed.
D. As she heard a signal, the source lamp flashed.

23. A. Every one of the time records have been initialed in the designated spaces. 23.____
B. All of the time records has been initialed in the designated spaces.
C. Each one of the time records was initialed in the designated spaces.
D. The time records all been initialed in the designated spaces.

24. A. If there is no one else to answer the phone, you will have to answer it. 24.____
B. You will have to answer it yourself if no one else answers the phone.
C. If no one else is not around to pick up the phone, you will have to do it.
D. You will have to answer the phone when nobodys here to do it.

25. A. Dr. Barnes not in his office. What could I do for you? 25.____
B. Dr. Barnes is not in his office. Is there something I can do for you?
C. Since Dr. Barnes is not in his office, might there be something I may do for you?
D. Is there any ways I can assist you since Dr. Barnes is not in his office?

26. A. She do not understand how the new console works. 26.____
B. The way the new console works, she doesn't understand.
C. She doesn't understand how the new console works.
D. The new console works, so that she doesn't understand.

27. A. Certain changes in my family income must be reported as they occur. 27.____
B. When certain changes in family income occur, it must be reported.
C. Certain family income change must be reported as they occur.
D. Certain changes in family income must be reported as they have been occurring.

28. A. Each tenant has to complete the application themselves. 28.____
 B. Each of the tenants have to complete the application by himself.
 C. Each of the tenants has to complete the application himself.
 D. Each of the tenants has to complete the application by themselves.

29. A. Yours is the only building that the construction will effect. 29.____
 B. Your's is the only building affected by the construction.
 C. The construction will only effect your building.
 D. Yours is the only building that will be affected by the construction.

30. A. There is four tests left. 30.____
 B. The number of tests left are four.
 C. There are four tests left.
 D. Four of the tests remains.

31. A. Each of the applicants takes a test. 31.____
 B. Each of the applicant take a test.
 C. Each of the applicants take tests.
 D. Each of the applicants have taken tests.

32. A. The applicant, not the examiners, are ready. 32.____
 B. The applicants, not the examiners, is ready.
 C. The applicants, not the examiner, are ready.
 D. The applicant, not the examiner, are ready

33. A. You will not progress except you practice. 33.____
 B. You will not progress without you practicing.
 C. You will not progress unless you practice.
 D. You will not progress provided you do not practice.

34. A. Neither the director or the employees will be at the office tomorrow. 34.____
 B. Neither the director nor the employees will be at the office tomorrow.
 C. Neither the director, or the secretary nor the other employees will be at the office tomorrow.
 D. Neither the director, the secretary or the other employees will be at the office tomorrow.

35. A. In my absence, he and her will have to finish the assignment. 35.____
 B. In my absence he and she will have to finish the assignment.
 C. In my absence she and him, they will have to finish the assignment.
 D. In my absence he and her both will have to finish the assignment.

KEY (CORRECT ANSWERS)

1.	B	11.	A	21.	A	31.	A
2.	B	12.	D	22.	D	32.	C
3.	C	13.	C	23.	C	33.	C
4.	B	14.	B	24.	A	34.	B
5.	C	15.	A	25.	B	35.	B
6.	C	16.	C	26.	C		
7.	D	17.	B	27.	A		
8.	B	18.	D	28.	C		
9.	D	19.	B	29.	D		
10.	D	20.	B	30.	C		

TEST 2

DIRECTIONS: Each question or incomplete statement is followed by several suggested answers or completions. Select the one that BEST answers the question or completes the statement. *PRINT THE LETTER OF THE CORRECT ANSWER IN THE SPACE AT THE RIGHT.*

Questions 1-4.

DIRECTIONS: Questions 1 through 4 consist of three sentences each. For each question, select the sentence which contains NO error in grammar or usage.

1. A. Be sure that everybody brings his notes to the conference. 1.____
   B. He looked like he meant to hit the boy.
   C. Mr. Jones is one of the clients who was chosen to represent the district.
   D. All are incorrect.

2. A. He is taller than I. 2.____
   B. I'll have nothing to do with these kind of people.
   C. The reason why he will not buy the house is because it is too expensive.
   D. All are incorrect.

3. A. Aren't I eligible for this apartment. 3.____
   B. Have you seen him anywheres?
   C. He should of come earlier.
   D. All are incorrect.

4. A. He graduated college in 2022. 4.____
   B. He hadn't but one more line to write.
   C. Who do you think is the author of this report?
   D. All are incorrect.

Questions 5-35.

DIRECTIONS: In each of the following questions, only one of the four sentences conforms to standards of correct usage. The other three contain errors in grammar, diction, or punctuation. Select the choice in each question which BEST conforms to standards of correct usage. Consider a choice correct if it contains none of the errors mentioned above, even though there may be other ways of expressing the same thought.

5. A. It is obvious that no one wants to be a kill-joy if they can help it. 5.____
   B. It is not always possible, and perhaps it never ispossible, to judge a person's character by just looking at him.
   C. When Yogi Berra of the New York Yankees hit an immortal grandslam home run, everybody in the huge stadium including Pittsburgh fans, rose to his feet.
   D. Every one of us students must pay tuition today.

6. A. The physician told the young mother that if the baby is not able to digest its milk, it should be boiled. 6.____
   B. There is no doubt whatsoever that he felt deeply hurt because John Smith had betrayed the trust.
   C. Having partaken of a most delicious repast prepared by Tessie Breen, the hostess, the horses were driven home immediately thereafter.
   D. The attorney asked my wife and myself several questions.

7. A. Despite all denials, there is no doubt in my mind that 7.____
   B. At this time everyone must deprecate the demogogic attack made by one of our Senators on one of our most revered statesmen.
   C. In the first game of a crucial two-game series, Ted Williams, got two singles, both of them driving in a run.
   D. Our visitor brought good news to John and I.

8. A. If he would have told me, I should have been glad to help him in his dire financial emergency. 8.____
   B. Newspaper men have often asserted that diplomats or so-called official spokesmen sometimes employ equivocation in attempts to deceive.
   C. I think someones coming to collect money for the Red Cross.
   D. In a masterly summation, the young attorney expressed his belief that the facts clearly militate against this opinion.

9. A. We have seen most all the exhibits. 9.____
   B. Without in the least underestimating your advice, in my opinion the situation has grown immeasurably worse in the past few days.
   C. I wrote to the box office treasurer of the hit show that a pair of orchestra seats would be preferable.
   D. As the grim story of Pearl Harbor was broadcast on that fateful December 7, it was the general opinion that war was inevitable.

10. A. Without a moment's hesitation, Casey Stengel said that Larry Berra works harder than any player on the team. 10.____
    B. There is ample evidence to indicate that many animals can run faster than any human being.
    C. No one saw the accident but I.
    D. Example of courage is the heroic defense put up by the paratroopers against overwhelming odds.

11. A. If you prefer these kind, Mrs. Grey, we shall be more than willing to let you have them reasonably. 11.____
    B. If you like these here, Mrs. Grey, we shall be more than willing to let you have them reasonably.
    C. If you like these, Mrs. Grey, we shall be more than willing to let you have them.
    D. Who shall we appoint?

12. A. The number of errors are greater in speech than in writing. 12.____
    B. The doctor rather than the nurse was to blame for his being neglected.
    C. Because the demand for these books have been so great, we reduced the price.
    D. John Galsworthy, the English novelist, could not have survived a serious illness; had it not been for loving care.

13. A. Our activities this year have seldom ever been as interesting as they have been this month. 13.____
    B. Our activities this month have been more interesting, or at least as interesting as those of any month this year.
    C. Our activities this month has been more interesting than those of any other month this year.
    D. Neither Jean nor her sister was at home.

14. A. George B. Shaw's view of common morality, as well as his wit sparkling with a dash of perverse humor here and there, have led critics to term him "The Incurable Rebel." 14.____
    B. The President's program was not always received with the wholehearted endorsement of his own party, which is why the party faces difficulty in drawing up a platform for the coming election.
    C. The reason why they wanted to travel was because they had never been away from home.
    D. Facing a barrage of cameras, the visiting celebrity found it extremely difficult to express his opinions clearly.

15. A. When we calmed down, we all agreed that our anger had been kind of unnecessary and had not helped the situation. 15.____
    B. Without him going into all the details, he made us realize the horror of the accident.
    C. Like one girl, for example, who applied for two positions.
    D. Do not think that you have to be so talented as he is in order to play in the school orchestra.

16. A. He looked very peculiarly to me. 16.____
    B. He certainly looked at me peculiar.
    C. Due to the train's being late, we had to wait an hour.
    D. The reason for the poor attendance is that it is raining.

17. A. About one out of four own an automobile. 17.____
    B. The collapse of the old Mitchell Bridge was caused by defective construction in the central pier.
    C. Brooks Atkinson was well acquainted with the best literature, thus helping him to become an able critic.
    D. He has to stand still until the relief man comes up, thus giving him no chance to move about and keep warm.

18. A. He is sensitive to confusion and withdraws from people whom he feels are too noisy. 18.____
    B. Do you know whether the data is statistically correct?
    C. Neither the mayor or the aldermen are to blame.
    D. Of those who were graduated from high school, a goodly percentage went to college.

19. A. Acting on orders, the offices were searched by a designated committee. 19.____
    B. The answer probably is nothing.
    C. I thought it to be all right to excuse them from class.
    D. I think that he is as successful a singer, if not more successful, than Mary.

20. A. $360,000 is really very little to pay for such a wellbuilt house. 20.____
    B. The creatures looked like they had come from outer space.
    C. It was her, he knew!
    D. Nobody but me knows what to do.

21. A. Mrs. Smith looked good in her new suit. 21.____
    B. New York may be compared with Chicago.
    C. I will not go to the meeting except you go with me.
    D. I agree with this editorial.

22. A. My opinions are different from his. 22.____
    B. There will be less students in class now.
    C. Helen was real glad to find her watch.
    D. It had been pushed off of her dresser.

23. A. Almost everyone, who has been to California, returns with glowing reports. 23.____
    B. George Washington, John Adams, and Thomas Jefferson, were our first presidents.
    C. Mr. Walters, whom we met at the bank yesterday, is the man, who gave me my first job.
    D. One should study his lessons as carefully as he can.

24. A. We had such a good time yesterday. 24.____
    B. When the bell rang, the boys and girls went in the schoolhouse.
    C. John had the worst headache when he got up this morning.
    D. Today's assignment is somewhat longer than yesterday's.

25. A. Neither the mayor nor the city clerk are willing to talk. 25.____
    B. Neither the mayor nor the city clerk is willing to talk.
    C. Neither the mayor or the city clerk are willing to talk.
    D Neither the mayor or the city clerk is willing to talk.

26. A. Being that he is that kind of boy, cooperation cannot be expected. 26.____
    B. He interviewed people who he thought had something to say.
    C. Stop whomever enters the building regardless of rank or office held.
    D. Passing through the countryside, the scenery pleased us.

27. A. The childrens' shoes were in their closet. 27.____
    B. The children's shoes were in their closet.
    C. The childs' shoes were in their closet.
    D. The childs' shoes were in his closet.

28. A. An agreement was reached between the defendant, the plaintiff, the plaintiff's attorney and the insurance company as to the amount of the settlement. 28.____
    B. Everybody was asked to give their versions of the accident.
    C. The consensus of opinion was that the evidence was inconclusive.
    D. The witness stated that if he was rich, he wouldn't have had to loan the money.

29. A. Before beginning the investigation, all the materials related to the case were carefully assembled. 29.____
    B. The reason for his inability to keep the appointment is because of his injury in the accident.
    C. This here evidence tends to support the claim of the defendant.
    D. We interviewed all the witnesses who, according to the driver, were still in town.

30. A. Each claimant was allowed the full amount of their medical expenses. 30.____
    B. Either of the three witnesses is available.
    C. Every one of the witnesses was asked to tell his story.
    D. Neither of the witnesses are right.

31. A. The commissioner, as well as his deputy and various bureau heads, were present. 31.____
    B. A new organization of employers and employees have been formed.
    C. One or the other of these men have been selected.
    D. The number of pages in the book is enough to discourage a reader.

32. A. Between you and me, I think he is the better man. 32.____
    B. He was believed to be me.
    C. Is it us that you wish to see?
    D. The winners are him and her.

33. A. Beside the statement to the police, the witness spoke to no one. 33.____
    B. He made no statement other than to the police and I.
    C. He made no statement to any one else, aside from the police.
    D. The witness spoke to no one but me.

34. A. The claimant has no one to blame but himself. 34.____
    B. The boss sent us, he and I, to deliver the packages.
    C. The lights come from mine and not his car.
    D. There was room on the stairs for him and myself.

35. A. Admission to this clinic is limited to patients' inability to pay for medical care. 35.____
    B. Patients who can pay little or nothing for medical care are treated in this clinic.
    C. The patient's ability to pay for medical care is the determining factor in his admission to this clinic.
    D. This clinic is for the patient's that cannot afford to pay or that can pay a little for medical care.

KEY (CORRECT ANSWERS)

1.	A	11.	C	21.	A	31.	D
2.	A	12.	B	22.	A	32.	A
3.	D	13.	D	23.	D	33.	D
4.	C	14.	D	24.	D	34.	A
5.	D	15.	D	25.	B	35.	B
6.	D	16.	D	26.	B		
7.	B	17.	B	27.	B		
8.	B	18.	D	28.	C		
9.	D	19.	B	29.	D		
10.	B	20.	D	30.	C		

FOLLOWING INSTRUCTIONS

COMMENTARY

An important part of every job is the ability to follow instructions.

This is especially true of postal service work in processing the mail. The distribution clerk sorts the mail (in some places by hand, in some paces by machine) and does other things to keep the mail moving.

Mail sorters must learn, commit to memory, and apply intricate sorting schemes that form the rationale of the physical movement of the mail.

Then, then, must sort the mail quickly, correctly, and efficiently.

In order to do this, they must be able to follow instructions punctiliously and swiftly.

This section will prepare you for the part of the Postal Service Examination called FOLLOWING INSTRUCTIONS.

It shows you how to do the different kinds of questions.

It offers you an extended opportunity for practice and drill.

It gives you a chance to test yourself with tests just like those used in the examination—same kinds of questions, same difficulty, same length.

The material is arranged so that you can study by yourself. Read the explanation, try the questions, check your answers. For the questions you get wrong, try to figure out why the correct answer is right and why you made a mistake.

EXAMINATION SECTION

TEST 1

DIRECTIONS: Read carefully so that when you take the examination you will remember HoW to do the test.

FINDING TRAIN NUMBERS:

Below are a Sorting Scheme and a Key. In the Sorting Scheme is a list of post offices. Each post office is followed by a letter. For example, after "Guilford" is the letter "F." This "F" refers to the Key at the right which reads "F Atlantic 6." Mail for "Guilford" is sent by way of "Atlantic on Train 6." ALWAYS BEGIN WITH A POST OFFICE IN THE SORTING SCHEME AND FIND THE TRAIN NUMBER IN THE KEY.

SORTING SCHEME

Atlantic	F	_____
Bloxam	T	_____
Greta	O	_____
Groton	K	_____
Guilford	F	_____
Hopeton	K	_____
Hopkins	I	_____
Kane	G	_____
Keller	J	_____
Mears	U	_____
Melfa	G	_____
Nandua	M	_____
Nelson	F	_____
Oak Hill	H	_____
Onley	S	_____
Painter	I	_____
Parksley	S	_____
Paulson	H	_____
Quimby	U	_____
Sanford	S	_____
Shields	J	_____
Silva	O	_____
Tangier	J	_____
Tasley	G	_____
Withams	P	_____

KEY

Mail sent by way of:

F	Atlantic	6	_____
G	Melfa	2	_____
H	Oak Hill	7	_____
I	Hopkins	3	_____
J	Tangier	8	_____
K	Hopeton	5	_____
M	Painter		_____
O	Greta	9	_____
P	Keller		_____
S	Sanford	4	_____
T	Groton		_____
U	Parksley		_____

NOTE: Do not make any marks in this Sorting Scheme or Key before you read the directions below.

BEGIN HERE: Do not skip any part of these directions. Work with a pencil so that if you want more practice you can erase the work.

COMPLETING THE KEY:

Look at "Painter" in the KEY. It is not followed by a number. Write after it the letter which you find after "Painter" in the Sorting Scheme. Your KEY should now read "M Painter I." Find the letters after "Keller, Groton, and Parksley" in the Sorting Scheme and write them after those post offices in the Key.

RECORDING ANSWERS:

In each question below a post office name is followed by five train numbers. Use the Sorting Scheme and Key to find the correct train number. Then see what Column (A, B, C, D, E) the correct train number is in, and mark this letter in the space at the right.

For Example: In the Sorting Scheme, "Painter" is followed by the letter "I." This tells you to look at "I" in the Key, which reads "Hopkins 3," and means that mail for "Painter" is routed by way of Hopkins on Train 3. The number 3 after "Painter" below is in Column B.

QUESTION NO.	POST OFFICE	A	B	C	D	E
1	Painter	2	3	5	7	9
2	Paulson	3	4	5	7	8
3	Mears	2	3	4	5	7
4	Kane	2	3	4	5	6

Mail for "Mears" is sent by way of "U Parksley S" through "S Sanford" on Train 4, which is in Column C.

MAKING CHANGES IN THE SORTING SCHEME AND KEY:

Never put numbers in the Sorting Scheme. Make changes from the Bulletins EXACTLY as they direct you to.

Never cross out names in the Sorting Scheme.

BULLETIN NO. 1
Changes in Routing

NOTE: When changing Sorting Scheme, change Key too if the name is in the Key. Note that the names in the Sorting Scheme are in alphabetical order, but those in the Key are not.)

Silva by way of I	Painter by way of K
Shields by way of O	Change Key G to Read: G Train 10
Guilford by way of P	Melfa by way of H

To make the change for "Silva," cross out the "O" after Silva in the Sorting Scheme and write "I." Now your Sorting Scheme for Silva should read, "Silva ~~O~~ I. This means that mail for Silva is now sent by way of I, that is, through "Hopkins on Train 3."

To make the change for "Painter," cross out the "I" after "Painter" in the Sorting Scheme and write "K." Then find Painter in the Key and change the "I" after it to "K." Mail for Painter will now go through "K," that is, through "Hopeton on Train 5." To change Key G, cross out "Melfa 2" and write "Train 10." Make the other changes ordered.

Select the letter showing the train on which you should put mail for:

QUESTION NO.	POST OFFICE	A	B	C	D	E
5	Tasley	2	3	7	8	10
6	Nandua	2	3	5	8	9
7	Withams	4	6	8	9	10

NOTE: In answering Question 6 for "Nandua," did you start to mark C for Question 5 because you were thinking of Train 5?

BULLETIN NO. 2	
Offices Established (Add to Sorting Scheme)	Changes in Routing (When changing Sorting Scheme, change Key too, if the name is in the Key.)
Saxis by way of F Talbot by way of H	Paulson by way of G. Parksley by way of O. Change Key J to read: J Tangier 2.

NOTE: To add "Saxis" to the Sorting Scheme, write "Saxis F" on the first line at the end of the Sorting Scheme. To change Key J, cross out "8" after "J Tangier" and write "2." Make the other changes ordered.

QUESTION NO.	POST OFFICE	A	B	C	D	E
8	Mears	4	5	7	9	10
9	Silva	2	3	5	7	9
10.	Guilford	2	6	8	9	10
11	Painter	2	3	4	5	6
12.	Parksley	3	4	5	7	9
13.	Shields	2	3	5	7	9
14.	Talbot	3	4	7	9	10
15.	Melfa	2	3	5	7	10

NOTE: If you have chosen "4" for "Mears," you have not made the change for "Parksley" in both the Sorting Scheme and Key. Mail for Mears should be sent through "U Parksley O" by way of "O Greta" on "Train 9."

BULLETIN NO. 3	
Offices Established (Add to Sorting Scheme)	Changes in Routing (When changing Sorting Scheme, change Key too, if the name is in the Key.)
Somerset by way of G Elkton by way of W	Oak Hill by way of W. (Be sure to change Oak Hill in the Key.) Add to Key: W Train 12 Change Key F to read: F Atlantic 3. Parksley by way of K.

NOTE: To make the addition to the Key, write "W Train 12" on the first line at the end of the Key. Select the letter showing the train on which you should put mail for:

QUESTION NO.	POST OFFICE	A	B	C	D	E
16.	Parksley	4	5	7	8	9
17.	Talbot	3	6	7	10	12
18.	Somerset	2	4	8	10	12
19.	Saxis	3	4	5	6	8
20.	Paulson	2	4	7	10	12
21.	Elkton	2	4	7	10	12

BULLETIN NO. 4
Changes in Routing

NOTE: When changing Sorting Scheme, change Key too if the name is in the Key.

Painter by way of O Hopkins by way of J Kane by way of P	Change Key S to read: S Melfa. (Cross out Sanford 4 in the Key.) Sanford by way of H.

NOTE: To complete the change for Key S, you must refer to the Sorting Scheme to find the letter which should be written after Melfa. Select the letter showing the train on which you should put mail for:

QUESTION NO.	POST OFFICE	A	B	C	D	E
22	Sanford	2	4	7	10	12
23	Nandua	3	5	8	9	10
24	Hopkins	2	3	4	6	8
25	Kane	2	4	6	8	10

Note: If you have chosen "Train 5" for "Nandua," you have not made the change for "Painter" in both the Sorting Scheme and the Key.

KEY (CORRECT ANSWERS)

SORTING SCHEME

Atlantic	F	
Bloxam	T	
Greta	O	
Groton	K	
Guilford	~~F~~	P
Hopeton	K	
Hopkins	I	J
Kane	~~G~~	P
Keller	J	
Mears	U	
Melfa	~~G~~	H
Nandua	M	
Nelson	F	
Oak Hill	~~H~~	W
Onley	S	
Painter	I	~~K~~ O
Parksley	~~S~~	~~O~~ K
Paulson	~~H~~	G
Quimby	U	
Sanford	~~S~~	H
Shields	~~J~~	O
Silva	~~O~~	I
Tangier	J	
Tasley	G	
Withams	P	

KEY

Mail sent by way of:

F	Atlantic	~~6~~	3
G	~~Melfa~~	~~2~~	Train 10
H	Oak Hill	~~7~~	W
I	Hopkins	~~3~~	J
J	Tangier	~~8~~	2
K	Hopeton	5	
M	Painter	I	~~K~~ O
O	Greta	9	
P	Keller		J
S	~~Sanford~~	~~4~~	Melfa H
T	Groton	K	
U	Parksley	~~S~~ ~~O~~ K	
W	Train 12		

1.	B	6.	C	11.	D	16	B	21.	E
2.	D	7.	C	12.	E	17.	E	22.	E
3.	C	8.	D	13.	E	18.	D	23.	D
4.	A	9.	B	14.	C	19.	A	24.	A
5.	E	10	A	15.	D	20.	D	25.	A

TEST 2

DIRECTIONS: Using the following Sorting Scheme and Key, answer the problems below by writing the number of the train on which you would send mail for each of the places named.

SORTING SCHEME

Ingram	_____	C	_____
Madill	_____	G	_____
Moore	_____	D	_____
Tatum	_____	G	_____
Crane	_____	F	_____
Houston	_____	A	_____
Rotan	_____	B	_____
Walters	_____	A	_____
Hooker	_____	E	_____
Preston	_____	J	_____
Coyle	_____	E	_____
Ferris	_____	F	_____
Paige	_____	A	_____
Marlow	_____	B	_____

KEY

A	Houston	_____	9	_____
B	Rotan	_____	3	_____
C	Preston	_____		_____
D	Coyle	_____		_____
E	Hooker	_____	6	_____
F.	Crane	_____	7	_____
G	Marlowe	_____		_____
J	Ferris	_____		_____

PROBLEM I: Write the number of the train on which you would send mail for each of the following offices.

Preston	_____	Ferris	_____	Rotan	_____	Marlow	_____
Ingram	_____	Moore	_____	Walters	_____	Hooker	_____
Coyle	_____	Paige	_____	Houston	_____	Madill	_____

BULLETIN NO. 1

Add to Sorting Scheme	Changes in Routing
Taylor by way of J Burton by way of R Add to Key R Train 8	Preston by way of F Rotan by way of A Change Key D to read: D Coyle 2 Change Key J to read: J Train 4

PROBLEM 2: Write the number of the train on which you would send mail for each of the following offices.

Rotan _____	Coyle _____	Burton _____	Marlow _____
Preston_____	Moore _____	Ingram _____	Ferris _____
Tyler _____	Tatum _____	Crane _____	Walters _____

BULLETIN NO. 2
Changes in Routing

Tatum by way of J
Marlow by way of A
Hooker by way of R
Moore by way of E
Rotan by way of D

PROBLEM 3: Write the number of the train on which you would send mail for each of the following offices.

Madill _____	Marlowe_____	Crane _____	Tyler _____
Moore _____	Tatum _____	Paige _____	Houston _____
Hooker _____	Rotan _____	Coyle _____	Ingram _____

KEY (CORRECT ANSWERS)

SORTING SCHEME

Ingram	C
Madill	G
Moore	~~D~~ E
Tatum	~~G~~ J
Crane	F
Houston	A
Rotan	~~B~~ ~~A~~ D
Walters	A
Hooker	~~E~~ R
Preston	~~J~~ F
Coyle	E
Ferris	F
Paige	A
Marlow	~~B~~ A
Tyler	J
Burton	R

KEY

A	Houston _____	9 _____
B	Rotan _____	~~3~~ ~~A~~ D_____
C	Preston _____	~~J~~ F_____
D	Coyle _____	~~E~~ 2 _____
E	Hooker _____	~~6~~ R_____
F.	Crane _____	7 _____
G	Marlowe _____	~~B~~ A _____
J	~~Ferris _____~~	~~F~~ Train 4
R	Train 8	

PROBLEM 1

7 7 3 3
7 6 9 6
6 9 9 3

PROBLEM 2

9 6 8 9
7 2 7 7
4 9 7 9

PROBLEM 3

9 9 7 4
8 4 9 9
8 2 8 7

TEST 3

NOTE: This is a test of your ability to follow instructions. All directions must be followed exactly as shown below.

DIRECTIONS: Below, at the left, is a list of post offices called a Sorting Scheme. After each of these offices is a letter. For example, after "Butler" is the letter "A." This refers to the "A" in the Key at the right, which reads "A Gould 2." The "A" after "Butler," therefore, means that mail for Butler is routed by way of Gould. The numbers after ——— the names in the Key indicate the trains on which mail for those post offices must be placed. After "Gould" in the Key you will find the number 2. This means that mail for Gould is sent on Train 2. Since mail for Butler is routed by way of "Gould," mail for Butler would also be sent on Train 2.

SORTING SCHEME

Adair	_____	B	_____
Butler	_____	A	_____
Calvin	_____	B	_____
Durant	_____	I	_____
Enid	_____	E	_____
Fargo	_____	B	_____
Gould	_____	A	_____
Lawton	_____	D	_____
Newkirk	_____	H	_____
Osage	_____	C	_____
Snyder	_____	C	_____
Tyrone	_____	A	_____

KEY

Mail sent by way of _____

A	Gould	_____	2	_____
B	Calvin	_____	4	_____
C	Osage	_____	3	_____
D	Tyrone	_____		_____
E	Adair	_____		_____
F.	Newkirk	_____	5	_____
H	Marlowe	_____		_____
I	Fargo	_____		_____
	_____	_____		_____
	_____	_____		_____

NOTE: You must follow directions exactly as given. Make your numbers and letters clear, to avoid mistakes.
Look at the name "Tyrone" in the Key. It is not followed by a number. Write after it the letter which you find after Tyrone in the Sorting Scheme. Your Key will now read "D Tyrone A." Find the letters after "Adair" and "Fargo" in the Sorting Scheme and write them after those names in the Key.

NOTE: Never put numbers in the Sorting Scheme. On the line after each of the following offices, write the number of the train on which you would send mail for that office.

To find the number which should be written after "Snyder," look for Snyder in the Sorting Scheme. After it is the letter "C." This refers to Key "C Osage 3," and means that mail for Snyder is routed through "Osage on Train 3."

After "Enid" is the letter "E." This refers to Key "E Adair B," and means that mail for Enid is routed through "Adair" by way of "B," and Key B reads "Calvin," on "Train 4." Therefore, you write "4" after Enid in the list below.

Now write the train numbers after the others.

Snyder	3	Butler	____	Newkirk	____
Enid	4	Durant	____	Lawton	____

If you have followed directions, you will find that the CORRECT answers are:

3 2 5
4 4 2

CHANGES IN ROUTING

Changes in train schedules or other changes affecting train service, such as accidents, floods, etc., may require the re-routing of mail. Such changes in routing are indicated in "Bulletins" issued to the post offices affected.

You now receive BULLETIN NO. 1:

Tyrone by way of C
Adair by way of A

To make the change for "Tyrone," cross out the "A" after Tyrone in the Sorting Scheme and write "C." Then your Sorting Scheme for Tyrone should read "Tyrone C." This means that mail for Tyrone is now sent by way of "C Osage 3." Next look for Tyrone in the Key and change the "A" after it to "C." Next, make the change for "Adair" so that your Sorting Scheme will read: "Adair ~~B~~ A," and the Key will read "E Adair ~~B~~ A."

Never change the letter BEFORE the name in the Key. When a letter or number is changed, it is always the letter or number AFTER the name.

Make changes in both the Sorting Scheme and Key if the names are in both.

After making the above changes, write the number of the train on which you would send mail for each of the following offices:

Tyrone	____	Osage	____	Fargo	____
Gould	____	Calvin	____	Adair	____

If you have followed directions, you will find that the CORRECT answers are:

6 3 4
2 4 2

Next, you receive Bulletin No. 2.

BULLETIN NO. 2 Changes in Routing (Make changes in both Sorting Scheme and Key, if the names are in both) Change Key C to read: C Osage 6 Change Key A to read: A Train 7

To make the change for Key C, cross out the "3" after "Osage" in the Key and write "6," because the train for Osage has been changed from "3" to "6."

To change Key A, cross out "Gould 2" and write "Train 7." This means that mail for offices marked A is no longer sent through "Gould' but is routed direct on Train 7.

Now write the number of the train on which you would send mail for:

Butler	_____	Gould	_____	Durant	_____
Fargo	_____	Enid	_____	Tyrone	_____

The CORRECT answers are:

7 7 4
4 7 6

BULLETIN NO. 3	
Offices Established (Add to Sorting Scheme)	Changes in Routing
Charter by way of C Noble by way of H	Add to Key: R Train 2 Change Key D to read: D Train Change Key E to read: E Butler Durant by way of R Calvin by way of H

NOTE: To add "Carter" to the Sorting Scheme, write "Carter C" on the first blank at the end of the Sorting Scheme. Next, add "Noble H."
To add "K Train 2" to the Key, write "K Train 2" on the first blank line at the end of the Key.
To make the change for Key E, cross out "Adair A" in the Key and write "Butler." Then find the letter after Butler in the Sorting Scheme and write it after the name in the Key.
To make the change for "Calvin, cross out the "B" after Calvin in the Sorting Scheme, and write "H." Then, in the Key, cross out "4" after Calvin and write "H."
Make the other changes ordered.

Write the number of the train on which you would send mail for:

Carter	_____	Enid	_____	Calvin	_____
Durant	_____	Gould	_____	Lawton	_____
Osage	_____	Adair	_____	Snyder	_____
Noble	_____				

The CORRECT answers are:

6 7 5
2 7 4
6 7 6
5

KEY (CORRECT ANSWERS)

SORTING SCHEME

Adair	_____	~~B~~ A_____
Butler	_____	A _____
Calvin	_____	~~B~~ H_____
Durant	_____	~~I~~ R_____
Enid	_____	E _____
Fargo	_____	B _____
Gould	_____	A _____
Lawton	_____	D _____
Newkirk	_____	H _____
Osage	_____	C _____
Snyder	_____	C _____
Tyrone	_____	~~A~~ C_____
Carter	_____	C _____
Noble	_____	H _____

KEY

Mail sent by way of _____

A	~~Gould~~	_____	~~2~~ Train 7
B	Calvin	_____	4 H_____
C	Osage	_____	~~3~~ 6_____
D	Tyrone	_____	A ~~O~~ Train 4
E	Adair	_____	~~B~~ A Butler 4
F.	Newkirk	_____	5 _____
I	Fargo	_____	B _____
R	Train	_____	2 _____

TEST 4

DIRECTIONS: In the Sorting Scheme below, each square represents a box for mail going to the cities named in that square. You will be required to study the Sorting Scheme and then write after each city in the following list the number of the box in which you would put mail for that place. Look at the first name in the list, "Worth." The number "4" is written after it because Worth is in the box numbered "4." "Rio" is in box number "7," so "7" should always be written after Rio.

Work straight down each column, taking the cities in order. You will receive no credit if you skip cities and scatter your answers.

Study the Sorting Scheme for 10 minutes, to get it thoroughly in mind before beginning to write. You may look back at the Sorting Scheme as often as you wish.

You may not have time to finish the test. Do as much as you can in the time allowed.

SORTING SCHEME

Box	Cities
1	Adams, Eagle, Temple
2	Dublin, Gail, Roscoe
3	Delhart, Austin, Orange
4	Worth, Rodney, Stout
5	Pecos, Midland, York
6	Denver, Rome, Clayton
7	Rio, Dallas, King
8	Welch, Jasper, Miles
9	Davis, Shary, Garner
10	Gorman, Caddo, Bowie

GROUP 1

CITY	BOX NO.
Worth	4
Rio	7
Dublin	______
Caddo	______
Orange	______

GROUP 2

CITY	BOX NO.
Austin	______
Rodney	______
Rome	______
Denver	______
Gorman	______

GROUP 3

CITY	BOX NO.
King	______
Bowie	______
Miles	______
Eagle	______
Gail	______

GROUP 4

CITY	BOX NO.
Adams	______
Stout	______
Temple	______
Pecos	______
King	______

GROUP 5

CITY	BOX NO.
Welch	______
Delhart	______
York	______
Midland	______
Shary	______

GROUP 6

CITY	BOX NO.
Bowie	______
Davis	______
Clayton	______
Dallas	______
Roscoe	______

GROUP 7

CITY	BOX NO.
Eagle	______
Welch	______
Jasper	______
Adams	______
York	______

GROUP 8

CITY	BOX NO.
Austin	______
Dublin	______
Miles	______
Denver	______
Rio	______

GROUP 9

CITY	BOX NO.
Gorman	______
Gail	______
Rodney	______
Caddo	______
Midland	______

GROUP 10

CITY	BOX NO.
Adams	______
Rio	______
Rodney	______
Delhart	______
Davis	______

GROUP 11

CITY	BOX NO.
Austin	______
Garner	______
Clayton	______
Midland	______
Gail	______

GROUP 12

CITY	BOX NO.
York	______
Dublin	______
Welch	______
King	______
Stout	______

GROUP 13

CITY	BOX NO.
Eagle	______
Caddo	______
Pecos	______
Clayton	______
Midland	______

GROUP 14

CITY	BOX NO.
Bowie	______
Worth	______
Shary	______
Austin	______
Garner	______

GROUP 15

CITY	BOX NO.
Jasper	______
Delhart	______
Davis	______
Rome	______
Stout	______

GROUP 16

CITY	BOX NO.
Roscoe	______
Dallas	______
Orange	______
Temple	______
Denver	______

GROUP 17

CITY	BOX NO.
Miles	______
Worth	______
Welch	______
Rio	______
Rodney	______

GROUP 18

CITY	BOX NO.
Rome	______
Austin	______
Gail	______
Bowie	______
Delhart	______

GROUP 19

CITY	BOX NO.
Midland	______
Adams	______
Gorman	______
Jasper	______
Dallas	______

GROUP 20

CITY	BOX NO.
Clayton	______
Eagle	______
Caddo	______
Pecos	______
Denver	______

KEY (CORRECT ANSWERS)

GROUP 1
4
7
2
10
3

GROUP 2
3
4
6
6
10

GROUP 3
7
10
8
1
2

GROUP 4
1
4
1
5
7

GROUP 5
8
3
5
5
9

GROUP 6
10
9
6
7
2

GROUP 7
1
8
8
1
5

GROUP 8
3
2
8
6
7

GROUP 9
10
2
4
10
5

GROUP 10
1
7
4
3
9

GROUP 11
3
9
6
5
2

GROUP 12
5
2
8
7
4

GROUP 13
1
10
5
6
5

GROUP 14
10
4
9
3
9

GROUP 15
8
1
9
6
4

GROUP 16
2
7
3
1
6

GROUP 17
8
4
8
7
4

GROUP 18
6
3
2
10
3

GROUP 19
5
1
10
8
7

GROUP 20
6
1
10
5
6

TEST 5

DIRECTIONS: In the Sorting Scheme below, each square represents a box for mail going to the cities named in that square. You will be required to study the Sorting Scheme and then write after each city in the following list the number of the box in which you would put mail for that place. Look at the first name in the list, "Mingus." The number "7" is written after it because Mingus is in the box numbered "7."

Work straight down each column, taking the cities in order. You will receive no credit if you skip cities and scatter your answers.

Study the Sorting Scheme for 10 minutes, to get it thoroughly in mind before beginning to write. You may look back at the Sorting Scheme as often as you wish.

You may not have time to finish the test. Do as much as you can in the time allowed.

SORTING SCHEME

Box	Cities	Box	Cities	Box	Cities	Box	Cities	Box	Cities
1	Canton Moffett Dawson	2	Frost Kyle Marlin	3	Kemp Albany Salina	4	Grove Stanton Handley	5	Chilton Perry Keota
6	Tipton Omaha Lyons	7	Booker Mingus Hedley	8	Newark Sonora Laredo	9	Norman Helena Chelsea	10	Apache Dayton Menard

GROUP 1

CITY	BOX NO.
Mingus	______
Stanton	______
Frost	______
Lyons	______
Newark	______

GROUP 2

CITY	BOX NO.
Albany	______
Canton	______
Laredo	______
Apache	______
Chelsea	______

GROUP 3

CITY	BOX NO.
Helena	______
Dawson	______
Omaha	______
Keota	______
Kyle	______

GROUP 4

CITY	BOX NO.
Dayton	______
Sonora	______
Norman	______
Mingus	______
Kyle	______

GROUP 5

CITY	BOX NO.
Booker	______
Tipton	______
Hedley	______
Perry	______
Grove	______

GROUP 6

CITY	BOX NO.
Marlin	______
Chilton	______
Menard	______
Albany	______
Keota	______

GROUP 7

CITY	BOX NO.
Apache	______
Booker	______
Grove	______
Canton	______
Chilton	______

GROUP 8

CITY	BOX NO.
Helena	______
Omaha	______
Albany	______
Kyle	______
Lyons	______

GROUP 9

CITY	BOX NO.
Laredo	______
Keota	______
Marlin	______
Salina	______
Mingus	______

GROUP 10

CITY	BOX NO.
Newark	______
Frost	______
Grove	______
Kyle	______
Tipton	______

GROUP 11

CITY	BOX NO.
Sonora	______
Booker	______
Norman	______
Mingus	______
Kyle	______

GROUP 12

CITY	BOX NO.
Laredo	______
Kemp	______
Chilton	______
Canton	______
Mingus	______

GROUP 13

CITY	BOX NO.
Chilton	______
Sonora	______
Lyons	______
Marlin	______
Moffett	______

GROUP 14

CITY	BOX NO.
Newark	______
Hedley	______
Grove	______
Keota	______
Marlin	______

GROUP 15

CITY	BOX NO.
Booker	______
Menard	______
Kyle	______
Omaha	______
Handley	______

GROUP 16

CITY	BOX NO.
Norman	______
Menard	______
Hedley	______
Handley	______
Dawson	______

GROUP 17

CITY	BOX NO.
Helena	______
Chelsea	______
Lyons	______
Salina	______
Frost	______

GROUP 18

CITY	BOX NO.
Chelsea	______
Laredo	______
Keota	______
Marlin	______
Perry	______

GROUP 19

CITY	BOX NO.
Keota	______
Frost	______
Helena	______
Lyons	______
Handley	______

GROUP 20

CITY	BOX NO.
Sonora	______
Moffett	______
Menard	______
Marlin	______
Kemp	______

KEY (CORRECT ANSWERS)

GROUP 1
7
4
2
6
8

GROUP 2
3
1
8
10
9

GROUP 3
9
1
6
5
2

GROUP 4
10
8
9
7
2

GROUP 5
7
6
7
5
4

GROUP 6
2
5
10
3
5

GROUP 7
10
7
4
1
5

GROUP 8
9
6
3
2
6

GROUP 9
8
5
2
3
7

GROUP 10
8
2
4
2
6

GROUP 11
8
7
9
7
2

GROUP 12
8
3
5
1
7

GROUP 13
5
8
6
2
6

GROUP 14
8
7
4
5
2

GROUP 15
7
10
2
6
4

GROUP 16
9
10
7
4
1

GROUP 17
9
9
6
3
2

GROUP 18
9
8
5
2
5

GROUP 19
5
2
9
6
4

GROUP 20
8
1
10
2
3

TEST 6

DIRECTIONS: In the Sorting Scheme below, each square represents a box for mail going to the cities named in that square. You will be required to study the Sorting Scheme and then write after each city in the following list the number of the box in which you would put mail for that place. Look at the first name in the list, "Pawnee." The number "3" is written after it because Pawnee is in the box numbered "3."

Work straight down each column, taking the cities in order. You will receive no credit if you skip cities and scatter your answers.

Study the Sorting Scheme for 10 minutes, to get it thoroughly in mind before beginning to write. You may look back at the Sorting Scheme as often as you wish.

You may not have time to finish the test. Do as much as you can in the time allowed.

SORTING SCHEME

Box	Cities	Box	Cities	Box	Cities	Box	Cities	Box	Cities
1	Miami Kermit Mission	2	Genoa Canyon Argyle	3	Bivins Pawnee Devers	4	Elgin Groves Nixon	5	Vernon Ranger Prairie
6	Gilmer Mason Hunter	7	Locus Nash Olton	8	Ralston Wallis Forney	9	Baird Ponca Yukon	10	Lehigh Calvert Slaton

GROUP 1

CITY	BOX NO.
Pawnee	______
Mason	______
Ponca	______
Genoa	______
Vernon	______

GROUP 2

CITY	BOX NO.
Groves	______
Nash	______
Calvert	______
Bivins	______
Gilmer	______

GROUP 3

CITY	BOX NO.
Ranger	______
Wallis	______
Miami	______
Elgin	______
Locust	______

GROUP 4

CITY	BOX NO.
Lehigh	______
Slaton	______
Olton	______
Nixon	______
Canyon	______

GROUP 5

CITY	BOX NO.
Baird	______
Yukon	______
Hunter	______
Devers	______
Kermit	______

GROUP 6

CITY	BOX NO.
Ralston	______
Forney	______
Prairie	______
Argyle	______
Genoa	______

GROUP 7

CITY	BOX NO.
Miami	______
Elgin	______
Locust	______
Lehigh	______
Calvert	______

GROUP 8

CITY	BOX NO.
Canyon	______
Prairie	______
Wallis	______
Ponca	______
Groves	______

GROUP 9

CITY	BOX NO.
Devers	______
Hunter	______
Yukon	______
Forney	______
Canyon	______

GROUP 10

CITY	BOX NO.
Prairie	______
Argyle	______
Yukon	______
Ralston	______
Elgin	______

GROUP 11

CITY	BOX NO.
Elgin	______
Miami	______
Ralston	______
Forney	______
Groves	______

GROUP 12

CITY	BOX NO.
Bivins	______
Lehigh	______
Olton	______
Wallis	______
Nixon	______

GROUP 13

CITY	BOX NO.
Pawnee	______
Mason	______
Lehigh	______
Genoa	______
Devers	______

GROUP 14

CITY	BOX NO.
Nash	______
Calvert	______
Hunter	______
Kermit	______
Wallis	______

GROUP 15

CITY	BOX NO.
Miami	______
Elgin	______
Argyle	______
Canyon	______
Groves	______

GROUP 16

CITY	BOX NO.
Baird	______
Slaton	______
Vernon	______
Nash	______
Gilmer	______

GROUP 17

CITY	BOX NO.
Bivins	______
Calvert	______
Genoa	______
Slaton	______
Olton	______

GROUP 18

CITY	BOX NO.
Locust	______
Prairie	______
Ponca	______
Nixon	______
Wallis	______

GROUP 19

CITY	BOX NO.
Ponca	______
Argyle	______
Lehigh	______
Prairie	______
Locust	______

GROUP 20

CITY	BOX NO.
Kermit	______
Yukon	______
Calvert	______
Olton	______
Bivins	______

KEY (CORRECT ANSWERS)

GROUP 1
3
6
9
2
5

GROUP 2
4
7
10
3
6

GROUP 3
5
8
1
4
7

GROUP 4
10
10
7
4
2

GROUP 5
9
9
6
3
1

GROUP 6
8
8
5
2
2

GROUP 7
1
4
7
10
10

GROUP 8
2
5
8
9
4

GROUP 9
3
6
9
8
2

GROUP 10
5
2
9
8
4

GROUP 11
4
1
8
8
4

GROUP 12
3
10
7
8
4

GROUP 13
3
6
10
2
3

GROUP 14
7
10
6
1
8

GROUP 15
1
4
2
2
4

GROUP 16
9
10
5
7
6

GROUP 17
3
10
2
10
7

GROUP 18
7
5
9
4
8

GROUP 19
9
2
10
5
7

GROUP 20
1
9
10
7
3

TEST 7

DIRECTIONS: In the Sorting Scheme below, each square represents a box for mail going to the cities named in that square. You will be required to study the Sorting Scheme and then write after each city in the following list the number of the box in which you would put mail for that place.
Work straight down each column, taking the cities in order. You will receive no credit if you skip cities and scatter your answers.
Study the Sorting Scheme for 10 minutes, to get it thoroughly in mind before beginning to write. You may look back at the Sorting Scheme as often as you wish.
You may not have time to finish the test. Do as much as you can in the time allowed.

SORTING SCHEME

Box	Cities	Box	Cities	Box	Cities	Box	Cities
1	Abilene Holyoke Kettering Oak Park Stockton	2	Decatur Clifton Lancaster Wilmington Tyler	3	Sioux City Lynn Tampa Newport News Pensacola	4	Knoxville Covington Somerville Albuquerque Malden
5	Lorain Sunnyvale Terre Haute Muncie Aurora	6	Joliet Hialeah Lake Charles Odessa Lubbock	7	Pasadena Lima Springfield, Mo. Rockford San Mateo	8	Ogden Meriden San Bernardino Bakersfield Anaheim
9	Chicopee Springfield, Ill. Dearborn Amarillo Lakewood, Calif.	10	Bayonne Albany, Ga. Kalamazoo Lakewood, Ohio Shreveport				

GROUP 1

CITY	BOX NO.
Anaheim	_______
Lynn	_______
Lakewood, Ohio	_______
Tyler	_______
Lorain	_______

GROUP 2

CITY	BOX NO.
Springfield, Ill.	_______
Hialeah	_______
Wilmington	_______
Somerville	_______
Kettering	_______

GROUP 3

CITY	BOX NO.
Pensacola	_______
Odessa	_______
Lancaster	_______
Bayonne	_______
Malden	_______

GROUP 4

CITY	BOX NO.
Lubbock	_______
Pasadena	_______
Chicopee	_______
Clifton	_______
Muncie	_______

GROUP 5

CITY	BOX NO.
Kalamazoo	_______
Newport News	_______
Oak Park	_______
Albany, Ga.	_______
Loraine	_______

GROUP 6

CITY	BOX NO.
Covington	_______
Tampa	_______
Dearborn	_______
San Mateo	_______
Ogden	_______

GROUP 7

CITY	BOX NO.
Shreveport	_______
Oak Park	_______
Knoxville	_______
Terre Haute	_______
Decatur	_______

GROUP 8

CITY	BOX NO.
Meriden	_______
Sunnyvale	_______
Stockton	_______
Lakewood, Calif.	_______
Malden	_______

GROUP 9

CITY	BOX NO.
Amarillo	_______
Pensacola	_______
Odessa	_______
Clifton	_______
Springfield, Mo.	_______

GROUP 10

CITY	BOX NO.
Lake Charles	_______
Knoxville	_______
Lima	_______
Sioux City	_______
Holyoke	_______

KEY (CORRECT ANSWERS)

GROUP 1
8
3
10
2
5

GROUP 2
9
6
2
4
1

GROUP 3
3
6
2
9
4

GROUP 4
6
7
9
2
5

GROUP 5
10
3
1
10
5

GROUP 6
4
3
9
7
8

GROUP 7
10
1
4
5
2

GROUP 8
8
5
1
9
4

GROUP 9
9
3
6
2
7

GROUP 10
6
4
7
3
1

TEST 8

DIRECTIONS: In the Sorting Scheme below, each square represents a box for mail going to the cities named in that square. You will be required to study the Sorting Scheme and then write after each city in the following list the number of the box in which you would put mail for that place.
Work straight down each column, taking the cities in order. You will receive no credit if you skip cities and scatter your answers.
Study the Sorting Scheme for 10 minutes, to get it thoroughly in mind before beginning to write. You may look back at the Sorting Scheme as often as you wish.
You may not have time to finish the test. Do as much as you can in the time allowed.

SORTING SCHEME

Box	Cities
1	Abilene Holyoke Kettering Oak Park Stockton
2	Decatur Clifton Lancaster Wilmington Tyler
3	Sioux City Lynn Tampa Newport News Pensacola
4	Knoxville Covington Somerville Albuquerque Malden
5	Lorain Sunnyvale Terre Haute Muncie Aurora
6	Joliet Hialeah Lake Charles Odessa Lubbock
7	Pasadena Lima Springfield, Mo. Rockford San Mateo
8	Ogden Meriden San Bernardino Bakersfield Anaheim
9	Chicopee Springfield, Ill. Dearborn Amarillo Lakewood, Calif.
10	Bayonne Albany, Ga. Kalamazoo Lakewood, Ohio Shreveport

GROUP 1

CITY	BOX NO.
Muncie	______
Kettering	______
Rockford	______
Lynn	______
Meriden	______

GROUP 2

CITY	BOX NO.
Sunnyvale	______
Lubbock	______
Lima	______
Joliet	______
Lakewood, Calif.	______

GROUP 3

CITY	BOX NO.
Somerville	______
Lancaster	______
Shrevenport	______
Tyler	______
Hialeah	______

GROUP 4

CITY	BOX NO.
Springfield, Mo.	_______
Terre Haute	_______
San Bernardino	_______
Chicopee	_______
Decatur	_______

GROUP 5

CITY	BOX NO.
Stockton	_______
Amarillo	_______
Lorain	_______
Covington	_______
Odessa	_______

GROUP 6

CITY	BOX NO.
Bakersfield	_______
Tampa	_______
Sunnyvale	_______
San Mateo	_______
Malden	_______

GROUP 7

CITY	BOX NO.
Kettering	_______
Kalamazoo	_______
Aurora	_______
Pensacola	_______
Meriden	_______

GROUP 8

CITY	BOX NO.
Aurora	_______
Knoxville	_______
Shreveport	_______
Muncie	_______
Anaheim	_______

GROUP 9

CITY	BOX NO.
Albany, Ga.	_______
Holyoke	_______
Ogden	_______
Albuquerque	_______
Lubbock	_______

GROUP 10

CITY	BOX NO.
Lynn	_______
Hialeah	_______
Wilmington	_______
San Bernardino	_______
Knoxville	_______

KEY (CORRECT ANSWERS)

GROUP 1	GROUP 2	GROUP 3
5	5	4
1	6	2
7	7	10
3	6	2
8	9	6

GROUP 4	GROUP 5	GROUP 6
7	1	8
5	9	3
8	5	5
9	4	7
2	6	4

GROUP 7	GROUP 8	GROUP 9
1	5	10
10	4	1
5	10	8
3	5	4
8	8	6

GROUP 10
3
6
2
8
4

TEST 9

DIRECTIONS: In the Sorting Scheme below, each square represents a box for mail going to the cities named in that square. You will be required to study the Sorting Scheme and then write after each city in the following list the number of the box in which you would put mail for that place.
Work straight down each column, taking the cities in order. You will receive no credit if you skip cities and scatter your answers.
Study the Sorting Scheme for 10 minutes, to get it thoroughly in mind before beginning to write. You may look back at the Sorting Scheme as often as you wish.
You may not have time to finish the test. Do as much as you can in the time allowed.

SORTING SCHEME

Box	Cities
1	Abilene Holyoke Kettering Oak Park Stockton
2	Decatur Clifton Lancaster Wilmington Tyler
3	Sioux City Lynn Tampa Newport News Pensacola
4	Knoxville Covington Somerville Albuquerque Malden
5	Lorain Sunnyvale Terre Haute Muncie Aurora
6	Joliet Hialeah Lake Charles Odessa Lubbock
7	Pasadena Lima Springfield, Mo. Rockford San Mateo
8	Ogden Meriden San Bernardino Bakersfield Anaheim
9	Chicopee Springfield, Ill. Dearborn Amarillo Lakewood, Calif.
10	Bayonne Albany, Ga. Kalamazoo Lakewood, Ohio Shreveport

GROUP 1

CITY	BOX NO.
Newport News	______
Lake Charles	______
Wilmington	______
Sioux City	______
Amarillo	______

GROUP 2

CITY	BOX NO.
Terre Haute	______
Somerville	______
Dearborn	______
Decatur	______
Covington	______

GROUP 3

CITY	BOX NO.
Lima	______
Clifton	______
Ogden	______
Abilene	______
Bayonne	______

GROUP 4

CITY	BOX NO.
Odessa	_______
Pensacola	_______
Anaheim	_______
Muncie	_______
Oak Park	_______

GROUP 5

CITY	BOX NO.
Lakewood, Ohio	_______
Lynn	_______
Meriden	_______
Lake Charles	_______
Stockton	_______

GROUP 6

CITY	BOX NO.
Hialeah	_______
Lorain	_______
Malden	_______
Chicopee	_______
Rockford	_______

GROUP 7

CITY	BOX NO.
Tyler	_______
Aurora	_______
Lancaster	_______
Knoxville	_______
Springfield, Ill.	_______

GROUP 8

CITY	BOX NO.
Clifton	_______
Ogden	_______
Hialeah	_______
Shreveport	_______
Loraine	_______

GROUP 9

CITY	BOX NO.
Albuquerque	_______
Decatur	_______
Bakersfield	_______
Lakewood, Ohio	_______
Covington	_______

GROUP 10

CITY	BOX NO.
Dearborn	_______
Muncie	_______
Kettering	_______
Malden	_______
San Mateo	_______

KEY (CORRECT ANSWERS)

GROUP 1	GROUP 2	GROUP 3
3	5	7
6	4	2
2	9	8
3	2	1
9	4	10

GROUP 4	GROUP 5	GROUP 6
6	10	6
3	3	5
8	8	4
5	6	9
1	1	7

GROUP 7	GROUP 8	GROUP 9
2	2	4
5	8	2
2	6	8
4	10	10
9	5	4

GROUP 10
9
5
1
4
7

TEST 10

DIRECTIONS: In the Sorting Scheme below, each square represents a box for mail going to the cities named in that square. You will be required to study the Sorting Scheme and then write after each city in the following list the number of the box in which you would put mail for that place.
Work straight down each column, taking the cities in order. You will receive no credit if you skip cities and scatter your answers.
Study the Sorting Scheme for 10 minutes, to get it thoroughly in mind before beginning to write. You may look back at the Sorting Scheme as often as you wish.
You may not have time to finish the test. Do as much as you can in the time allowed.

SORTING SCHEME

Box	Cities
1	Abilene Holyoke Kettering Oak Park Stockton
2	Decatur Clifton Lancaster Wilmington Tyler
3	Sioux City Lynn Tampa Newport News Pensacola
4	Knoxville Covington Somerville Albuquerque Malden
5	Lorain Sunnyvale Terre Haute Muncie Aurora
6	Joliet Hialeah Lake Charles Odessa Lubbock
7	Pasadena Lima Springfield, Mo. Rockford San Mateo
8	Ogden Meriden San Bernardino Bakersfield Anaheim
9	Chicopee Springfield, Ill. Dearborn Amarillo Lakewood, Calif.
10	Bayonne Albany, Ga. Kalamazoo Lakewood, Ohio Shreveport

GROUP 1

CITY	BOX NO.
Oak Park	_______
Sunnyvale	_______
Somerville	_______
Newport News	_______
Chicopee	_______

GROUP 2

CITY	BOX NO.
Malden	_______
Stockton	_______
Lynn	_______
Amarillo	_______
Clifton	_______

GROUP 3

CITY	BOX NO.
San Mateo	_______
Lima	_______
Lorain	_______
Holyoke	_______
Meriden	_______

GROUP 4

CITY	BOX NO.
Lakewood, Cal.	________
Decatur	________
Aurora	________
Pasadena	________
Wilmington	________

GROUP 5

CITY	BOX NO.
Lancaster	________
Sunnyvale	________
Malden	________
San Mateo	________
Joliet	________

GROUP 6

CITY	BOX NO.
San Bernardino	________
Decatur	________
Knoxville	________
Dearborn	________
Kalamazoo	________

GROUP 7

CITY	BOX NO.
Holyoke	________
Chicopee	________
Covington	________
Tampa	________
Springfield, Mo.	________

GROUP 8

CITY	BOX NO.
Lima	________
Tyler	________
Meriden	________
Odessa	________
Rockford	________

GROUP 9

CITY	BOX NO.
Tampa	________
Decatur	________
Lorain	________
Ogden	________
Knoxville	________

GROUP 10

CITY	BOX NO.
Wilmington	________
Aurora	________
Bakersfield	________
Lake Charles	________
Oak Park	________

KEY (CORRECT ANSWERS)

GROUP 1	GROUP 2	GROUP 3
1	4	7
5	1	7
4	3	5
3	9	1
9	2	8

GROUP 4	GROUP 5	GROUP 6
9	2	8
2	5	2
5	4	4
7	7	9
2	6	10

GROUP 7	GROUP 8	GROUP 9
1	7	3
9	2	2
4	8	5
3	6	8
7	7	4

GROUP 10
8
5
8
6
1

www.ingramcontent.com/pod-product-compliance
Lightning Source LLC
Chambersburg PA
CBHW080321020526
44117CB00035B/2458
9781799316091